ADVANCE PRAISE FOR *MEGA MILK*

"This surreal, horny, and gloriously grotesque investigation of milk will suck you in and surprise you, again and again. I will forever suckle at the teat of Megan Milks's magnificent mind. They are a poet of the sensate, a weird queer pilgrim at the altar of the udder, asking how we might be kinder to each other, human and cow. Why can't more books be like this?"

—SABRINA IMBLER, author of *How Far the Light Reaches: A Life in Ten Sea Creatures*

"*Mega Milk* is the kinkiest book I've ever read. A work of udder genius!"

—MYRIAM GURBA, author of *Creep: Accusations and Confessions*

"Kin to a cattle farmer, I grew up with an entire butchered steer in our family freezer. Bumping past the deep freeze daily, I was horrified; unlike me, the thing was packed. In other words, never, in my most miserable trans kid yearning, did I realize the zaps of pleasure, relief, and swelling recognition I'd feel reading *Mega Milk*. These aren't essays so much as vast vats of stretchy, generous, perv-a-palooza-ing, world-porous wisdom. In true Milks-ian form, *Mega Milk* is completely unafraid to be weirder than any/all proffered containers. Beginning in the confusing vault of queer Virginian adolescence and spraying everywhere, Megan Milks's cowdungsroman is so profoundly outside (everything) that it's deeply interior, so intestinal it's already in the field fertilizing. OF COURSE bovine anuses, neurodivergence, adjuncting, romance novels, human nethers, bull semen straws, cross-species kinship, and the tragically disappeared

Frog Bra go together. Each swill-y sentence increases my metabolic capacity one billion percent. A genre unto itself, *Mega Milk* has no ilk, no comparison. My hooves are sweating in admiration. This is a Milks world, and we're just lucky to be in it!"

—JESS ARNDT, author of *Large Animals: Stories*

"Milk is just the beginning of this book. Cows are just the beginning. Animal rights, factory farming, capitalist desecration, human-animal relations ranging from cruelty to tenderness, Megan's own autobiography—are just the beginning. *Mega Milk* is a feat of literary virtuosity, a kaleidoscope of eros that left me gasping."

—DODIE BELLAMY, author of *Bee Reaved*

"Inquisitive, rigorous, aberrant—in other words, enthrallingly queer—*Mega Milk* leads readers on a visceral romp through family, identity, sex, the bodies of actual cows, and the whole of the dairy industry. Often tantalizing and occasionally lovingly confounding, Milks's first essay collection is nothing short of astounding. There are few books I can shove in the hands of both theorist pals and farm friends across the gender spectrum and tell them honestly: 'Read this. It will change your life.'"

—ANNE ELIZABETH MOORE, author of
Body Horror: Capitalism, Fear, Misogyny, Jokes

"Megan Milks is the most interesting prose writer working today. There! I said it."

—ANDREA LAWLOR, author of
Paul Takes the Form of a Mortal Girl

MEGA MILK

ESSAYS

MEGAN MILKS

Published in 2026 by the Feminist Press
at the City University of New York
The Graduate Center
365 Fifth Avenue, Suite 5406
New York, NY 10016

feministpress.org

First Feminist Press edition 2026

This book is made possible by the New York State Council on the Arts with the support of the Office of the Governor and the New York State Legislature.

This book is supported in part by an award from the National Endowment for the Arts.

This book was published with financial support from the Jerome Foundation.

First printing January 2026

Cover design by Xander Marro
Text design by Drew Stevens

Library of Congress Cataloging-in-Publication Data is available for this title.
ISBN 978-1-55861-358-4

PRINTED IN THE UNITED STATES OF AMERICA

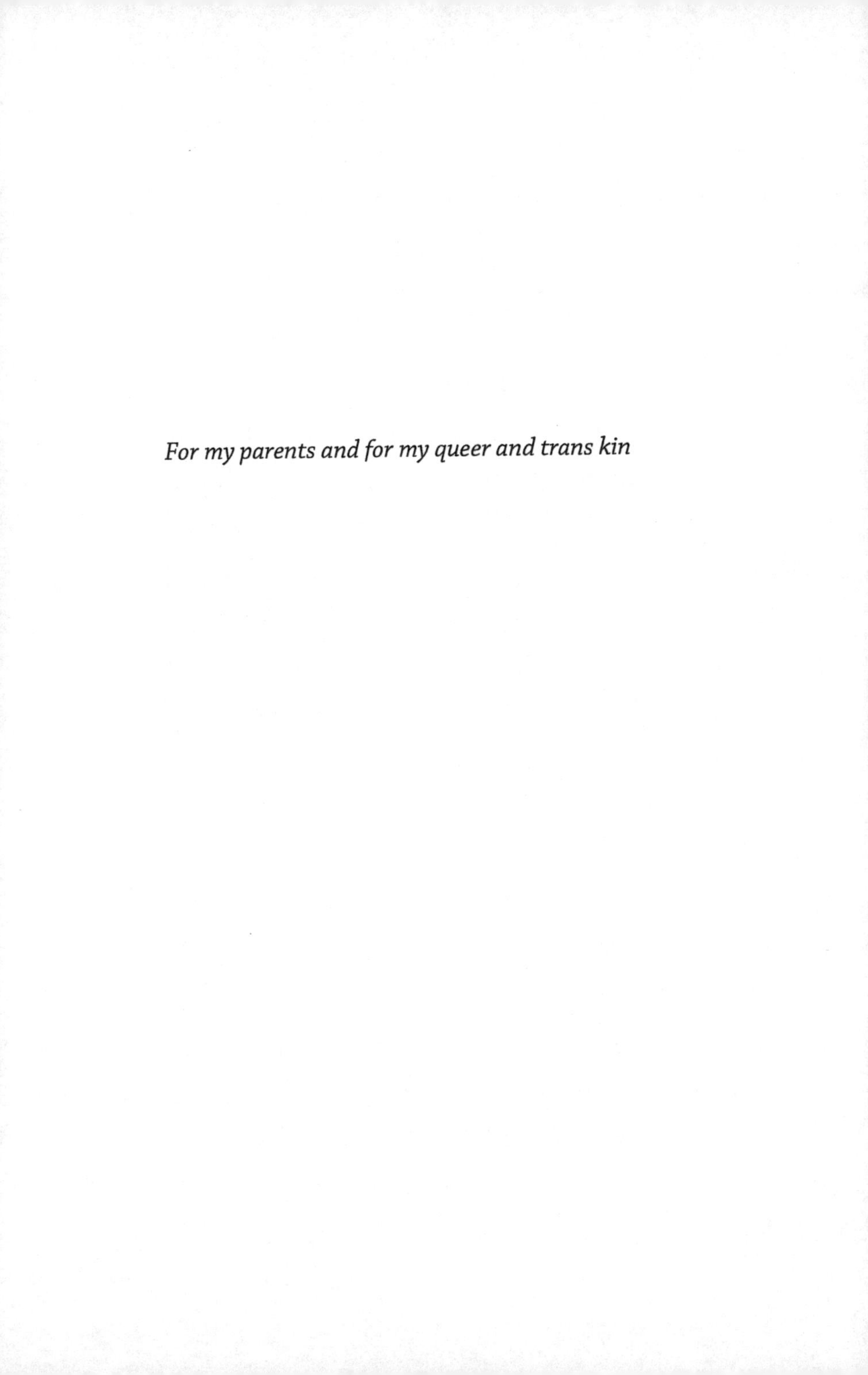

For my parents and for my queer and trans kin

Out of milk arises all imagination.
—MELANIE JACKSON and ESTHER LESLIE,
Deeper in the Pyramid

I got up, drank some milk and wrote to you.
—FRANZ KAFKA, *Letters to Milena*

CONTENTS

No More Cows

— 1 —

MOST EVENINGS I drank a tall glass of 2% milk while being watched by cows. Boxy Holsteins grazed on pastoral landscapes above the kitchen cabinets. On the counters beneath them, one cow leered with wooden spoons and rubber turners sprouting from her back. Another cow rested on the bread box. When twisted, her body measured time. A third stood stoic beside her, waiting for one of us to lift a square in her back, permitting speech (*muhh*).

The cows kept to the kitchen, witness to the sun's daily reaches and recessions through large bay windows, witness to the rhythms of my family's everyday life. The five of us rushing in and out, separately and together, fridge open, fridge shut, pantry open, pantry shut, the gasp of a can's opened mouth, cat kibble barrage on plastic, click of dog nails on the vinyl, bang of the cabinet doors, toaster spring, knife scrape, cyclops eye of the television blinking alive, our small movements, tinks and clinks, sniffs and gulps, faucet on, faucet off, TV off, dishwasher staggering through its phases. The door to the garage flung open, shut, open, shut. Quiet. The cows: grinning, grazing. They chewed.

When we ate together, we'd gather around the oblong table, which would be draped in a seasonal tablecloth, plasticky, kid-proof. We seated ourselves on wooden chairs with green vinyl cushions, a few split from wear, the yellow foam peeking through. My place was opposite my brothers. Mom at my left, Dad at my right. My back to the baker's rack, where a cat-sized cow stuffie slumped, her stare drilling into my head. On the wall beside it a wire cow hung with tiny bells dangling from her hooves and belly. She had no eyes, but her presence brooded all the same.

I faced the kitchen: the stovetop island, the sink, the cabinets, fridge, and pantry. I could see most of the cows. They could see me.

They watched as I lifted each clear glass of cold, pasteurized, homogenized, partially skimmed milk to my lips, tilting it up and in. They observed as I closed my mouth over spoonfuls of emulsified ice cream. Smooth lumps of fermented, vanilla-flavored yogurt. Wet mounds of milk-drunk Raisin Bran. Mugs of scalded hot chocolate, milk skin floating on the surface.

Occasionally, steak. Pink juices spilling past the seat of a (cheddar-topped) baked potato to flavor the (butter-logged) brussels sprouts too.

Did the cows watch in judgment as we buried their bodies in ours? Did they strain in protest within the confines of their paralysis? Perhaps they preferred this new domestication to the lives they would have lived on a farm, popping out calves and pumping out milk. Perhaps they grasped it wasn't *their* milk in our mouths. Perhaps they possessed no sentience.

I was eight years old, then eleven, then thirteen, sixteen, eighteen. My own gaze trained inward and registered little outside my concerns: Write back to Kim; why do I have to do dish duty; but I *need* to go to the Bush concert. The cows blended into the countertops and disappeared into the wallpaper. They became part of the everything that formed our home.

Not just cows. We had dish towels and pot holders patterned with cow print. Wood art in the shape of a milk bottle. Jesus Christ on the cross, bleeding out. We ate of his body, too, at Mass every Sunday.

We lived in Chesterfield, Virginia, twenty miles south of the Philip Morris plant where our next-door neighbors worked. I associated Philip Morris with cigarettes and factories. I didn't know that the company had just merged with Kraft and now sold a third of the nation's cheeses.

It was the era of "Got Milk?" and "Milk. It Does a Body Good."

It was the era of Kelis's hit "Milkshake."

It was the era of osteoporosis awareness.

My brothers and I drank a lot of milk in that kitchen. We went through two gallons a week. Maybe more. From Ukrops or Food Lion or Giant, our three supermarkets. Store-brand milk with nondescript labels. No images of cows, whether cartoonish or pastoral. I didn't think much about the origins of the milk that I was swallowing, though I had only to look around me, and there they (sort of) were.

I didn't think much about our last name, either, except when introducing myself, except when it prompted reactions. *Milks? You must be in dairy.* Wink. Then I thought about it glumly. What a weird, maybe gross thing to be named after.

MILK: FLUID SECRETED from the mammary glands. Milk: what makes mammals mammals. Though some features of

Linnaeus's classification system have been phased out, like the *Homo monstrosus* category, and despite evidence that animals from other kingdoms produce forms of milk—a worm-like amphibian, for instance, cockroaches, and some spiders, who might also have fur—this distinction for mammals has held on. Mammals make milk.

Milk supports the nutrition and development of mammalian young—exclusively, for variable durations of time across species. The shortest lactation period is the four days hooded seals nurse their young. The orangutan's seven years is the longest.

Milk: the living fluid. Milk: the first vaccine. Milk grows organs and calibrates metabolism, gut health, and immunity. Milk is the medium for a feedback loop of signals between nursing parent and nursling. Milk is biodynamic. Full of protein. Hormones. Antibodies. White blood cells. Fat. Magic. Life.

A liquid with fluctuating properties, milk is thus doubly fluid. Its volume, content, and thickness change according to the rhythms of the day and the year, according to the rhythms and needs of the nursing parent and suckling child.

Milk is notable for its "capacity to be various, to be other to itself, to be always made anew."[1] London's Milk Street was formerly known as Melecstrate, Melchstrate, Melkestrate, Melcstrate, Melkstrete, Milkstrete, and Milkstrate. The Milks family (plural) was formerly known as the Milk family (singular). The "s" got added in 1875 by an in-law, Sarah Matilda Milks née Smith, who felt "Milks" had more class than "Milk." Now, when the "s" gets dropped on mailers, it's as though the word is migrating back to its source.

LIKE THE DRINK—I say over the phone or at the counter, in the pharmacy or at the box office, to my students on the first day. *Like a glass of milk. But plural.* This has always been my last name, and so I have always had a close and at times uncomfortable relationship with the substance and its associations. Like breasts and udders. Like cows—mainly Holsteins, those hefty white rectangles with black splotches and skinny legs, the most popular dairy cows of America. Like Big Dairy and its ubiquitous ad campaigns. Like the swirl of celestial bodies we know as the Milky Way, or the candy bar named after it, three textures in one, a small galaxy of flavors. Like coconut milk, almond milk, soy milk, oat, cashew, macadamia. Like my father's side of the family and our roots in early American settler colonialism. Like the "wholesome" white American nuclear family that cow milk has come to symbolize. Like white nationalists chugging gallons of milk to troll an anti-Trump art installation: "We must secure the future of our diet and the future for milk drinking!" Like the rapid proliferation of alternative milks and non-white, non-nuclear families that threaten this white supremacist vision. Like former San Francisco city official Harvey Milk (unrelated), with whose post-Stonewall gayness I've developed a queer kinship. Like the two other Megan Milkses, both of whom, I've learned, are queer; one of whom is also gender nonconforming—she's in Florida, a mixed martial artist and the cover model of the 2014 *It's All Butch* calendar.

I'm often asked whether my family—the Milks side of it—has a history of dairy farming. The answer is not that we know of. The name's origins are unknown and may be Slavic or German in nature. *Melk*: Slavic for border. *Milch*:

German for milk. We apparently have German ancestry, but the traceable lineage starts in sixteenth-century Norfolk, England. While I can find dairy people in the Milk-Milks genealogy, any correspondence between the Milks patrilineage and dairying is weak.

The first milk comes from the breast. The first culture to milk domesticated animals was likely the Sumerians. The first cows to live in what is now the United States were shipped here in 1624, their presence contributing to the swift decline of the bison population.

The first American Milk is John Milk, son of Robert John, son of John. He arrives in 1662 to settle on Massachusett, Pawtucket, and Naumkeag territory, in the colonial town of Salem, where he is appointed town cowherd. I imagine John has had little to no experience with cows and is given this appointment because of his surname. He also works as a chimney sweep. Eventually John buys a lot near the river, builds a home, and marries a Sara Weston, one of several who lived in this region at the time. When he dies, he leaves behind Sara, two children, and a cow.

John begets John begets John. John Jr. moves to Boston and becomes a shipbuilder and neighbor to Paul Revere. John III begets a daughter, Jane, who marries a member of the Boston Tea Party. That's all we have about Jane.

I know all this because my dad has also been working on a Milk book. His is called *From England to America: A Short but Comprehensive History of One Ancestral Line of the Milk-Milks Family from the 1600s to Present Day*. It updates an existing two-volume genealogy prepared by distant relatives.

My dad's Milk-Milks book ends with him and us, his family. Though it's hardly a complete record, we are fortunate to be able to trace our lineage as extensively as we can, when many people cannot due to histories of family separation, lost or destroyed archives, enslavement, colonialism, genocide, other violences. Our "one ancestral line" is, of course, an approximation at best, not a line but a mess of branched veins, incompletely mapped and entangled with other maps, all of which chart familial bonds by patrilineage. One joins the map through wedlock, recognized birth, state-sanctioned adoption. Whoever doesn't neatly, officially link up gets lopped off the map.

Dad's account of himself numbers ten pages (some filled with photographs) and includes his high school basketball rebound statistics, his many professional titles and achievements, and his current golf handicap.

My mother's biography is made up of three sentences. I assume he gave her the opportunity to write her own, as he did for me after offering his version, which stated my name and academic degrees; that was it. I corrected some incorrect details and added my book titles (my children) and a note about my use of they/them gender pronouns. It didn't occur to me to take up ten pages.

Legally, I have stayed Megan Milks since birth. Unlike my brothers, whose names I have changed in this book, I wasn't named after anyone. And because I was assigned female at birth, I have never been expected to carry on the family name. This has been, in some sense, a freedom. Now I live at an odd, queer angle to the family, to our line. I'm there and not there, a childless, quivering bulb at the end of one small capillary, destined to shrivel up without spreading.

A status I've chosen. I have no impulse to procreate or parent. I don't much care about the map or the name—so I think, so I tell myself. Yet here I am begetting this book.

IT STARTED AS a question about names. I started thinking about changing my first name, then wondering about changing my last.

I changed my first name. I changed it again, changed it again, I changed it back.

I changed it.

I changed it back.

These name changes were social, not legal, and for a variety of reasons didn't stick.

I became obsessed with names and started a column named Name Tags for a quarterly newsmagazine in Chicago. I wrote the first column, which functioned as both a call for pitches and an exploration of my own name, then edited one guest writer's essay per issue. In that first column, I wrote:

> *A name marks, abbreviates, begins.*
>
> *A name is a failure, always already inadequate to describe that which it purports to name.*
>
> *A name is a tool for giving instruction, that is to say, for dividing being. (Socrates in Plato's* Cratylus*)*
>
> *We are given some names; we take others.*
>
> *What is your relationship to your name(s)?*[2]

When the publication folded, I resuscitated the column for an online website. The pitches rolled in until that publication ceased running and I let the column die.

I could write a whole book about names, I thought. My name. I could use the writing to make myself decide on a new name.

It started when, as a Halloween costume, I cut out the title from the title page of Ariana Reines's *The Cow* and taped it to a dangly earring so that my face—black splotch painted over one eye and a cheek—read *Megan Milks: The Cow*. White T-shirt. Black jeans. My best and laziest costume.

It started when grade school classmates started calling me Megan Milks the Cow.

Or when my friends started singing "Megan Milks, Megan Milks" when they saw me in the hallways at school, as if one name couldn't live without the other.

SOCRATES: Take courage then and admit that one name may be well given while another isn't.[3]

It started as a joke to myself. What if I wrote a book about . . . milk?

It started with *milk*. Which was among the first words that I learned. How confusing to try to understand that I was a Milks, that Dad was a Milks, that Mom had become a Milks, that there were many other Milkses, and that we may or may not have been named after this white stuff that we drank. Did families take their names from beverages?

Milks. I'm ambivalent. I dislike the sound. Voiced out loud, it's clunky in the mouth, clotted up with too many consonants. It doesn't lilt or sway, or declare itself with confidence. It's inelegant, unwriterly, embarrassing. But it's distinctive—in a mundane way. This makes it both memorable and easily spelled and pronounced.

I ask my family what they think.

My dad: "I'm proud of the name."

I ask him about nicknames, and he shrugs. "People said stuff in school, but I pretty much ignored them."

Mom: "I would say it's pretty neutral. It's kind of a cool name, actually. It's different. It's short. Easy to write." Shorter than her maiden name by three letters.

"The funny thing is, I don't like milk," she says. "Even when I was a child. I never liked it."

A cousin: “It’s very unique and I like it the older I become. However, as a kid I hated it.” His nicknames: “Milksy, Milks, 1% Milk, Got Milks, [First Name] Milks a Cow. He also mentions “lots of milking or milk jokes in the sexual nature.”

I ask my younger brother Derek—annoying nicknames? Not really. “It’s probably worse for girls.” He’s thinking about boob jokes. No one made that kind of joke to my face, though I’m not sure it would have registered if they had. I was willfully oblivious about that whole world.

Derek brings up one of my childhood friends, whose given name was Smelley. We are agreed: At least our last name wasn’t that.

My older brother Michael doesn’t want to speak with me about it. He needs to protect the family name—from me, I guess.

IT STARTED WHEN I saw Jordan Peele’s *Get Out* and found myself implicated in the milk moment. It’s that scene where the Black protagonist’s white girlfriend is sipping a large glass of thick milk while trawling a dating site for her next mark. It’s milk as a symbol of whiteness. I took in this scene with the tingling creep of self-recognition. Uh-oh, I thought. Is that me? I’m white, but not *that* kind of white—right? I haven’t drunk cow milk in years. Which was beside the point. *Get Out* effectively implicates all white people in anti-Black racism, and I, a white person named Milks, felt the implication pointedly.

I started researching, learning, researching more. My interest began to shift from names to the thing itself.

Milk: It’s everywhere, in everything. Bodies and bottles and family and history and dairy and whiteness and cows. Our mammalian kin, plus the spiders and that one lactating amphibian. Gender and hormones and climate change. Trains, refrigeration technology, plastic. I pluck off the cap and the milk spills out, flowing in all directions. Milk as soft global power. Milk as colonial force. Milk as symbol of increasingly entrenched cultural divide. I walk by a giant "Milk. It Does a Body Good" campaign featuring Olympic athletes. I watch Aubrey Plaza in a "Wood Milk" ad paid for by the Milk Processor Education Program. I watch tradwife influencers cradle mason jars of creamy raw milk. I get the news alerts: Wildfires in Texas kill more than seven thousand beef and dairy cattle; bird flu confirmed in cattle in two states, then several, then sixteen. I stop in the dairy aisle and survey the options: whole milk, skim milk, 1/2%, 1%, 2% in pints, quarts, gallons. Half and half. Creamer. Cream. Caffeinated. High protein. Soy.

It shows up in my reading, shimmering on the page when it does. *Achilles milks the spear's poison.* Two pints become crucial evidence in the first essay of Joan Didion's *Slouching Towards Bethlehem. The moon is milky. His skin is milky. She smiles, milkily.*

— 2 —

SINCE I'M WRITING about milk, I'm writing about my family name.

Since I'm writing about my family name, I'm writing about family.

Let me tell you about mine. I'll start with me. I'll take up ten pages. Maybe more.

Find me tucked into the long side of the kitchen table, which I have just set: five plates, five forks, knives, spoons, paper napkins. I've put out the butter, the salt and pepper, our salad dressings—Italian for everyone but Dad, who prefers ranch or sometimes the orange stuff. I've poured three glasses of milk. Unsweetened iced tea for our parents.

If I'm in elementary school, my long hair is pulled back by the neon pink scrunchie headband I so love. I am done with my dinner and impatient for Derek to finish his so we can move on to dessert. I need to do my math homework and practice for the spelling bee. I aim to win. At school I am called the expected things: Nerd. Brownnoser. Dorkus porkus. Megan Milks the Cow.

That one's the stickiest. I interpret it as a comment on my fatness: Megan Milks, the Cow. *The* as in singular. The one and only cow (fat girl) of the third-grade classroom. Then fourth grade. Then fifth. Later, as an adult, when someone who doesn't know me as fat or as formerly fat accurately guesses my childhood nickname, my first impulse is to assume they're calling me fat. But the context—a small group of kind, anti-fatphobic friends—will lead me to check myself and, pulling the logic backward, wonder if my younger peers were simply verb-ing my last name.

But I had never milked a cow and to be called a cow, *the* cow, made more sense.

Green's online Dictionary of Slang compares its entry on *Cow (n.)* to those of *Bitch (n.)* and *Sow (n.)*. When applied to humans, these words are typically used to describe "a woman," especially an unpleasant or unattractive one. *Cow* and *sow*, but not *bitch*, are used to call a woman fat.

Cow has also been used as slang for prostitute; for "an awkward or stupid person"; for "an objectionable thing" or "horrendous situation" (as in, *it's going to be a cow of a day*); and more. In the 1950s it was used in the US to describe an effeminate male homosexual. At the same time, to be *cow-simple* in queer parlance was to be a man attracted to women.

One can be *cow-cunted* or *cow-faced*. I don't know which is better.

I don't know which is worse, for women to be associated with cows or for cows to be brought into cis men's misogyny.

Though the word has become laden with insult and moral judgment, there's nothing inherently negative about fatness. (Fat activists have been telling us this for decades.) Still, it's inaccurate to describe cows in this way. A cow is a block of muscle containing a large and complex digestive system inside which grasses and feed convert to milk and meat. Cows are bulky, boxy, solid. Not *fat*. I guess they are *heavy*. *Hefty*. *Massive*. Terms also wielded as insults against people, especially women, of size.

So, then, as a child, I know to be insulted by "Megan Milks the Cow." At the same time, my life is much bigger than my feelings around this epithet, and I enjoy it overall. I have my own rosy bedroom and a weekly allowance that I save up to buy My Little Ponies and Mariah Carey cassettes. I have a bike and friends who live in biking distance. A mom who takes me to the library every two weeks. My brothers are annoying but bearable. I can eat pretty much whatever and whenever I want. It's a fine middle-class life in semirural central Virginia.

I spend most of it reading. On summer days I stretch out on the sunroom futon with a stack of books. Sometimes Tiger, our cat, permits me to read to him. The French doors shut the world out, though behind their glass I am lit up for anyone in the family room to see. I hide my face behind my book and pretend to be unseeable. As the sun heats up the closed room, I become aware of my body and other disappointing intrusions. I prefer to live in story.

Michael raps on the door. Dinnertime. (Tonight it was his turn to set the table.)

I sit down in my best shirt, an oversized button-down in soft silk, a gift from my favorite aunt. The back of my bra is itching where it hooks. I'm in eighth grade, my bangs swooped up and sprayed rigid. These days I am boarding the earlier bus to high school in the morning because I'm in accelerated math and my middle school has run out of curriculum. I take math and science at Michael's school, then another bus ferries me to mine. In his school my brother does not know me, though I'm showing him up in his—our—algebra class.

On the high school bus the first day, I sit in the only open stretch of seats, unaware—no thanks to Michael—they've been left empty for a reason. These seats, I soon learn, are the territory of the four Black boys who board the bus a few stops later, who own the bus because they act like they do. While the rest of the mostly white kids cram together in twos and threes, these kids each claim their own row.

"Who's this bitch in my seat?" *Moi?* I turn to face my interrogator. As he slides in next to me, I hug the window, unsure whether I'm expected to respond. "Yo, what is your *name*, bitch?" I don't remember if he asks for my last name, too, or if I just introduce myself in full like a dork. He—and I forget his name now, though he shared it, while shaking my hand—starts calling me Cereal Baby and greets me as such every morning. Though I would not say we are friends, at one point he informs me I look like a Christmas tree. Holiday sweatshirts and light bulb earrings are socially acceptable, even approved of, in middle school. But not in high school. I retire my holiday flair. He is a friend to let me know.

By dinner I'm wiped and I still have to practice my oboe.

Or I'm sweaty and dusty from softball, settling down with microwaved leftovers, back late after a game. I've freed my ponytail to cover my ironed-on "nickname" with my hair. I'm not sure why my dad signed me up for this team, but I'm playing with girls I don't know who all know each other. They have tried to include me but I'm shy, aloof, and also gay, obliviously; they've stopped trying. When the coach says we can put our nicknames on our jerseys instead of our last names, my teammates cheer and I panic. Everyone has a good nickname but me. I want to fit in, so on the shirt sheet I write *Milkyway*, which is clever, I hope. It will give the impression that I can hit the ball to a galaxy far, far away, that I am a real slugger.

When I show up thus named, my teammates are perplexed. "Do people call you that?" the pitcher ("Mandy-pants") asks. I shrug, tongue-tied and embarrassed. When I go up to bat, no one knows how to rally for this unknown, suspect person. My dad's voice rings out clear and strong and humiliating: "Go Milky! Hustle, Milky!" He doesn't know how to cheer for me either.

I sit down at the kitchen table. I take a sip of milk.

Now I'm in high school and blurrier by the day. Receded, subdued, over it, get me out. If I'm seventeen, I've replaced milk with water for weight-loss purposes. I will eat little, return to my room, flip the cassette to record the second side of a Tori Amos bootleg while finishing my AP Calc homework, then creep down to the garage for my cardio time, during which I blast pop music and fling myself around in a loose approximation of aerobics. It is the highlight of my day. If anyone opens the door and intrudes on this party, I freeze in place and wait for them to leave.

For now I'm sixteen. I'm drinking my milk. I'm telling you about my family. Mom is on my left, setting down lasagna on a trivet in the center of the table. No, not lasagna, something simpler because she's in college now. She didn't finish her BA the first time around; she got her MRS degree instead (she jokes). She met my dad at a frat party at Virginia Tech, the story goes. My mom, drunk—it was her birthday—pointed to a tall stranger across the room and declared she would marry that man. They've been together ever since. After his junior year, they married and lived in a trailer until he graduated. She (a school year behind) chose not to reenroll, taking a job at the college instead.

She has been mostly happy to be a stay-at-home mom, but now that we're older she's completing her degree. The change has been good for her. She is reminded of how smart she is, a quick learner and likable: Her younger classmates all want her in their project groups. She's studying information systems at VCU. I like this new version of Mom, but I'm too self-obsessed and perpetually irritated to tell her.

I'm also big on academic achievement, so this would be the first detail I share. My mother has always been smart, likable, and good at what she does. She runs the house and manages our lives and gets us where we need to be: in my case, to the library, to jazz and tap classes, to short-lived riding lessons when they replace dance, to Girl Scouts until I quit, to symphonic band until I can drive. Mom is fun, silly, a talker with an easy sense of humor, often the good-natured butt of our jokes. After meeting her on parents' night, my fifth-grade teacher tells me I have a great mom. I'm miffed to hear her mom-ness so casually appraised, but it's true. Mom is great.

Dinner is pork chops and canned green beans with mushrooms. She scoops some beans onto her plate and passes the dish to Derek. He sets it down. He's not ready yet for the beans.

My younger brother by five years is painfully shy and slow to speak, to put on his shoes, to tie them. Slow to eat. Finicky. For years he asserted a rejection of pizza until the Teenage Mutant Ninja Turtles made him rethink. Right now he is fixated on removing the fat and gristle from his chops, so he is holding up the beans. He chews slowly. Swallows slowly. Has to be goaded into finishing. We are always waiting on Derek. But his language is rhythm: On his drum set he's fast, nimble, a force. He's taken over the sunroom with it. Which is fine. These days I read in my room.

"Derek," Mom chides. He sets down his fork and knife reluctantly and dumps some beans next to the meat on his plate. Passes them to Michael.

Michael has a hat on, camo print. Mom made him take it off, then relented after beholding the greasy gloss of his hair. He's fifteen months my elder. We were once close, but our lives have been going so differently. I'm flourishing in a magnet program twenty-five miles away; he's at the less-resourced local school and struggling. Now that he can drive, he is drinking and driving. Skipping school. Our parents have made him take up a sport to keep out of trouble. He chose wrestling, which has required him to exert control over his diet and body, and he has risen to this challenge in ways I could not have predicted, diminishing himself in a matter of months from ruddy and robust to svelte, cut. He's got a girlfriend now, too, and a hunting gun, a chewing tobacco habit, and new Confederate signage. Not long ago he dropped a weight on his face, an accident that left his front teeth dead and brown. He's stopped smiling. Occasionally he'll bring home a deer carcass and hang it from the hind legs by a hook in the garage to bleed out. Then I can't use the space for my cardio routine, and I'm mad but keep my feelings to myself. We all keep our feelings to ourselves.

Dad goes for a second chop. He's changed out of work clothes into a Hokies shirt and has one eye on the TV behind my head. We're watching the football game or the basketball game or the six o'clock news. The stories of our time are Rodney King, the Gulf War, the Bosnian War, Clinton's impeachment, Matthew Shepard, Columbine. Lorena Bobbitt: a Virginia story. Dad cheers for his team. Mom tsks her reactions to tragedy and war. Dad travels frequently for his job in the Defense Department and brings home free swag: seasonal candy, duffel bags with company logos (Keebler, Hershey's). When he's home, he goes to bed at 9 p.m. and we turn the TV down. Except on Fridays when he stays up for *The X-Files*, which is our thing (me and Dad's). On weekends he mows the lawn and weeds the flower beds, checks on the vegetable garden in the backyard. He is quietly pleased when I ask him to take me to the park to practice basketball. He drives us to church every Sunday, and to Northern Virginia to see family on holidays, and if we're not in the van at the designated time, he will pretend to be leaving us. It's usually Mom who's late, still in the bathroom. Or Derek, putting on his shoes. The license plate reads 5 MILKS.

Back to me. The pork is dry and I force it down with a gulp of milk.

No more pork. I'm vegetarian.

No more milk. Water. I'm seventeen and I don't want to be here anymore. I've eaten in this kitchen, lived in this house, for nine years, the longest I've lived anywhere. Soon I will leave, and my family will move, but I return in my mind all the time.

It's the last time we all share a home. Soon Michael will enlist in the army and leave for basic training. Soon I'll leave for my parents' college pick, their alma mater, where I'll spend two unhappy semesters keeping empty days full with crew practice, an impossibly heavy course load, and binge eating; soon I'll have totaled two (used) cars. Soon Derek will go silent when our parents tell him they are moving to California. Soon the house will be packed up, the kitchen dismantled. Soon we'll all be elsewhere.

I DIDN'T MILK any cows growing up, but they gathered in that kitchen.

Their origin story is simple enough. My mom saw a cow item while shopping one day, a decorative dish. She thought it would be funny to display in the Milks kitchen, and it fit the kitchen's country-style aesthetic, the buttery cabinets, the bay windows with ruffled bangs. She bought it. The first cow.

The first cow was installed on the wall above one of the cabinets, where she stared down at us, a soothing solidity in the most chaotic room in the house. Her shining eyes beseeched us: More cows, please, she needed company. My mom asked family and friends to keep a lookout for cow décor, initiating years of such gifts. In no time, we had amassed a whole herd.

After a few years of these cow gifts, my mother started to weary of the theme, or so I thought. Unwrapping a stuffed cow from Harrods, a gift from my aunt, I read her enthusiasm as feigned, her laughter forced. "Another cow?!"

I remember her expressing relief at leaving behind the country aesthetic when my family packed to move for California in my college years. "No more cows," she declared, dropping a stuffie into a giveaway box, its tiny bell dinging dully.

Upon examination, this memory collapses. I couldn't have witnessed this scene; I was in Charlottesville, not present when she packed for this move.

Maybe I'm remembering my first visit to their new home in Rocklin? I can see her now, introducing me to that Spanish-style kitchen, where country aesthetics wouldn't jive. "See?" she says with a triumphant flourish of the hand. "No more cows."

I sit down with my mom now and ask her about it. Did she resent the endless supply of cows that people kept giving her? No, she says. She started it. She invited it. It was a big country kitchen, and she thought cow and milk items worked well. In the new house in California, dairy kitsch didn't fit.

Derek, passing by, chimes in. "You got sick of them," he says.

Maybe, she allows. But she saved them all.

We're at the high square table in their kitchen in Chester, where they live now, not far from where I grew up. Their current home is less milked out. My mom says she gave most of the cow décor to Michael when he and his wife bought a home, and she put the rest in storage. No more cows.

As we're talking, I spot a ceramic Holstein above the kitchen cabinets, in profile, more rustic. My mother laughs. The cookie jar. She forgot about it. "The battery is dead, but it used to go moo. Oh! There's another thing." She disappears into the dining room, still talking, to retrieve a cow reindeer Christmas decoration: that is, a cow with an udder and reindeer horns, leading a sleigh. "Oh!" She heads to the family room to grab a cow stuffie from the mantle. She holds it out, happy to help. "Want to take a picture?" I do.

— 3 —

I BREAK AWAY from my writing to attend a rough-cut screening of my friend Madsen's new film about Fakir Musafar, the extreme body modification artist. Fakir documented his life meticulously, and the film is comprised largely of material from his vast archives, collaged together with voice-over from archival and original interviews. I'm touched by footage of Fakir as an adult and fully formed freak visiting his parents and siblings in Aberdeen, South Dakota. With his dweeby haircut and thick-rimmed glasses, he fits in, and doesn't, with his wholesome-seeming kin. This far into the film, we've seen what's underneath his normy clothes: stretched nipples, dramatically cinched wasp waist, slits in the meat of his pecs to fit daggers and hooks. I imagine Fakir and his folks don't have much to say to each other and are smiling gamely through mutual bewilderment. I'm maybe 20—okay, 10—percent of the freak Fakir was, but I am at home with him in these images.

The family photo that Dad chose as the cover image for his *Milk-Milks* book was taken at the hotel reception after my mom's dad's funeral a few years ago. We are arranged by height with apex Dad in the back, flanked by Michael and Derek. I'm in the front next to short queen Mom. She's bleary-eyed from grief, and the overhead lighting throws the distorted cast of her head along her teal sweater—her shadow-self haunting the photo, or maybe it's Granddad.

Michael has his usual closed-mouth frown-smile, a relic of the years spent hiding his teeth. Dad looks like he always does in photos: tall, broad, blank grin, wispy hair gleaming white. Derek, still in his suit, is captured mid-snicker. My blazer and pants don't match—I haven't updated my more formal attire since starting hormones, and nothing fits right. I'm in a striped shirt, no tie, boots. When I stepped out of the elevator, Dad squinted at me as if he wanted to tell me something about menswear but thought better of it. In the photo my hair is thinning and sparse: I want to blame the hideous lighting but it's the testosterone, and the botanical shampoo recommended by Jordy that I don't realize is making it worse. I have no idea that this unfiltered, unedited photo will be enlarged and plastered across the cover of a family genealogy or that I'll be describing it here. But my smile is easy and open, as if to assure future generations: trans and happy, queer and proud.

A corner of my cell phone peeks out of my blazer pocket, and I remember my friend Liz and B, my sort-of boyfriend, checking in. I'd asked them for support, and it's helping. I haven't seen many of these people since starting T, and it's been a bit weird but okay. I got to be a pallbearer—Mom's attempt to affirm my gender. After we take the photo, I'll head to my room to FaceTime with B before they head to a play party. I'll tell them about the limo ride to the cemetery, among the guys. Michael, who has problems with trans people, problems with me, said nothing to me. Did I say a thing to him? I think I did. Maybe I didn't. B and I try to make sense of a second cousin's confounding and probably offensive Nazi joke, but neither of us can, so we decide he wanted to say a "bad" word and see how I flinched. When I return to the reception, my eighty-year-old great-uncle from

Mississippi will make an effort to use they/them pronouns. A younger cousin plants herself next to me, eager to tell me she's bi, and maybe her boyfriend is . . . Her voice drops. We don't know yet.

THE FAMILY I dropped into in the 1980s was prototypically suburban American and from an earlier era: breadwinner dad, stay-at-home mom, detached house, mom-cooked meal eaten together most nights, church (Mass) every Sunday, extended family a few hours away. Prototypical and no longer typical. The cultural dominion of this form of family was short—lasting from 1950 to 1965, when a whopping 77 percent of children were parented by couples in heterosexual marriages, which the majority of adults were in.[4] Blended and extended families are now more prevalent, more people are forming chosen and forged families, more parents are single, more adults are choosing not to marry, and more married couples have pets than children (which is selfish, according to the pope[5]).

Despite its blippy status, the nuclear family looms large in the US cultural imagination, where it's often held up as the healthiest and socially and morally best kind of family—the one Christian conservatives see themselves rescuing in their crusade to "save America's families" and cycle us back to a pre–New Left life when the white Christian family reigned and the average American consumed a liter of milk a day.

When I began this book project in 2022, a parallel trajectory had long been established: As the nuclear family waned, fluid milk consumption declined alongside it. Since the 1940s, milk drinking has trended downward, increasing in pace from the late 1950s on. Between 1978 and 2008, preadolescent milk consumption dropped by a third; in the same period, teen and adult milk consumption fell by a quarter.[6] In the new century, the downturn has steepened further,[7] prompting alarm among those with vested interests in Big Dairy, namely milk producers, their legislators, lobbyists, and the USDA.

Who was to blame? Maybe, they said, it was Michelle Obama's fault: She'd made public schools replace whole milk with less tasty low-fat options. Maybe it was the fault of plant-based milks, or "mylks," which the dairy industry argued shouldn't be allowed to compete on the milk market. Or it was the fault of competition from other beverages and from cereal alternatives like breakfast bars and other options. No, Gen Z was to blame.[8] No, it was demographic shifts: Because white people are the biggest milk drinkers, milk consumption was declining as the nation became more diverse.

In fact, no one person, entity, or trend was more at fault for the decline than Big Dairy itself. Blame overproduction. Blame the "get-big-or-get-out" mentality that has ruled the industry and the sustainability problems it has created. Blame greater awareness of inhumane treatment of animals in factory farming and persuasive arguments about the superior sustainability of plant-based diets. Blame dairy allergies, or the rise in these due to traces of gluten in milk, now that wheat is being increasingly used as feed for dairy cows. Blame the USDA, whose recommendation of three cups of dairy a day is simply not beneficial for all bodies and actually harmful to many.

Among all the alarm and blame, few media reports ventured to suggest that a decline in milk consumption might actually be a good thing: that the protein and calcium one might get from dairy can be attained through other foods, or that a better source of vitamin D may be sunlight . . .

I could go on. But while the continuation of this downturn seemed inevitable when I began my research, data suggest it may be starting to reverse. In 2024, fluid cow milk consumption in the US rose by about 1.9 percent. If this seems like a trivial amount, it's not: It marks only the second time in half a century that milk sales have gone up, not down. Notably, whole milk consumption floated up even more (3.2 percent), and sales of raw milk surged by 17.6 percent, a response to the growing influence of the raw milk movement. By contrast, plant-based milk sales are trending down.[9]

This reversal may or may not last. If I'm receiving the news of it with an odd sort of validation (and it is with some discomfort that I report that I am), this has more to do with the evidence it presents of milk's abiding relevance, I think, than with any sense of triumph over how many more people are drinking it. When I first started talking about writing this book, I had trouble interesting people in the topic. This probably had something to do with my own hesitancies; I wasn't sure I wanted to devote years of my life to milk or that anyone would want to read a whole book about it. But some internal herdsperson guided me forward, and once I started researching and writing in earnest, it seemed I might never stop. The book swelled and swelled, getting bigger and more mega, until it started to seem like it just might live up to its cheeky title—which is the same title it's always had, though, like myself, I've repeatedly tried and failed to rename it. At various points, I've thought: I could just keep writing more milk essays; the subject doesn't want to dry up. But there is such a thing as a firm deadline, and by the time mine loomed close, milk seemed to be on everyone's minds.

MILK: THE JUICE that makes fitter families fit. It's the perfect food supporting the best bodies supporting a wholesome and healthy America.

There is nothing more American than milk. A French Reddit user asks if we drink as much milk as our media suggests. "Watching American TV shows and movies, it is very frequent to see characters (grown-ups) drinking whole glasses of milk without anything else on the side, and at any time of the day. Is it actually a thing?" Yes, the comments confirm. "Milk is my water," one user responds. Another user's husband drinks so much of it he "is basically a bovine."

But this is a limited sample and the comments aren't a consensus. Another user detests the substance: "It's like drinking snot."

I'm an occasional milk consumer with a strained relationship to family. It's hard to imagine a scenario where I would be able to chug down cow milk or traditional family values and not bring the bulk of it back up.

But these are not the only things milk and family can mean. I'm interested in that other space—the queer capacities of family, the trans potentiality of milk. I'm interested in what we can learn about, not family per se, but kinship—that "radical and open-ended field of relational experimentation"[10]—through milk. Who and what nourishes us? Mothers and other nurses. Cows and goats and sheep and yaks. Nuts and soy and oats. Farmers. Teachers. Our forged and chosen families. Animal intimates and companion species. Friendship as a way of life. Our lovers. Language. Story. Art. Am I proposing a kind of milk kinship? Maybe. Provisionally. I'm also interested in kinship's milkiness: its fluidity and malleability, its leaky excesses, its variable shelf lives and propensities to sour.

I approach these ideas with ambivalence and curiosity. I'm accustomed to being the fly in the milk, the agent of queer disruption sullying my family's wholesome vibes. Or maybe the more apt metaphor would call me a fermenting presence. I should like to transform our prototypically familial milk into something else, like yogurt. Cottage cheese. But my family has never been interested in reconstituting themselves according to my agenda. I've reached my forties; by now I have other families, other kin. Still, I cling to this first one, hanging out on the edge of the meniscus, floating at the boundary between inside and out, and sometimes I sip the milk.

The editors of *Reading Autobiography* observe that the late twentieth and early twenty-first centuries have been characterized by "an outpouring of memoirs about family and filiation for an audience seeking cohesion." They understand this flood as a response to the dissolution of the family as an institution.[11] With this book, I'm not trying to scratch any itch for cohesion; I might rather the institution would dissolve.[12] My agenda is essays: an assembly of attempts at that slippery short form that, collected together, might reflect the gorgeous mess of my many attachments, familial and not, at the same time as each offers a fluid container for some of what I have learned about milk. As Phillip Lopate puts it in his introduction to *The Art of the Personal Essay*: "The essay form allows the writer to circle around one particular autobiographical piece, squeezing all possible meaning out of it, while leaving the greater part of his [sic] life story available for later milking."[13] In these essays, I'm milking milk.

When I tell a friend, a fellow writer, what I'm working on, she leans in with delight. "Sometimes," she says, "the subject chooses you."

Leaky nipple, greedy mouth.
I've taken the subject and latched on.

WELCOME TO MY milk book.

Though I prefer an oat latte, I've gone back to consuming cow milk while writing this, occasionally, with cereal. It's sweeter and silkier than nondairy, and I slurp up what's left in the bowl.

I'm not here to make a case for or against dairy farming or cow milk consumption. I'm on the side of udders and mothers and tits, cows and farmers and workers, cheese and semen and milk of most kinds.

I have no cows in my kitchen. Yet in my workspace, the milk and cow stuff accrues. Wade has gifted me two milk bottle art objects he's made with the word *MILKS* on them. They sit across from the milk carton Erin sent me, which has *MILKS* painted on all sides, in front of which sits a tiny glass cow from Italy, a gift from B, along with a vintage dairy token from D and T, and a cow coloring book from Anne. Upon my sternum rests an antique cow charm from Dodie—an amulet, she guides me as I write.

I'm following in my mother's footsteps, it seems. I've assembled my own herd.

NOTES

1. Melanie Jackson and Esther Leslie, *Deeper in the Pyramid* (Banner Repeater, 2018), 4.
2. Megan Milks, Name Tags, *The Land Line*, January 2012.
3. Quoted in Milks, Name Tags.
4. Prior to 1950, most people lived in extended family structures. Since 1965, the nuclear family has weakened its stronghold and gradually been supplanted by other

structures. By 2016, the number of families made up of married couples with children had become half what it had been in 1970. David Brooks, "The Nuclear Family Was a Mistake," *The Atlantic*, March 2020, 57–58.

5. In 2022, Pope Francis declared pet keeping "a form of selfishness . . . a denial of fatherhood and motherhood [that] diminishes us, takes away our humanity." Harriet Sherwood, "Choosing Pets over Babies Is 'Selfish and Diminishes Us,' Says Pope," *The Guardian*, January 5, 2022, https://www.theguardian.com/world/2022/jan/05/pope-couples-choose-pets-children-selfish.
6. Hayden Stewart, Diansheng Dong, and Andrea Carlson, "Is Generational Change Contributing to the Decline in Fluid Milk Consumption?," *Journal of Agricultural and Resource Economics* 37, no. 3 (2012): 439.
7. The 2000s saw an average 1 percent decline per year; by the 2010s, that average per-year decline had risen to 2.6 percent. Hayden Stewart et al., *Examining the Decline in US Per Capita Consumption of Fluid Cow's Milk, 2003–2018*, ERR-300, US Department of Agriculture, Economic Research Service (October 2021), 28.
8. The so-called "Not Milk" generation, Gen Z drinks 20 percent less than the national average. Stewart et al., *Examining the Decline*; Kim Severson, "Got Milk? Not This Generation," *New York Times*, April 4, 2023, https://www.nytimes.com/2023/04/04/dining/milk-dairy-industry-gen-z.html.
9. Julia Moskin, "Got Weird? Milk Is Headed for Its Strangest Year Yet," *New York Times*, February 6, 2025, https://www.nytimes.com/2025/02/06/dining/milk.html/.
10. Tyler Bradway and Elizabeth Freeman, "Kincoherence / Kin-aesthetics / Kinematics," in *Queer Kinship: Race, Sex, Belonging, Form*, ed. Tyler Bradway and Elizabeth Freeman (Duke University Press, 2022), 2.
11. Julia Watson and Sidonie Smith, *Reading Autobiography: A Guide for Interpreting Life Narratives*, 2nd ed. (University of Minnesota Press, 2010), 154–55.
12. For more on family abolition, see Sophie Lewis's *Abolish*

the Family: A Manifesto for Care and Liberation (Verso, 2022) and M. E. O'Brien's *Family Abolition: Capitalism and the Communizing of Care* (Pluto, 2023).

13. Phillip Lopate, *The Art of the Personal Essay: An Anthology from the Classical Era to the Present* (Anchor, 1995), xxix.

Dear Dairy I: A Visit to the And-Hof Animal Sanctuary

December 2022

I'm reading a book called *Milked*, about the economic interdependence of Wisconsin dairy farmers and Mexican-born farmworkers, with B, my sort-of boyfriend, next to me on the couch. We're in Kingston, New York, at the bookstore that is also a coffee bar. "This seems like a moment," B observes. "Megan Milks reading *Milked*."

I'm a few pages in when a friend DMs me a meme of Kafka's best quotes about milk. *Milk is very good* (1924). *Drinking down with milk the boredom of six hours work* (1908). *However I will now drink my milk and go to sleep. Keep well* (1920). I'm sipping a mint chocolate latte with oat milk. B is drinking milk-cloudy tea. I put the book down and pick up my phone to research the farm animal sanctuary we'll visit tomorrow. I want to make a list of questions to ask our guide.

"Uh-oh," I mumble as I scroll down their page. "Looks like there are no cows at this sanctuary."

B gives me a bemused look over a copy of Hilton Als's *My Pinup*. "Wasn't meeting cows the whole point?"

It was. I'm building up to visiting dairy farms. I want to meet some cows and maybe, ideally, learn how to milk. B has graciously agreed to accompany me on this trip, a month after our original plan to go to a larger, more well-known animal sanctuary got scuttled when I came down with COVID. That place is now closed for the winter, so my friend Diana suggested we go to And-Hof instead. Her friend Ryder volunteers there and would be down to give us a tour.

I'm sheepish to learn there are no cows, but oh well. There are other animals, and I'm sure I'll learn a lot regardless. I'm just dipping my toes into this world, I remind myself. The prospect of this kind of research is daunting, as my life is so removed from farm culture. I'm lacking basic knowledge of its vocabularies and cadences, its pressures and challenges, and there's only so much that reading can give me. This will be a first step, cows or no cows.

DIANA DRIVES US to Catskill to pick up Ryder, a lithe weirdo artist whose steampunk-fae aesthetic suits them perfectly. Ryder directs Diana to a farm stand on the way, where we pick out kale, spinach, and berries for the birds. Inside, Ryder asks me who I am when I'm not visiting an animal sanctuary.

"I'm a writer and teacher," I tell them. "I'm working on a book about milk."

They grimace. "We don't have any cows," they say apologetically. The owner used to have one but found her another home. Ryder says that's a good thing. Cows are a lot of work.

I assure them I know about the cowlessness. "I'm just dipping my toes in," I say, I keep saying. "Trying to enter the world of farms."

"We do have goats and sheep," they go on. "But we don't do any milking." There's no consumption of animal products at this sanctuary. No commerce. The hens' eggs are up for grabs, but Ryder is vegan, and they're not grabbing.

Back in the car, they bring up cow insemination. There's someone whose job is solely to slide sperm up cows' vaginas.

With cautious enthusiasm, I mention my research on the bovine semen industry. "It's fascinating," I say.

"I guess fascinated is a good way to be," they respond slowly.

They're not intending to chasten me—I think they really mean to convey a respect for my fascination, not imply that their own sense of being deeply disturbed is the only acceptable response. I'm chastened all the same.

Diana parks at the lot and we start up the snowy path, talking about milk. Diana and I both consume dairy products, but no one in our group drinks cow milk on its own, Ryder as a rule, the rest of us out of taste or lactose intolerance. B's mother hated milk and drank cereal with orange juice. We break into pairs as we walk, stepping into icy tire treads.

"I see the hog hut!" Ryder cheers. We approach a wood structure with a wire fence. Loud grunts precede the animal. This long, beautiful hog emerges as if its body won't end. When it's all out—huge! The hog's hide is a mottled black and pink, lightly hairy. Its nose seeks upward like the finger of an elephant's trunk. Soon come the snorts, the heavy body of a second hog tottering heavily from the hut. Then a third. And a fourth. They've been sleeping hard, it seems, in a cuddle pile. It's cold. Winter. The first snowfall two nights ago has stuck. Their eyes are tiny and squinting, maybe from the brightness, the sun on snow. The oldest is shivering and seems to have a hard time balancing. They're all hoping for food. But we only have treats for the birds, not for the hogs. Sorry, hogs.

We proceed down the slippery path, where two alpacas await us, one with a shaved face. They're friendly, aggressively so. We're eye to eye, their heads bobbing on skinny necks. They're a little intimidating, to be honest. They don't respond well to pets, Ryder tells us. They might spit, but if they do, they'll arch their necks, that's the warning. The more assertive one nibbles the edge of my coat. Comes for my hat.

Most animals here are free to roam at will. The sanctuary's mission supports permaculture, a holistic approach to ecological management. "Rather than being contained in pens, our animals enjoy as much freedom and autonomy as is safe," the mission statement reads. "We then nurture them to follow their instinctual habits and build on that to create a healthier ecosystem."

We meet some goats. Some bellowing geese. We squeeze through a gate into the duck pond, where wild turkeys strut, iridescent feathers shining in the bright day. Many of them are rescues from Staten Island, relocated several years ago as part of efforts to manage their overpopulation. The turkeys hang out on an iced-over pond. Some ducks nap on its snowy edge. Others sleep standing on the ice. There's a shed on the other side. The donkeys come out of it to say hi. They protect the birds from predators, Ryder says. Their braying keeps the wildcats away.

They all want treats. A donkey nibbles at the brown bag of veggies and fruits I'm holding, tears a rip down the side. Eats the paper until Ryder takes it from me. We slide back out of the gate. The geese nip at our shoes and ankles.

There's Hugo, the antagonistic ram. Wants to charge us with his flat-iron head, wants to play or assert dominance or both. I make the mistake of direct eye contact. He's intent on headbutts. Ryder grips him by his fleece and tells him, "No, no, these are my friends." They shoo us around the house quickly.

A gang of goats and sheep intercepts us on the way to the chicken coop, interested in whatever food we must have.

We push them away and scurry down a trail and through the fence.

Many of the chickens and turkeys here are rescues from factory farms, where they were raised on hormones designed to plump them up as much as possible. As a result, their legs struggle to hold their bodies up. Many have trouble walking and seem unsteady on their feet.

B stays outside—it smells, they say. I don't notice after a bit. Ryder and Diana and I feed the birds kale—they peck at the voluminous leaves we hold out to them. Then blueberries—Ryder shows us how to cradle the orbs in our palms and hold them out for the birds to peck. "It doesn't hurt," they assure us. One of the turkeys is older and going blind. Anticipating a berry, he pecks at the meat of Diana's hand, drawing blood. We scatter spinach leaves in the dirt. Two bags of veggie slaw. We smush up strawberries and toss them to whoever's fast.

Once we've exhausted our treats, we head back up and around the house the other way. The sheep and goats greet us again. Hugo wants to fight. Another ram intervenes and butts Hugo away. He doesn't listen. Fight! Fight! Ryder does their best. Diana, B, and I escape the scene one by one, each with our own strategies. I'm the last to break free. We feel guilty leaving Ryder, who can clearly fend for themself, but this ram will not leave them alone. We sequester ourselves in the donkey and duck pen as Ryder and Hugo circle a tree stump. "No, Hugo, no. We're friends." After a while, Ryder's rubbing his head, scratching behind his ears. Then he's ramming again. Ryder hides behind a tree and waits for him to get bored and forget about them. Finally Ryder escapes.

The alpacas escort us back up the trail, first leading, then following. When we reach the hog hut, they lose interest and fall back.

"The energy there was really intense," B says. "There were so many needs."

And it was cold. The animals have shelter but it's unheated shelter. We're bummed thinking about it. Resolved: I will cancel my dating app subscription and reroute that money into a monthly donation to And-Hof. I don't know. It's something to do.[1]

We drop Ryder off and find food in Kingston. Diana has a burger. B has duck. I choose steak au poivre.

We talk about this. How do we justify eating dead animals after spending the afternoon at a farm animal sanctuary? Our answers are shrugging at best. I like eating meat and I don't want to stop. In my teens and early twenties I abstained from lots of foods, and now any restriction I make is tied up with disordered eating practices. I try to choose food items with an awareness of context. This meat comes from local animals raised on small sustainable farms; supporting these farms feels like the right ethic.

One of my oldest vegan friends used to tell me to *see the cow* when she was in an evangelizing mode. The cow is the one common farm animal I haven't yet seen—not up close, in living flesh. But she's in my mind and on my plate. Actually this steak was probably not a cow, but a steer. I see the steer. I honor the steer. I enjoy the steer. I take the leftovers home.

NOTE

1. In late 2024, And-Hof was forced to close due to a lack of financial resources. All animals have since been relocated to other homes and sanctuaries.

Muscle Milk

I was kidding about the protein shakes, I tell B as we mount the steps exiting the station. Earlier I said I would have some on hand for the circuit training scene we have planned. B confesses disappointment, so we stop at the corner store to see what they have.

The options: vegan smoothies in bottles and cans, Nesquik chocolate milk, and Muscle Milk. You should write about Muscle Milk for your project, B suggests, referring to the book about milk I keep saying I'm writing. I totally should. I consider purchasing a bottle, but I'm full from our meal. B selects a plant-based chocolate milk stuffed with protein.

We head to my place to feed my cat, then to Liz's place upstairs. She's gone for the week and said I could have a date over if I want. I want—the privacy and the sectional. The ottoman we'll convert to a weight bench.

This summer I'm taking Dodie Bellamy's workshop, and our weekly assignment is this: Write against progress. As I brainstorm ways to respond, I'm reminded of a quote from Shunryu Suzuki: *In the beginner's mind there are many possibilities; in the expert's mind there are few.* I encountered this in Alison Bechdel's book on exercise and clung on. In writing, in intimacy, and in exercise, it seems I am always beginning, and I have trouble balancing all three. I've been viewing this as a problem, but maybe it could be something else, like personal wisdom.

This week I've written little, having funneled my creative energy into this scene, which I've fed with some time at the gym. I've fantasized and I've prepared. Earlier I brought up my yoga mat and ab roller, one heavy dumbbell. Toys and towels. A change of sheets. My outfit: a cropped sleeveless hoodie and bike shorts under running shorts with a harness in between.

We talk it over. We execute. It's fun and very hot. We're the only two guys in the gym. We complete two-minute rounds at the stations we've created, ramping things up as we go—erotically speaking. Wall sits, sit-ups, tricep dips, bench press, some cooldown yoga, finishing with a shoulder stand. Perhaps this setup was overly elaborate, I'm reflecting now—for all the planning we did for each station, we ought to have repeated the circuit. Did we heat things up too early, drop a cock out too soon? I did that, that was me. Though at the time I was too exuberantly present to worry about my performance, I'm assessing it now with a critical eye. I broke character, laughed a lot. I couldn't decide if my character was straight or gay. I didn't have a character beyond repetitions of *dude* and *man*, so I guess I played it straight. B played way gay in bright, tiny shorts and strappy singlet with Day-Glo cuffs. I should have bought the Muscle Milk, to incorporate it as prop, for character. Then I would have all these plant-based milk proteins speeding through my bloodstream to find and support my muscles. I would have gym buddies on both the outside and the inside.

Muscle Milk makes me think of the well-known "Got Milk?" campaign created for the California Milk Processor Board in 1993. In the original ad, titled "Aaron Burr," the protagonist is unable to vocalize the answer (Aaron Burr) to a radio trivia game because he doesn't have the milk he needs to wash down the peanut butter he's eaten. The ad, which has since been inducted into advertising's prestigious Clio Hall of Fame, was directed by Michael Bay, later known for blockbusters like *Transformers*. Michael Bay also directed the video for Meat Loaf's "I'd Do Anything for Love," as well as a Meat Loaf documentary. As a kid in Central Virginia, I regularly ate meatloaf with milk, which we drank daily. In eleventh grade I repurposed the "Got Milk?" campaign to run for office in the National Junior Council League. At the annual convention, my speech was terrible, but my posters were fine. At first I considered the tagline "MEGAN MILKS. She [sic] does the NJCL body good." You can see why I went with "Got Milks?" instead. I didn't win.

Usually milk comes *from* the thing it's named after. Oat milk comes from oats. Soy milk, from soy. Muscle Milk does not come from muscles. What kind of milk would that be? Sweat? No, that's unscientific. True muscle milk would involve adenosine triphosphate (ATP) and lactic acid. Yum. Oh, of course. Muscle Milk is milk *for*, not *from*, your muscles. It's liquid protein. Twenty-five grams.

Got muscles? There are more than six hundred in the human body, and their strength can be measured in various ways. By weight, the strongest would be the masseter, located in the jaw and used primarily to chew. The masseter can close the teeth with a force as great as two hundred pounds on the molars, much more than I can lift with my arms. Then there's endurance: Our most tireless muscles are the tongue and the heart. The heart pumps blood every beat; the tongue is used in mastication, vocalization, and the constant shoveling of saliva down the throat.

B and I use these and many more muscles in our circuit training scene. Though our scene was by any measure a success, I have a compulsion to revise it, do it better, get it right.

ON SUNDAY AND Monday I am having hard gay t4t sex. Now it's Wednesday and I am on the train to Richmond, Virginia, for a weeklong visit with my family, which we'll launch with a trip to Chincoteague. B requests a video of me getting off in public. *This may take me a few days*, I reply, imagining myself improbably hiding out in the forests and marshes of Virginia. Two hours later I'm in the Amtrak bathroom: Is this public enough? Assignment complete. I request a video of them in turn.

And I've arrived. At home my parents have a "Got Milk?" bumper sticker affixed to the door into the house from the garage. I had hoped this one-week trip, unusually long for me, would give my family—my parents and younger brother and I, at least—an opportunity to really connect. To grow and build our intimacy. To make progress. So far that's not happening. The next day we leave at 9 a.m. and drive four hours, no music, to the Eastern Shore. I flee to the hotel fitness room the first chance I get.

In Chincoteague we drive by a gym named Hubbmuscles. Gay content! I snap a photo. We head to Assateague and drive through the National Wildlife Refuge. In the visitor's center I read about their progress growing the populations of rare birds and squirrels. We take the lighthouse trail. The lighthouse is closed due to COVID.

In the distance we spot two herds of wild ponies; I take a halfhearted photo. These photos aren't assignments. With no anticipated recipient, there is no charge. I think of Bruce

Boone's entropic poems, how they're held together by the magnetism of desire. The exhilaration of his writing about his lover, this explosion of language floating out from the center. How the erotic sustains in the entropy.

I want another assignment but don't request one from B, who is busy at a residency. Instead I request thirty minutes of alone time from my family. My request is granted and I use it to respond to Dodie's prompt. Perched on the small balcony of our hotel room with the door shut behind me, I attempt to write against progress.

What can I say? Although my younger brother and I are adult children, my middle-class parents are paying for the whole trip. It's class regress. I can't imagine being able to afford this kind of vacation for four. My mother made the small request that my brother and I each pay for one meal. I charge Thursday's dinner to my credit card. I've just gotten this account down so it's easy to justify adding more debt. This breaks the seal on my credit card purchases.

At the T-Shirt Factory I charge two tank tops and point out a racist T-shirt to my mom. The shirt depicts a white soldier kneeling to aim his firearm against an American flag backdrop; the caption reads *This is how we take the knee*. My mom nods, whispers she knows. She doesn't want me to be loud about it. When we get home, she'll ask me to shave my mustache off to make my queer appearance more palatable to my older brother, who would probably buy that T-shirt. I'll say no. Absolutely not. I understand I embarrass her. They all embarrass me. Because they embarrass me, I've never brought a lover home. Because I've never brought a lover home, my family has not witnessed me being loved or desired.

The gulls circle and shriek as the sun sets. They float down the bay or swoop near my perch. They laugh at us (they're laughing gulls). A white man holds French fries in his fist and the gulls frenzy to snatch them. I watch, disapproving.

When my thirty minutes of alone time are up, I extend them by fleeing again to the fitness room. On the elliptical machine I revert to my seventeen-year-old self, pumping my legs furiously while listening to mid-'90s PJ Harvey. I lift some weights, make my own circuit. Count. Sweat. Do ab work. I have been doing versions of this same workout for twenty-four years yet somehow I'm always beginning. In more motivated phases I push myself harder, to do it better, get leaner or stronger, to make progress. Most of the time I don't.

Milking the Bull

I don't want your future / I'm never ever coming home
—ANOHNI, "Why Did You Separate Me from the Earth"

Remember, an open cow makes no milk or money.
—BRUCE POULIN, "Semen Tank Management: A Dozen Do's and a Few Don'ts"

When I see the container in which my bull semen order has been shipped, I want to laugh. I had no idea what to expect, and it's not this: a girthy blue cylindrical tank in the shape of R2D2, the Cattle Visions logo blaring from the front. Among the stacks of Amazon and Chewy boxes in the lobby of my building, it's comically incongruous. And tall—rises past my knee.

The doorman asks no questions.

I lug it by the metal bucket handle into the elevator, then down the hall to my apartment, where I heave it onto the kitchen table.

King George has arrived.

PROVERBIALLY, "milking the bull" means to undertake a futile endeavor. The idiom rests on the assumption that bulls cannot be milked. Whoever originated this proverb didn't anticipate an industry based on bull semen collection, a practice that involves the milking of bull penises with what are called "artificial vaginas," not so dissimilar from the milk pumps attached to cows' teats. A typical bull donor can produce anywhere from ten to sixty billion sperm per week. From this haul, breeders create "doses" (aka "straws") of about twenty million sperm apiece that are sold online to beef and dairy farmers who use them to inseminate their cows.

In the dairy world, cows who are not pregnant are called "open cows": Producers strive to maintain the tightest lactation cycles possible in order to maximize their production of salable milk. In the world of bovine semen, the parallel goal is to maximize bulls' production of salable straws by keeping them virile and pathogen-free. Breeding the natural way, a bull might be expected to sire two hundred calves in his lifetime. Through artificial insemination, the same sire could hypothetically produce hundreds of thousands of calves in the same period—or beyond. The record holder for semen sales is a Holstein bull known as Toystory, who produced 2.4 million units and sired half a million calves (and counting). Bulls like Toystory belong to what's known in bovine genetics as the "millionaires club."

King George is not part of this club. I found him last summer while at a residency in Memphis, searching Maps for dairy farms in the area. I zoomed out once, twice, five times. There were farms, but none that seemed promising for a research trip. Then I clicked on something called Cattle Visions, a name that brought to mind handsome animals reclining on fluffy pink clouds. Cattle Visions bills itself as "home to the HOTTEST sires!" The bull sires catalogued on the company's website stood on hay or grass against fencing. Each was posed in profile to exhibit the bigness of his testicles, the tightness of his sheath, the lumpy slopes of his formidable musculature. The copywriting fused enthusiastic adspeak and insider lingo. This or that bull was *faultless, big footed, sound as a cat. Moves with ease, comfort, and authority.* Others had *great scrotal genetics* and *excellent genomic data*. Mr. H Bogota Manso was an *excellent semen producer*. Play It Safe *scream[ed] female maker*. (Female calves are more economically viable for a dairy farm to make.) Plum Creek Paradox demonstrated an *uncanny ability to stamp his calves with long extended fronts, huge bone and foot size, and hair like a Heat Wave*.

Based in Clark, Missouri, Cattle Visions is one of a few dozen national bovine semen distribution centers in the US that store cryogenically frozen semen in liquid nitrogen freezers and ship orders on dry ice. I envisioned myself calling up Cattle Visions and asking if I could, as a writer—no, I would say journalist—tour the facilities and set up some interviews. I mapped the drive. Six hours. I could rent a car but I was low on funds. Halfway through my three-week residency, I was low on time, too.

My visions of Cattle Visions fogged.

There must be other ways in, I thought. I kept thinking.

ON THE PHONE with B, I shared my plan. I'm going to order some bull semen, I shared, proud of this creative approach.

Oh? they replied. What will you do with it?

I wasn't sure yet. My best idea was to eat it mixed with ice cream served with chocolate sprinkles on top. In this way I would "impregnate" myself with the bull's experiences—an embodied experiment that would grant me a kind of insider's access to the cattle genetics industry.

Hmm, they said, swishing the idea through their performer mind. I think you should take more risk.

I deflated. We'd been seeing each other more than a year, and I was coming to understand that no matter what level of creativity I demonstrated, they would remain unimpressed, if available and attractive as ever. More attractive. A challenge. But I saw their point.

You mean actually inseminate myself? I had thought of that, but—I explained about the unknown pathogens that bull semen can carry into the body. On the one hand, sires are thoroughly genetically screened and kept in immaculate health: One would expect the product to be pristine. On the other hand, the product is not necessarily screened for all elements that could potentially be harmful to humans.

Like I said—risk, B repeated. I heard metal scraping ceramic and pictured them at home in their studio apartment. They would be seated with excellent posture at their small wooden multipurpose table, savoring the extravagant meal they'd prepared, the contents of which they'd described in detail. They would be bringing their long-tined fork to their plush lips. They had me on speaker. Doesn't the semen get deep freezed?

Yes, but cryogenic freezing doesn't actually kill pathogens, I said. That's why it's used to keep the semen viable.

So use a barrier, they said. I heard them chewing, and I got up from the couch to start preparing my own meal: a burger (turkey) and greens.

Wouldn't that defeat the purpose? I liked my idea better. I could boil the semen and kill the risky things. Then chill and ingest risk-free, bringing it into my body through dairy, which would be funny: two forms of milk at once. Get it?

But you'd kill the semen too, they said. Wouldn't that defeat the purpose?

True. What was my purpose? I wasn't sure.

Think of the scene, they said. They had some experience with insemination, having assisted a few friends who were trying to get pregnant. They'd be happy to help me with this.

You *are* a Taurus, I pointed out. I was not one to miss an opportunity to erotically collaborate with B. And they were an excellent bull sire candidate. Their build was faultless. They moved with ease, comfort, and authority. I couldn't recall the size of their feet, but their hair glowed and flowed; it could be said to be *like a Heat Wave*.

We brainstormed. They would be the bull and I would be the cow. Or they would be the bull and I would be a teaser steer. I explained about teaser steers, castrated male cattle used as mount animals instead of teaser cows. Many farmers prefer steers to avoid the risk of accidental impregnation or spreading venereal disease (to cows, I suppose, since steers, too, can contract STIs). Whether cow or steer, the teaser animal is positioned with their backside before the bull, taunting him with their smells and holes. As soon as the bull mounts, the handler guides the erect penis into a rubber sleeve known as an artificial vagina—which could just as easily be called an artificial anus, or just a rubber sleeve.

My purpose was starting to clarify. I wanted to become a receptacle for the semen and take it into my body in some hot, creative, and maybe uncomfortable—risky—way.

I needed to be not the teaser steer, but the cow, I thought.

But I'd technically be a heifer, since a cow becomes a cow after giving birth to her first calf.

I'd start the scene as heifer. Then the act of creative impregnation would facilitate my transition into cow. Through this scene, I would at last step into the destiny of my childhood nickname: Megan Milks, the Cow.

I had it: the concept, the purpose, the arc.

B, never one to miss an opportunity for group sex, suggested we find a third, a co-top. They were thinking of logistics: one top could handle the semen, the other could do sexy things to the cow.

Another Taurus, I said. I'll draft the Lex ad tonight.

I DIDN'T DRAFT the Lex ad. I rolled around in anxiety instead. After hours of warmth and connection, B and I had ended our call coolly.

We've been on the phone for a really long time, I'd croaked, having lost my voice.

Just two lonely people whiling away the night, they'd said.

That was a little more general than I felt. So I'd countered. Or . . . two people who really like each other?

They neither confirmed nor denied this assessment. I cringed. I had been too cloying. Too open. Too something.

We ended the call. As though a door in my chest had flung loose, lonesomeness rushed in, a swift and bitter wind suggesting (according to Google's dictionary) not just aloneness but sadness or dejection over a lack of companionship; a feeling of separation from others.

When I feel lonesome, I think of Lonesome George, the giant Pinta tortoise who died in 2012, a conservation icon notable for having expressed little to no interest in mating. Lonesome George is what is considered an endling: the last of his kind. He was taken from his island in the Galapagos in 1972 and lived out the remainder of his life at the Charles Darwin Research Station on nearby Santa Cruz Island.

I first learned about Lonesome George at an asexuality studies conference, where the scholar Nicole Seymour read his sexual disinclination through an asexual lens. He's stayed with me ever since. Back home post-conference, I read everything about him that I could find. He'd lived a rich, full life of many chapters: taken from his home by conservationists, threatened with death by local fishermen, sexually stimulated by a graduate student in an effort to encourage mating. No wonder that, for much of his century on earth, Lonesome George preferred solitude.

So did I, often. But not that night, after an hours-long call with B. I set down my phone and grimaced, taking in my aloneness, this whole cute house I had to myself. But I missed B, I missed my cat, I missed my friends. I didn't want to work or write a Lex ad. I wanted to feel loved, or else to wallow in lonesomeness.

I started searching for the perfect bull donor to pass the time.

SOME OF MY friends who've perused human sperm donor profiles online have told me they had a strong feeling when they stumbled onto "the one." I saw my bull donor's photo and just knew.

PHF/DC King George 725 lives and grazes on a farm in southeastern Ohio. His semen is stored at and available for purchase from Cattle Visions. He is a handsome guy, deep-chested and solidly muscled, but so are all the advertised sires. In comparison to some other, much bigger bulls producing costlier semen, King George's size is modest. The most expensive units on Cattle Visions are five hundred dollars apiece. Their source, a pristine white Charolais bull named M&M Outsider 4003 PLD, has produced multiple show champions. But despite his magnificence, I was unmoved by M&M Outsider, whose head was tiny and countenance smug, and I definitely couldn't afford him.

By contrast, King George was humbler, his expression

shy and skeptical. A common American Angus, his coat was midnight and sleek, his dense muscularity softened by a thick layer of fat. I was compelled by his shine, his resignation, and his price tag—one unit of his semen sold for forty dollars. This is about average for bulls.

According to his donor page, King George's pedigree is "loaded with success":

> Limited use of King George has produced big results. His calves have added frame size, extention [sic] through their front one third and are extremely square and sound at the ground. He will work in a variety of situations and make females that can compete at any level.
>
> Has been used on heifers with no reported issues.[1]

King George's genetic merit was ample. He was free of undesirable genetic conditions, and his progeny were expected to exceed other Angus cattle (on average) in many of the desirable categories, including body weight, weaning weight, maternal milk, carcass weight, and marbling.

Bull sires are also called studs or donors, though the latter suggests voluntarism where it does not exist. Their lives vary significantly. I'm guessing from King George's affordability and the fact that his sperm is banked in another state that he lives on a smaller farm, where he may or may not have free range on pasture seasonally. At such a farm, a stud like King George might be led into the ejaculation stall one to three times a week, producing one to two spurts (or "collections") of semen each time.

At large breeding farms, a stud might be milked twice a day and never leave his stall. Bulls housed at distribution centers generally live out their lives inside barns, never leaving the enclosures due to health concerns. Some would say these animals lead pampered lives: They get air conditioning, mattresses, a balanced feed approved by nutritional scientists, an on-site vet, and frequent sexual stimulation.[2] One professor of dairy science who has otherwise been critical of the AI industry (artificial insemination, that is) has attested that there is no animal welfare issue at play in this setup.[3]

But I've seen a video of a four-year-old rescued bull stud being released into a field for the first time. You can measure the impact of his limited barn life by the euphoric intensity of his zoomies. He rushed, he bucked, he zigzagged. His hooves had never before touched pasture and the contact injected them with energy like fuel.

THE LEX AD would read something like this:

> Trans/nonbinary writer seeks second Taurus for co-topping scene involving bovine semen. You would not be handling the semen. Must be reliable with scheduling and okay with the scene being written about in a published essay. You would be pseudonymized. While your being a Taurus would add something special, please be in touch if you are interested in participating in this scene and yet are not a Taurus.

My Lex handle would be @bovinesemenexperiment, linked to a new Instagram account with the same handle and featuring King George's image as the profile pic and first and only post. I would wait to post until we had a sense of our time frame.

The plan was well laid. But that fall B and I were either in conflict or one of us was traveling. I thought we'd wait for Taurus season, but then we broke things off. The scene would remain fantasy.

I want to say I predicted this, though I can point to no evidence. I had taken the plan seriously and proceeded as if I believed we would execute it. But I'm not sure I fully bought into this particular cattle vision coming to fruition: me being co-topped, as a heifer, becoming cow. Was my imagination too puny? If I had been able to envision it more fully, more sharply, as a scene—here's me, kneeling in cow pose, on . . . my bed? B's? the floor? . . . big blank for the sexy things the faceless third party is doing to me . . . now I'm being entered from behind, muhh, by what? An insemination gun? A dildo? A fist? Would a stronger vision have pushed it into reality?

I had done enough role-play with B to expect a certain degree of disjunction between my visions and theirs. We'd agree on a scene, only for them to change it completely as we inhabited it. I'd show up ready to play the masseur only to learn they were a hustler I'd hired, which changed the dynamic completely. But I'm still the masseur? Yes, you've hired me as a body to massage. But shouldn't you be massaging me? I thought you wanted to be the masseur!

My favorite of our scenes were realized over text—writing being my safe space. The best was an ecosexual scene I helmed during a sext date while they were away. I had sketched out a loose, three-part structure beforehand; I did some research; and I visualized it—where would B's body be in time and space? where would mine be? from what vantage point would the scene be narrated? We started off with B in a forest clearing, sunbathing on a mossy slab. As their body heated up, excited moss tendrils began investigating their skin and hair. In Part 2, three small garter snakes dropped down from a tree branch above them. They slithered around B's nipples and cock while the moss continued to fondle them.

Then it was Part 3, and my turn. I slithered out from my hiding spot, revealing myself as the narrator taking pleasure in watching from the woods. My character was a giant milk snake, I announced: a subspecies of king snake with red, cream, and black bands. *i'm very hot and thick,* I wrote. *you may call me ssssir*. Before long my hemipenes emerged, and we were all having a very good time.

That was early in the relationship. A year later, we couldn't agree on the kind of relationship we wanted, just like we could never agree on our scenes. While this suggested a fundamental impasse, often enough we could reroute around that, find ways to live in the easy parts of our dynamic, in some unagreed-upon form of relationship that often functioned very well. But then we'd find our way back to the impasse, until one day we were stuck in the impasse all the time.

So we broke up. We never did the bull scene.

Is fantasy unrealized lesser than fantasy realized? Might both—like "artificial" and "real" vaginas, like "artificial" and "natural" insemination—claim status as some form of the real? We made a real thing together: the idea of a scene. That could be enough.

But I want the real material. I want King George's extracted matter. I want to feel what it's like to participate in the beef and dairy economy. In this way, I can get closer to the bull, and to the cow.

A year later, King George is as handsome as ever, and his samples are still available, still forty bucks a straw, though shipping costs have jumped to $120. If I'm going to pay that much for shipping, I think, I might as well buy two. I bump up my order.

I wonder what Cattle Visions thinks of my purchase. I doubt they ship such small quantities often, especially to apartments in Brooklyn. I wonder if they are noting my last name and making jokes to one another about the kind of milking I'll do.

"MILKING THE BULL" is also slang for masturbation (of a penis). Read together with the idiomatic meaning—an exercise in futility—the suggestion is that masturbation, being nonreproductive, is futile.

Writing about oneself is considered by some to be a masturbatory exercise: self-indulgent, unproductive, bad. I don't agree, obviously: my fiction is all Self, Self, Self, in messy wrapping, and here I am again, dressed in the personal essay.

To milk something means to extract from it as much as you can, whether that's milk, semen, or self. All of these are salable products.

Right now I'm milking the self while surrounded by mirrors. One wall of my new apartment is taken up by seven full-length mirror panels all lined up in a row; on another, two more panels, also full-length. (I didn't install these; they were here when I moved in.) All day long I walk beside myself while I'm taking a break from writing about myself. While I often enough like what I see, what I write, overall it's sometimes a bit much. I find I would rather be milking the cows. And the bulls. In this way I would escape myself and the obligations of the personal essay.

An essay can be anything, of course—the blank page an open cow, each word charging it up with genetic destiny.

This afternoon I'm eating lunch with a friend who's in town (she shares) to have dinner with her and her partner's future sperm donor. He agreed to take on this role some years ago, and now they're forming a plan.

I just ordered semen, I say, laughing. From a bull.

She wants to know how it works. The bull is masturbated, I say. Wait, that's not the right language. The bull is—the cock is stimulated. He's given a hand job? No. It's like a sleeve and a cup.

Thinking of the word "masturbated" reminds me of Lonesome George. Because he was an endling, conservationists at the research station encouraged him to mate with female tortoises close in species in order to preserve his line. He wouldn't do it. Lonesome George was uninterested in mating and ensuring the survival of his lineage. Perhaps, scientists speculated, he had sustained an injury to his genitals. Or maybe, they considered, he had lived such an isolated life, he simply didn't know what to do.

A Swiss graduate student, a woman named Sveva Grigioni, tried to teach him to use his penis by "touching him strategically" or "masturbating him" for a few hours a day, her hands covered with pheromones from the female tortoises' genital secretions.[4] Sveva stroked Lonesome George's penis with her hand on a regular schedule. They developed a special relationship. In this way she awakened his interspecies sexuality.

Then, after the end of her four-month research fellowship, she left.

Right, so, "masturbating" means either to stimulate one's own genitals for sexual pleasure, or to stimulate someone else's genitals for sexual pleasure. But even leaving aside the question of consent, the activities involving both Georges are designed not for sexual pleasure so much as for the reproductive extraction of semen.

Shortly before his death, Lonesome George reversed course and successfully mated with some of the female tortoises, but the resulting eggs weren't viable. Lonesome George's line died with him.

By contrast, King George's line will never die. His semen will be used to produce many offspring in his life and after his death, notwithstanding the units taken out of this economy and shipped to my city apartment.

THE TANK'S CONVEX lid is held down with a rubber clasp, tied firm with a zip tie. I clip off the tie with pliers and pull back the helmet-like top. Inside is another tank, this one more serious, with warnings: *LIQUID NITROGEN*.

I replace the cover. Everything I read about liquid nitrogen floods me with panic. Risk of explosion, of asphyxiation, death. Online tips suggest handling with a buddy. I'm alone. It's the middle of the night. Is this how I die? For a poorly planned erotic experiment? For art?

I pull up to the company's website and gather that the tank isn't splish-splashing with liquid nitrogen; rather, the inner canister has dry ice stored in the walls. Its lid is loosely attached to allow gas to escape, preventing buildup and explosion. But I need to keep it in a well-ventilated place because it eats up a room's oxygen, and I'll need that oxygen to breathe.

I move the tank to rest under an open window.

I wish briefly that B were here. Bullish, they'd know what to do. But I am not incapable, and I will do this myself. I ask the internet what happens if you transfer cryogenically frozen semen to a lay freezer. This won't keep the semen viable, but I find I don't care about its potentiality. I see nothing that suggests the tube will explode. I take my contacts out and put on my glasses. I tie back my hair and protect my body with boots and gloves. I grab tongs and the unused second tier of a new metal dish rack. I open the tank and cut a second zip tie on the lid of the canister. I pull the inner seal up and step back.

Vapor rises.

With tongs, I lift the metal hook that holds the interior basket: there it is, a thin tube of glass and metal, with *King George* on the label in childish handwriting. I let the tube fall back in and line the dish rack with paper towels. I reach in with my tongs and pull the sample out, dropping it on the paper towels. I seal the canister and close the tank. I cover the sample with another set of paper towels and set my timer for twelve minutes, during which the sample will thaw at room temperature.

The paper towels seemed important. They would prevent the glass from sticking to the metal.

When the timer goes off, I transfer the sample to the freezer, nestling it upright within the dish rack.

I try to go to sleep but can't, worried that the gas will seep into my throat and I will never wake up.

The bull semen is in my freezer, its contents dying. I make it through the night.

IN THE FREEZER it stays, locked upright by the grid of the dish rack.

It stays there and stays there. I travel to London and it stays there. I foster kittens; it stays there. I visit farms upstate; it stays there. I get through my semester; it stays there. I go to Portland for a teaching gig; it stays there. I write a bunch; it stays there. I open the freezer an average of six times a day; sometimes I say hi but more often forget that it's there.

It hits me one day, the lonesomeness. Or one day I have empty hours enough to feel it creeping in.

The time has come, I think, to busy myself with King George.

I EXTRACT THE glass wand from the freezer and warm it in a cold-water bath, then in warmer water.

Once warmed, I mix it with a squirt of lube in a small

bowl. I suck it up with a plastic syringe attached to the ejaculating dildo I bought months ago for this exercise.

I ready the dildo and position myself on hands and knees, waiting patiently as the bull approaches from behind.

I hear him, the soft snort, the pawing. Feel his breath hot on my backside. I lift my tail to send him my smells.

As the bull assumes position, my breathing quickens. Now his hooves are on my shoulders, his pizzle finds my hole. He's heavy. The shape is weird: long pole with an angled head. It's quick and mean and I think of the guy in the documentary film *Zoo* who died from penetration by a stallion. But that guy's not me, and I—I can take it. A few grunts and he spurts inside me—a fizzy feeling, a frrrpt. He licks my back—my skin shudders, then relaxes—and slides off.

I hold my ass up to keep it in because I just have this feeling. If I absorb King George's semen, I'll absorb his life.

And I'm right.

His story expands inside me.

*

*

*

*

*

*

*

* * *

* * * * * *

* * * * * * * * *

Rough laps: a sticky sound, a rhythmic pressure. Then my tongue, searching, leading the way. My field of vision blurs and I can't make sense of anything—my legs wobble, my throat vibrates. There it is, the sweetness. I tug until it streams down my throat.

The human punches a tag through one of my ears. Pressure, then a pop. Everyone else has a tag so I need one, too. I like fitting in with the herd. The sweetness I drink, it comes from my dam. Her name is Georgina—that's why I'm George. (Matriarchal society.) I don't know who my sire is, but I'll be one, too. Is that why I'm a king?

Breeding happens with human arms and some sort of tube. Georgina explained it, but I won't be a cow, so I've dropped it from my mind.

I won't be a steer either. I'm not sure why. One morning Velvet Machine and Total Recall get pulled from the herd and when they come back, they have cuts. I sniff Total's ointment and sneeze. Maybe the humans forgot about me. Maybe my understuff will transform to an udder.

That hasn't happened.

On the pasture I hang with Velvet and Total. We like to find our way out of whatever paddock we're in. There's usually a stretch where the fence is low enough to get over it or high enough to get under. We don't go far. Just hang around beyond the fence feeling free. I'll pretend not to hear Georgina's nasal drawl calling me back. When we see the human coming up on his four-wheeler we scatter. I think he likes the chase, zigzagging behind us. We like it too. The rush!

We're grazing on the high hill when we hear calls. We go still, turn our ears forward. Velvet looks scared. Total looks confused. I zero in on my dam's voice, a call I haven't heard before. It's a warning and, I think, a goodbye. I get close enough to see her loaded in with the others. I figure we'll be on the next truck, and we are, a few days later—but we never see the others again.

When the truck stops, the smells are all new. Humans we've never seen before unload us into a strange field, with strange heifers and strange steers and hay bales. We hang out by the lesser hay bale and wait for the others to invite us in.

I stay here for a while. Then I'm separated out and moved to the bull pen.

I've never seen a full-grown bull before. He's massive with a tiny head—like something pinched his ears in place and stretched out the rest of his body. The thick hump on his neck must store future bulk. He grunts in my direction and returns to his hay, spittle clinging to his mouth as he chews.

He is hulk and veins and spittle and hooves. Am I going to become like that? I don't want to. It's hard to imagine moving around under all that body.

Later I understand the appeal. When he stands broadside, flutters his muscles, and groans, the whole farm snaps to attention. His name is Midnight Magic.

Midnight teaches me everything I need to know about being a sire, the same way his former pen-mate taught him. It'll seem stupid, he says. But that's life.

It's usually the bigger human who works us out. Sometimes the narrower one. When it's my turn, I follow the human to the stall on the other end, where the dummy's set up, where we have a bit of privacy. The dummy is there to activate my impulses. I mount it and my underthing comes out.

At first I was nervous it wouldn't happen like Midnight said, but he had coached me through some practices, and I did fine.

Midnight is cranky but nice and he seems to like my company. I like having him around too. We nuzzle and maneuver around each other in the dirty hay. He's been trying to prepare me for what he calls his inevitable departure, but I can't believe it. He's always been here. How could he ever leave?

But he leaves and doesn't come back.

That's when the lonesomeness starts. And all my questioning.

Like: If I'm bred for this, does that mean I'm meant for it? Are the two the one and the same? And: If Midnight hadn't shown me, would I have known what to do?

I knew, somehow . . . something inside me knew. But how? How does a body decide what and when and how to mount, and where to put one's parts? When it happens, it's as though something inside me has taken over. Is that thing me or not-me?

When I enter the collection stall, I try to track the causal chain, hoping to isolate the trigger that signals my body to jump forward the way that it does. Is it the light whisper of the fan hitting my underbelly? The strength of Midnight's left-behind musk?

It seems like it's one thing, then another. Or it's a confusion. I just know that something happens. And I perform.

Sometimes I make up stories to improve the feeling. Like . . . now I'm being tickled by tall grasses. Or . . . now a human being is summoning me through writing.

That's not a story, is it? That's you.

You purchased my material, and now I'm giving you more.

I can feel you inside me while I'm inside you. Pretty trippy.

We have our animal connection. That's how we understand each other. We're talking in animal.

I wonder when it was that I expressed the semen you've brought into your body. I was here on this farm. No question about that.

It must have been after the encounter I had with another

visitor, also not of my kind. Since it's encoded into my matter, it's already happened.

I remember it. A low and dismal day. Cold, wet. Just me and my hay. Me and my heft. Me and my tub of water that tasted like my own spitty spit.

I didn't know what to do with all this me. It itched.

I couldn't remember the last time I'd seen pasture, or the herd—they had been moved further out, and I rarely caught glimpses of them. Without Midnight to rub against, I took to the scratching post more and more. That fateful day I closed my eyes, rubbed on that post, and let myself feel the lonesomeness.

A warm wind tickled my tail end. I heard an alien sound behind me, something between a bray and a squeal. I turned to find a shelled creature had appeared on the hay. An elder, kind of faded. Craggy smile. Two holes for a snout. Long searching neck, beaked mouth. Rough skin. Old, yet handsome. Dignified. Kind.

I lowered my head in a posture I hoped was curious, not threatening. I sniffed, but it came out like a snort.

The creature didn't flinch. In fact, he lifted himself off the ground—slowly, registering my wariness—and floated around to my front end. Soon he was hovering—though without anything like wings—in the air before my head. He looked into one of my startled eyes, then the other, then rubbed his bald head against the plane of my cheek.

Nervous, I stepped away, then changed my mind. This was the only company I would have until stall time.

I leaned into him and rubbed back.

He got a little excited then and moved to press his bulging body against my thick chest. I sidestepped, taken by surprise. He was heavier and harder than I expected. When he nuzzled my ear with his beak, I relaxed. Holding my ground, I pressed against him as he pressed against me. The pressure was nice.

My underthing was stretching forward, and my questions fired up. Why was my body doing that? What was it that activated this response? I was, without doubt, responding.

Registering the change in my body temperature or scent, he maneuvered around my other side and rubbed his rough shell down the length of my body. My questioning turned into something else, something like want. I shifted my weight toward him to improve the friction. When he got to the end, he took in a whiff and let out his alarming bark. I swiveled my neck back to see his tiny head bobbing in the air to meet my gaze. I snorted my desire.

The creature understood. He floated to an appropriate height, tilted his ridged belly against my back, and . . . but I lost my nerve and covered myself with my tail. He adjusted his position and patted my haunch. I breathed in. I felt safe. It felt right. I huffed an exhale, and I lifted my tail.

He entered me. The feeling was great. He pumped into my hole with an evenness that suggested patient industry. Right when I felt a kind of tightness and a lingering thrust, he pulled out. I heard the semen splat on the hay, and I came with a guttural moan that startled me.

Lonesome George—for that was his name—was not surprised. He nuzzled my back with his beak, then lowered himself to the ground. He held my gaze as he lapped up my semen with a long, red tongue. Then he vanished.

Immediately I was lonesome.

His milky substance pooled on the dirt. I brought my snout down and gave it a reciprocal lick. Brackish, like the sea, with a vegetal quality. It tasted ancient, fermented . . . lonesome. I slurped it up.

Soon his memories, his voice, his gruff baritone filled my mind. And then I was him, or he was me.

His story expanded inside me.

*

*

*

*

*

*

*

* * *

* * * * * *

* * * * * * * * *

There are many Georges, I have learned: Curious George, Boy George. King George. There are plain Georges too.

To most, my name is Lonesome George.

I am the last of the Pinta tortoises, and I'm dead.

Though I have come to know some human languages fairly well, it has taken me a long time to understand the word *lonesome*. For a while, I thought it was simply the name I was given; I did not know it had further meaning. "Are you Lonesome George? Are you Lonesome George?" visitors would ask, with condescending smiles. Yes, I thought back. That's what you're calling me.

What they were really asking was "are you lonesome, George?" After enough children asked their parents what *lonesome* meant, I understood. It meant I was alone, but more than that. It meant I was alone and yearned not to be.

Was I lonesome?

Am I?

Are you?

I WAS BORN on a different island, not that of the Research Station. My island had silty shorelines and skittery crabs. Splayed cactus fronds. Lush, delectable grasses. The brown finches that plucked ticks from my folds. Crevasses. The leathering sun. The sea. Home.

I would be, I knew, the last of my kind.

Had I always known this? I can't remember a time when I did not.

Time moves differently for tortoises. Our lives are longer than most. They stretch.

I had a family. My home was populous, busy, full. I haven't mentioned the barking sea lions, basking iguanas, and swooping, chattering gulls. The colonies of insects and their songs. Or the ocean. I could see it from almost anywhere. I could hear it everywhere. The roar still hums in my ears.

Then the beginning of great change. I saw my tortoise kin hunted. Slung on branches and taken to ships. I watched my mother get carted away. I watched my father spurn the other female on the island. Soon she was taken too.

We tortoises aren't built to fight. We're built to graze, to feel the sun on our shells, the cool mud on our cheeks. We're built to lumber, and shelter, and stay. We are the keepers of the island, holding its history in our hearts.

We could not anticipate the swiftness of change. My father passed on what knowledge he could. Then he too was captured.

I WAS OFTEN hungry.

We tortoises are great survivalists. We can persist without food or water for many months. But we would rather be eating than not.

Before, I spent my waking life in the grasses with which our island was once lushly abundant. I snacked on guava and splayed cactus fronds. I ambled, making my circuits. I rested in the safety of my shell.

Then the goats came, left behind by humans. They depleted the once-plentiful grasses.

There was a goat who licked the flat plane of my head. My companion. My friend.

Sometimes she would rest on my shell. Sometimes I would march with her perched on my back. I amused myself with seeing how far I could go without waking her.

Then my goat friend was shot.

More wardens returned to shoot more goats. When they spotted me surrounded by rocks and feeding at a tree, they pointed a rifle at me. Then they lowered it and pointed some blocky thing at me instead. I would come to know this as a camera. I've seen many different cameras in my time. That was the first.

One human left and the other stayed with me. I tried to lose him, but I am slow.

We tortoises are slow creatures. Time doesn't run out. We don't rush to eat, or to mate, or escape. We are the species most fit to survive. And yet we are dying. Or dead.

When they found me I thought, no more time.

I knew what would happen. I had seen it happen to my kin. Rolled onto their backs and slung onto branches.

The branch snapped, and I fell on my shell. The wardens unleashed me and I thought myself free. But they looped a rope around my back foot and tied me to a large cactus.

I marched off, first one way, then another. The rope kept stopping me short. I changed direction. I changed direction again. I could not escape.

I THOUGHT I'D be reunited with my kin. Would they recognize me? I'd grown so large.

No. Only me. Alone in my cage, then alone in my pen when we arrived at the research center. Was I lonesome then? Probably. Where were my finches? Where were the iguanas and lizards and ticks? My favorite cave? My memory falters.

EVENTUALLY THE PEN became my own. My home.

I had a new friend in Fausto, my human keeper, who came to see me on a schedule, to feed me and talk to me. I also met Sveva, my special friend. She massaged my penis once a day.

The research scientists had been mingling me with the other tortoises, the females, whom I spurned. I believe the scientists assumed I didn't know how to mate. Perhaps there is some truth to that. But more powerful was the distaste I felt for engaging in such behavior.

I had lived a long time. I was the last of my kind, and that was right. I wished they would leave me alone.

Then Sveva came, and she was wonderful. I snuffed up the strange elixir, the pheromones her gloves were bathed in comingling with her own unique scent profile.

After Sveva left, I was more lonesome than I had ever been before. So I tried. I really tried. I mounted the other tortoises. I ejaculated. First one of them, then the other laid eggs. None hatched.

There is no future for my species. I am the last and I accept this fate.

AFTER I DIED, the taxidermists stretched my neck far and high, a posture endearing to viewers. For me it recalls hard-to-reach fronds and cactus pads. The eager march toward Fausto on Mondays, Wednesdays, and Fridays, when he'd bring a branch and shake it aloft, teasing me and making me work. I'd raise my head obligingly, snatch a leaf. Chew.

I think of this ritual now and there's a phantom snap in my jaw.

They sculpted my wattle into artful striations. They emptied me of my organs and stretched my skin over plaster, but some part of me remains, attached to my shell. Alone in a glass box, with glass for eyes. My lids glued open, I'm frozen in time, watching them watching me, when I would more gladly be left alone.

They positioned me with a leg half lifted as though I'm on my way somewhere.

And I am. Time hasn't run out. In you, my life grows longer and longer.

In you, my story lives on.

NOTES

1. "PHF/DC King George 725," Cattle Visions, February 22, 2017, https://cattlevisions.com/phf-dc-king-george-725/.
2. Kirk Kardashian, *Milk Money: Cash, Cows, and the Death of the American Dairy Farm* (University of New Hampshire Press, 2012), 84.
3. Kardashian, *Milk Money*, 84.
4. "Tracking Giant Galapagos Tortoises," BBC Earth, YouTube, March 23, 2019, https://www.youtube.com/watch?v=rEp6pkkYOgE; Henry Nicholls, *Lonesome George: The Life and Loves of a Conversation Icon* (Macmillan, 2006), 26–32.

Cat-Cow

We start with cat-cow. I arch my back and tuck my head, curving into myself slowly and with control. I am concave, caved in, sort of; I can only approximate the feline so much. At the instructor's cue, I drop my back and broaden my chest, becoming cow. In some ways the posture is awkward, exposing—ass out, belly down—but the chest is strong and the head's held high. I find the solidity in it.

Arch. I am a cat, sinuous and supple.

Drop. I am a cow, a noble brick.

Inhale: cat.

Exhale: cow.

We stay here, alternating between these postures, for some time.

THE GYM ISN'T far, but Svetlana picks me up. I got Claude to eat something, I report in the car. A bisque for senior cats. He likes to lap. He's nineteen, I remind her. As if that says everything.

He's nineteen and has kidney disease and arthritis and a lingering respiratory infection. His kidney values were improved when I took him to the vet a few months ago, but suddenly he's not eating much. Last week I took a short trip upstate to visit an animal sanctuary. In my absence he had good support, or I thought he did, but he hasn't been the same since. I nearly took him to urgent care over the weekend, but he hates it so much. I hate it so much. Instead I bought him new foods and a microwave, finally, to warm up his meals. He seems to like some of it. A little. Then he vomits.

In the Pilates studio, we continue cat-cow, warming up the core and spine. I arch my back toward the ceiling and imagine myself as Claude. Lately when he stretches, he loses balance. I maintain mine. I shouldn't have gone to Kingston. I chose to visit an animal sanctuary as my own animal slid into decline. Now he's dying.

Maybe not. He still cuddles and communicates. Gives me long looks and slow cat eyes, tries to groom my head. He keeps us in our routine. In the mornings he sits beside my chair, waiting for me to finish my eggs and give him the okay to leap into my lap, something he still does with relative ease.

We agree that our TV hour is the best part of the day. His cue is the wedge pillow I set up tall-ways at the head of the bed, the laptop I drag over. While I prepare the viewing station, he waits on his pillow, alert and often impatient. I settle down. I pat his spot. He hops over, circles once, twice, then nestles into the crook of my knee, his body long, spread out on his side. He's an all-black American shorthair with deep green eyes; his goofy underbite is his most distinctive feature. As I scratch his tender underarm, he gazes up at me and yaps, his happy sound.

He must be doing better, I think. The new food is helping. We have time.

We settle on Andrea Arnold's documentary *Cow*.

LUMA, THE DOCUMENTARY'S subject, is in labor when we meet her.

She's in a muddy pen. Appears in distress. Two farmhands coax her into another area. We hear her snorting, see her ears twitching. Her water breaks with a gushing smack upon the ground.

Next we see hooves out, a thin rope of burlap tied around them. One farmhand pulls while the other tends to the emerging head. *Steady* . . . The calf's body drops to the ground, a slick and leggy bundle. Hay straws cling to the wet body as Luma turns and begins licking up the sticky afterbirth. Her tongue's strokes are rhythmic and tender, private seeming, intimate. The calf is staring wild-eyed at the camera, and I'm hoping we're zoomed in, that there's distance between these animals and the crew.

In the next sequence, the calf is standing, seeking her mother's teats. Her narrow tongue curls against Luma's underbelly. Now as Luma returns to the milking parlor, the calf is intercepted with a bottle of milk—but she's more solid now, more robust. Some days or months have passed. Again we see the calf being bottle-fed, this time with Luma looking on. She installs her body between the farmer and her calf, but the farmer nudges her away.

The calf is tagged at the ear—504481—and moved into her own pen, where she struggles to feed on a rubber teat. Luma snorts. Calls out to her calf. At the feeding trough, Luma refuses to eat, rests her head against another cow's belly. She is milked. She kicks off the machine.

When Luma is moving, the camera follows her closely from behind, giving us the feeling of inhabiting her perspective. From this view we see the bony, curvy back from which the majority of her body is slung. A cow like Luma weighs around 1,500 pounds, most of it in the belly, most of it water weight. During this one ten-month lactation period, Luma will produce much more than that in milk: something like 23,000 pounds.

CLAUDE IS DOWN to seven.

He lifts himself carefully, stretches—arch—and resettles in the other direction. I am simultaneously with Claude and in the world of the film. I rest my hand lightly on Claude's side, where he's fleshiest, and watch him fall into twitchy slumber. I imagine he's dreaming of my roommate's cat Menace, who spends her time pretending to hunt him until her fantasy tilts into the real. Then she's pouncing, hissing. She does not respect Claude's clearly expressed boundaries; he's feeble and therefore prey.

Maybe he's gripping her throat in his jaws until she submits or, better, dies.

Maybe she's morphing into Pinto, a former roommate's cat who was even more of a bruiser. Maybe Claude has gone to find Ari, his other favorite human, and has been intercepted by Pinto lying in wait behind the curve of the hallway, ready to pounce out and bully him back to our room.

Maybe Ari is rescuing him, comforting him, letting him lick her long hair.

Maybe the hair then morphs into fur—the long, abundant fur of his brother Elliott, who died five years ago. He's disciplining Elliott's fur with his rough tongue on my bed in our Madison apartment, then they're jumping through my open window and racing into the backyard raspberry bushes. They're chasing flying beetles; they're digging in the mulch and pissing and covering the smell. Maybe he's back in

Chicago now, roaming our dusty attic with Elliott, cobwebs stuck in his whiskers.

Or maybe he's dreaming of me. I have been trying to cede his dreamspace to a world without me, as though such a world could exist. I've been with him most of his life, my smells a constant presence. Now it's morning, and he's hopping over my hips in bed, back and forth, determinedly. Now he's jumping onto my desk and sauntering past my Zoom room, enjoying the admiration of viewers from many states. He's chasing the knotted shoelace as I swing it this way and that, nestling against me during TV time. He's settling on the pillow next to mine, where he is.

Which becomes the litter box he's straining to poop in, hind legs shaking. Which becomes the dreaded cat carrier. We drive to the vet, and the sun strobing through the mesh is the laser light he's chasing in circles on my bed. The red light slows, grows into a lumbering roach that is a dying sparrow that is Elliott after he got his lion cut and seemed to shrink by half. Elliott's fur is the rug and Claude is eating it, suckling it. Teat. Biscuits. Biscuits. His tail twitches. Rests.

His breathing cycle hitches, then restarts. Big full inhale. Deep exhale.

His mother. Maybe he's dreaming of her.

LUMA'S CALF IS put into a pen with two other calves. Her horn nubs are burned off. Eventually the three calves are led onto a truck that drives them to another farm, where they're deposited into another pen. They buck around and kick up hay.

We see a cow carcass in mud.

Back to Luma. A vet injects hormones into her flank to encourage cycling. Pretty soon she's in heat, agitatedly mounting other cows. She is led into a pen where a black bull awaits. The mating ritual is sensual: The bull sniffs her backside, nostrils flared with arousal, the ring on his nose flipping up as he inhales a long whiff. He nuzzles her and licks her haunch. She welcomes the attention. After, she rests her chin on the slope of his back.

The vet pushes an ultrasound wand into Luma's vagina while looking at a screen that hangs down from a visor. *And she is pregnant*, he announces.

A joyful phase: The cows are let to pasture for the season. Their glee is powerful, tangible, charged. They jostle each other in their impatience to get to the grass. Luma's chomping is as intimate and sensual as the shots of her licking up the afterbirth.

We see her drinking in the wide night sky, the twilight. And the sun.

She gives birth again, this time to an all-black calf. It's her sixth, we learn. Luma headbutts the camera.

As she's led from her calf to the milking parlor, she exhibits a frantic energy. When she returns, she watches her calf being moved out of the pen and bellows repeatedly.

Now it's Christmas. Luma seems not to be walking well. She staggers into the parlor and needs to be stabilized with wood planks.

Then she is woken at an odd hour and led out of the barn alone. Her swollen udder is low, close to dragging. It looks painful. She can barely walk on the cold cement. The farmer leaves her for a moment in an isolated pen, then returns with a yellow bucket of feed. She eats, tentatively at first, watching him. When he leaves, she noses into the bucket with more fervor.

THE GUNSHOT STARTLES us both. I jolt, and Claude sits up, alarmed.

THE DROP IS immediate, a heavy collapse. Fifteen hundred pounds slamming the floor. The last shot captures Luma's head on the concrete, her dark eyes unfocused and going glassy. She heaves an exhale. A shorter snort. A pause. A last long release. She's gone.

THE SCREEN GOES dark. I'm shaking. Claude knocks his head against my hand for pets. Eventually he flops down and sinks back to sleep. I need a chaser. *Inside the Mind of a Cat* is ultimately boring but its blandness soothes my system. I make some notes. Inhale. Exhale.

I set up Claude's night food and clean out the litter box, which I've pulled into my room to separate him from Menace. I turn off the light and slide under the covers, which is his cue to take a poop, which is my cue to get up, grab the poop with tissues, and bring it into the bathroom to flush. I wash my hands and return to bed. I'm still disturbed by the farmer's betrayal of Luma. And am I so different?

The wrong food: a betrayal. Nothing fresh; everything dead and processed. The wrong playmates: betrayal. Any visit to the vet, even when it has been essential for the continuation of his life. Each time I've forcibly held him and squirted medication into his mouth. All the times I've waited until he got comfy in my lap so I could squeeze his paws one by one and trim his nails. The cat sitter who didn't clean out the litter box once in my absence: betrayal. That awful year in which he was made to share space with a dog. Though he kind of loved being chased by the dog. The countless times he's been made to give up his pillow for my partners and dates. All the bonds he developed with people who swept in and out of his life without explanation or goodbyes. My love, I think, gazing at his scrawny, diminished body. How I've betrayed you.

I pat his side lightly. His eyes gleam at me in the dark. He mews. I scratch his head. We drop to sleep.

LUMA'S DEATH WAS humane. It takes me a second viewing of the film, and more research on farm practices, to understand this. Luma was not killed prematurely. Her body was wearing out and she was struggling to move. She was given a last pleasure—her favorite food—before being killed without suffering.

This farm, a midsize family farm in the UK, aims to give its animals good lives. Luma spent most of her life on pasture. In the cold months, she had warm shelter and attentive care. She lived among other cows and was bred naturally, with hired bulls. She was given ample water and food, and her health was monitored closely.

Culling on dairy farms means to get rid of cows. Farmers cull cows who are diseased, broken, lame, spent, or "open" for too long—which means they are not successfully breeding. Farmers take culling decisions seriously. Some cows are sent to sanctuaries. Some are sold to other farms. Some are sent to the slaughterhouse to be processed as beef. Others are killed on-site.

Most dairy Holsteins are considered spent when they are six years old. Luma was seven or eight. Yes. It's true that a cow like Luma could live from fifteen to twenty years if not subject to the life-shrinking conditions of the dairy farm, and if she were viewed as worthy of life beyond her production value.

But a cow is expensive to care for, requiring a vast amount of water, energy, labor, equipment, and land. Farmers who rely on dairy income must pay attention to their margins or their dairies will not survive. When dairies don't survive, their cows are sold or slaughtered.

I'M SUPPOSED TO be in Virginia this weekend seeing my family for Christmas. I cancel because Claude is in decline.

At the urgent care clinic, it's me and Claude. I'm wishing I had asked someone to come with us, but it seemed like too big of an ask. Carley offered and I said no, thanks, I'll be fine. I also have some shame. I don't want anyone to see how bad Claude is, how bad I've let him get before I've taken him in. That's not true. I've taken him in several times these past two years. And now, the urgent care folks do not think him so urgent. His vitals seem fine, so when other animals show up, we get bumped. There's a holiday staff party going on—I can hear laughter and chatter through the door. After an hour I text B: I'm considering leaving. I'm worried for Claude. He probably needs to use the bathroom. He probably needs water. B says to give it a bit longer. A half hour later, I advocate for us more firmly. My cat is old and in a lot of pain. When will we be seen?

He's taken back. I wait for a call from the doctor. After twenty minutes, no call, so I duck out to grab a bite, and the doctor calls while I'm across the street. It's windy and cold, and we're not communicating well by phone. When she asks why I brought him in, I say he has early stage kidney disease—but his values had been coming down—but now he's not eating. What are the options? He's nineteen, I tell her, it might be that time.

The doctor asks: Do you mean time to put him down?

I balk. No, no. I mean, it might be that time when—I'm flustered. I don't know what I mean. I mean it might be that time—like his kidney values are getting worse. Like he's at the next stage.

Oh, she says, still seeming confused. What are you hoping we can do?

I don't know, I reply, also confused. What are the options?

She'll run some tests and call me back.

When she calls back, she tells me his kidney values are so elevated they are unreadably high. The options: Leave him in the hospital for two to three nights for fluid therapy that won't do much to improve his condition, or euthanize.

What? I say. What?

I ask about cost. Three to eight thousand for hospital stay. Eight hundred for euthanasia.

She tells me to think about it and let the person at the desk know my decision.

At this point it's past midnight. I want counsel but I don't want to bother my friends, who are likely asleep. Keeping him here would cost money I don't have. We would be apart. And he's in so much pain.

Later I will wish I had seen the third option: to say no. To bring him home, schedule an end-of-life appointment, and let us have a few more days.

But there are no appointments. It's two days before Christmas. My usual vet is booked out till January. The earliest appointment I could get at a different clinic was for five days away. I don't think he'll make it that long.

Now I wish I had scheduled at-home euthanasia weeks before this. I didn't think to research pet death until he was dead.

We have ten minutes alone, together in the room. He

brightens and lifts himself up when he sees me, more alert than he's been in weeks. It's hard to reconcile that with the report of his unreadable kidney values.

The hardest part was when he crawled back into the carrier, ready to go home. He understood something wrong was going on and resisted. Also I kept inadvertently squeezing the needle taped to his forearm for the injection, causing him pain.

He had been declining for months. Years. He was aging. He was going to die.

We had to pull him out of the carrier in order to expose his leg so we could push the injection into the tube.

It was hard to distinguish his dead body from his live body. I didn't catch his last breath. When I shifted my hand from under his head, he didn't lift it. His cooling. His flaky fur—stress flakes. His eyes got very moist and dilated. I couldn't close them. Cats' eyelids aren't like ours.

I took a last photo of him, of us together, before the doctor came in. And a photo of his body. A little blood came out of his right nostril at the end.

SOME WOULD SAY death by gunshot is cruel and inhumane. Many would say it's a kindness. It's part of the responsibility a dairy farmer has to care for their cows. And it's not without cost.

There is an emotional cost to killing an animal you've cared for for many years.

There is a cost to removing the body.

It's possible Luma was processed, that is, butchered and prepared for human consumption. The market would not consider meat from a cow like Luma desirable: The longer a cow lives, the tougher the meat. Gamier cow meat might go into canned soups and stews or be processed as ground beef. In the UK, processing a cow like Luma would cost something like 2,800 pounds. Only about 40 percent of a cow carcass is edible. The rest is abattoir waste and goes to a rendering factory.

If not processed for meat, her body would have been disposed of through burial, incineration, composting, or rendering. Burial requires a trackhoe and an available and appropriately isolated plot of land where a carcass can decompose without polluting water sources. The United Kingdom, where Luma's farm is located, and where mad cow disease devastated the industry in the 1980s and 1990s, has banned the burial of fallen livestock in order to prevent the spread of disease, with exceptions in case of weather events and animal health crises. Incineration is more costly than burial and also comes with pollution risks. Composting, a newer alternative to carcass waste management, seems promising, but means that the hormones and antibiotics lingering in deadstock will seep into any soil it yields. Considered "the silent industry," rendering is a grisly business, yet among the most environmentally sustainable practices for deadstock disposal.

After Luma's body crashed to the ground, it was likely kept in isolation until a deadstock collector could pick it up in a leakproof vehicle. Her carcass would need to be available to the incineration or rendering crew for quick pickup, but also out of view of the public. Though they vary by location, regulations typically require farmers to dispose of carcasses within seventy-two hours. To ensure that her body would be disposed of in an appropriately timely fashion, this farmer probably scheduled a pickup before he shot Luma.

Workers at the rendering plant, if that's where she went, would have removed Luma's brain and spinal cord per guidelines designed to prevent the spread of mad cow disease. Her body would be cut and ground into small pieces, then blended and cooked at high temperatures to kill microorganisms. The resulting product would then be separated into fat, protein, and water and sterilized into final products and by-products. Luma's hide and bones might be used for collagen powder, maybe the same brand I stir into my coffee every morning. Other parts of her body would be used to make candles, fertilizer, lubricants, fuel, and pet food.

CLAUDE LIVED FOR many years on pet food produced in part through rendering plants. He mostly consumed fish and poultry by-products, not beef, though when Elliott developed food allergies, we tried pretty much everything. (I hasten to add that Claude spent most of his life eating all-natural and wheat-free food; still, some of it came from rendered products.)

If Claude had been found dead on the street, his body would have also wound up at a rendering plant. Instead, it has been incinerated. I paid the extra cost to receive ashes that are only his, as opposed to a mix of his and other animals' (though how would I know?). It seemed like the right choice, though now I wonder—have I, with this final decision, once again taken him away from his kin? But I am his kin, and he's mine.

He's gone.

I'm grateful to have other family. When I wake the next morning, I remember and weep. I text a few close friends. Some of them call, or offer to call. I'm crying and unable to talk but I appreciate the support. Liz is dog sitting at some artist couple's fancy apartment and invites me over for dinner. She and Wade are making rotisserie chicken soup and Jiffy cornbread. I bring two bottles of wine and wonder how old this chicken was. We toast to Claude and enjoy the soothing energy of the sweet elder dog Liz is caring for. His hips are failing, and some days he can't support himself. He will need to be put down soon.

On Christmas morning I wrench my back picking up a shirt off the floor. I do cat-cow to assuage the pain. I think of the cow, all bone and bloat, as I let my belly curve toward the floor. I think of the cat—sinuous and supple—as I arch up. Slowly and with a firm core, I drop my spine down, widen my shoulders, become cow. Become Claude as cow. As he aged, Claude's stance became more bovine. A frail, empty cow. Skin stretched tight over jutting hips.

Later I head back to the apartment where Liz is dog sitting. We complete a cat-themed jigsaw puzzle in four hours while eating delivery from Chinese Garden and listening to dating podcasts.

At home I feel Claude's absence. The blood-stained, fur-covered pillow, the shallow dent where his slight body lived.

I ask Chewy.com if I can return all the unused food I just bought, as my cat is no longer alive. A customer service rep tells me to donate it and offers me sympathies. The next day I receive a bouquet of condolence flowers from Chewy.com.

The clinic calls to tell me Claude's ashes are ready for pickup. They're in the basic wooden vessel I selected from the brochure. They come with a sympathy card and some seeds, so I can plant a tree in his memory. I place the vessel on the shelf above my grandfather's photo and lean Audra's small portrait of Claude against it, his eyes bright with glow-in-the-dark paint.

A month later I'm still finding traces of him. A folded-up Post-it from a vet: *Zyrtec (Cetirizine) – 10 mg tabs. Give a ½ tab by mouth once daily.* We tried this for his respiratory problems. No improvement.

Dark dots on the wall from sneezes that sprayed blood.

Pebbles of litter under the dresser.

His favorite shoelace, on a shelf.

I leave it, for now.

Dear Dairy II: LeMars, Iowa

May 2023

I pour Hiland 2% on my Raisin Bran and eat up while reading *Nature's Perfect Food* by E. Melanie DuPuis. Oat milk's my usual, but lately I've been feeling indebted to dairy—it's been giving me so much content. Cow milk is smoother and sweeter, and good. I forgot.

I'm in Nebraska City for a month-long residency, and today I'm headed northeast to Iowa to see some cows.

Before I leave, I send a note to a livestock rendering company requesting a tour of a nearby plant. I drafted the email yesterday, then paused, thinking I should send it from a new email account using a different, more mannish name, so as not to show up confusing people with my name and gender incoherence. But then, if I have to show an ID . . . I went for a walk to think about it, then thought about other things. This morning I remembered I needed to send the request, and went ahead as Megan.

Maybe I'll try another name when I meet farm folks today. Maybe I'll enlist Dave in coming up with options. My bowels creak. Maybe I'm more lactose sensitive than I thought.

After the bathroom, the media contact has replied. It's a sorry. No tours for safety and security reasons. Makes sense. Rendering plants must be full of potentially dangerous machinery. And my timing's not great: The Nebraska slaughterhouse industry is now under scrutiny due to a child labor exposé after migrant children showed up to school with chemical burns on their hands and knees from overnight sanitation shifts. It was a long shot. I don't press. I grab my journal, get in my rental, and go.

The last time I interacted with rural farmers it was years ago, as visiting faculty at a small liberal arts college in western Illinois. A lot of my students came from farm families, and most were hardworking, focused, open-minded, great. But there were a few who politely refused to read anything that had trans content, namely an essay by trans activist Julia Serano that I had assigned as a model of the evolving thesis. The essay went against their religious beliefs, they said, and they wanted to know if there would be any consequences for them not reading it. Because the course permitted each student to miss a few of the regular reading responses assigned, I told them this would count as one of their permitted missed responses. At the time, I was genderqueer and in a partnership with a trans person, and I was stung by these interactions, which are on my mind as I'm preparing for this trip.

Oh—and there was the family reunion I attended a few days ago, full of farmers and farmer-adjacent people who were generally great and just wanted to understand what a residency was. But when I introduced myself as Megan to one of my extended relatives, his expression slid firmly from open to closed.

The drive to LeMars is smooth, bright except for a short dunk in hard rain. The hills are rolling. So much farm.

I'm meeting a different extended relative today, my dad's cousin Dave, who's taking me on a tour of two farms in the area—he knows the owners, we can stroll right in. I remember Dave vaguely from my youth, but before the family reunion two days ago, we hadn't crossed paths in two decades.

"Hi, we emailed about farm visits," I'd said when I greeted him there. He did an exaggerated double take. "By god, Tom, I thought you had a daughter!" My dad chuckled. "This is my daughter." Another double take from Dave. "You got to prepare me for this!"

"I'm trans," I supplied quietly. He shook his head, bemused, then chilled out and treated me like any other person.

We meet at a Love's Travel Stop, a deluxe-sized gas station off Route 75. I've been told to wait until I get there to fill up: Dave has a 10 percent discount.

I'm nervous to spend the afternoon with Dave, but he seems to have recovered from the gender thing. Our first stop is the older of the two farms. Dave drives past it so I can see how long the barns are, then he makes a U-ey. He explains that the large mound in the front is silage feed, which is covered with white tarps held down by tires. From here it looks like dark dots on white; I don't see how the dots could be tires until we're in the driveway and I understand how massive the mound is.

We park. Dave stands, stretches, and tightens his belt. He's not being lewd, he tells me. He has a hernia. "I gotta adjust." No one's in the front office, so he leads me to a windowed door where we can observe the process.

On one side of the barn, cows are being machine-milked.

More enter on the other side, each turning efficiently into a stanchion. Four farmworkers zip from stall to stall, disinfecting cow teats one by one with a handheld device, then attaching the vacuum pumps. "These guys are from Oklahoma," Dave says with a wink. "That's what I was told, anyway." By which he means they're migrant workers, probably from the same country and family. Workers like these make up more than half of all labor in the US dairy industry. Nearly 80 percent of American milk is produced by farms that employ such workers.

The milk flows through rubber tubes to somewhere invisible to us. Monitoring devices measure the amount of milk collected. When there's no more milk, the pumps fall off, and the cows get released and exit the lane before the next group marches in. Repeat the process.

The cows' backsides are marked with blue. Dave says it's from the vet. Maybe something to do with who's pregnant or how far along. These cows get artificially inseminated once a year, right? "They might be on a closer cycle," says Dave. "Maybe once every ten months or so."

These are feedlot cows. They don't get let out to pasture. Their days are spent in the feedlot and the milking barn, and in the thrice-daily march between them.

The workers' lives are repetitive too. Clean the teats, cow by cow. Attach the milker, cow by cow. Check the monitors. Turn to the other row and nudge any cows that aren't finding their positions themselves. Let the first set of cows go. Hose the floors clear of manure. Clean the teats. Attach the pumps. Check the monitors. Hose. Let the next set in. We're there for an hour and neither the procession of cows nor the rhythm of labor ceases.

This operation has fifteen hundred cows, and milking takes place from 6 a.m. until 9 p.m. "Everything's about production," Dave says. "The most that they can get." The milk from this barn gets sold to Wells Blue Bunny, which produces Blue Bunny ice cream, Blue Bunny soft serve, Blue Bunny bars and cones.

A cow on the end notices us in the window. When her milking is done, she steps closer and lifts her head to take in as much of us as she can. For a long moment, she just looks, I think at me. Dave's fixed on something else. Are we having a connection? She's holding my gaze, steady, indecipherable, and I wonder what she sees.

"That one likes us," says Dave, finally noticing her. "She wants to be on your video. She thinks you're a TV reporter. She wants to be on the six o'clock news. Don't cha!" He waves at her. "Hello!"

We drive around to the feedlot: another long barn. A tractor has gone down the center corridor and dropped silage on each side. Some cows calmly ruminate on these small dumps of food. Some stand idly. Some are lying down. They seem calm and alert. Dave lowers the window so I can take a video. They gaze at us. They're beautiful.

Dave tells me dairy cows are probably the most well-cared-for animals of all farm animals: The happier they are, the more milk they produce. He may be responding to my evident gloom at the idea of cows without grass. Or maybe he's just saying it. He comes from a farm family, though he left farming to join the military. He says it was the better option.

We take the long way to the other farm. Dan admires a bean planter: twenty-four rows! He notices some hog barns and hangs a right to take a look. "See that?" he says. I missed it. He backs up, and on the side of the road I see a pile of five hog carcasses swarming with flies. A couple dead pigs is normal, he says, but five might be a sign of disease. He doesn't know of any cases of swine flu, but mad cow has been hitting deer in the area.

We pull up to two hog barns. They're much larger and more mechanized than the cozy wood shelters at And-Hof. Feed and water are automated; on-site cameras monitor the animals. Some guy might come by every few days, Dave says. They don't see humans much, and this may explain why they're frightened of us. At And-Hof, the hogs heard us coming and lumbered up to the fence to say hello. Here, as soon as one hog spots us, they sound the alarm, and it's like a bomb dropped where we stand: They scatter, barking like dogs.

THE OTHER DAIRY barn is more modern, featuring a rotary parlor that can hold eighty cows at once. No one's in the front, so we wander upstairs to a viewing station used for school field trips and visitors like us. This farm is big on education.

Below us, cows step on the carousel one by one. A farmworker slips vacuum pumps onto each cow's teats as they go around the slow-moving circle. It takes four to five minutes for the milking machine to empty an udder, eight minutes for the carousel to make a full revolution. When each cow gets to the end of her rotation, she backs up, steps off, and returns to the feedlot barn. The rotary parlor can milk 560 cows an hour. Their milk goes to Agropur, a cheese plant in Hull.

We try to guess, based on udder size, which milking pumps will drop first. Younger cows with smaller udders don't hold as much milk, so their pumps fall or get kicked off sooner. (The machine is attached by a thin rope that a cow can manipulate by kicking a hind leg back.) We generally guess right.

There are attendants here too, three of them. They stay busy disinfecting the teats, attaching the milk pumps, and monitoring the machine and the cows, but they seem more relaxed than their peers on the other farm. A few times the carousel stops; there's some glitch or delay or a cow doesn't step off right. Many of these cows have green marks on their backsides with the letter P, probably for "pregnant," but we're not sure.

As we leave, Dave mentions that when he was looking for the bathroom, he stepped into a room where bunks were set up. The workers must sleep here sometimes or rest between milkings. Many dairy workers put in twelve- to eighteen-hour shifts; on some farms, workers live in rooms like this.[1]

Time for ice cream. We head to town. On the drive Dave tells me he's become more lactose tolerant since he got COVID earlier this year. In the past he had a milk allergy: Drinking it gave him a sore throat and once even pneumonia, in addition to indigestion. But since his bout with COVID—a mild case—he's been eating ice cream every day with no problem. This sounds incredible to me, although maybe it tracks with COVID's many other mysterious lasting anecdotal effects.

In 1994, the Iowa state assembly named LeMars the ice cream capital of the world, and the city has leaned into this title, placing fifty sculptures of ice cream cones around town. I count twelve as we head to the Wells Blue Bunny Ice Cream Parlor and Visitor Center. Dave gets strawberry shortcake on a waffle cone. I order double chocolate and mint chocolate chip in a cup. We sit at a booth and talk about stockyards. His brother Joe worked at the Sioux City Stockyards, carving meat. Joe's union went on strike, and then everyone was fired and replaced with migrant workers. Dave is nonchalant. It's a fact, not an anti-immigrant screed. His wife is from Nicaragua. He's helped her and her kids, as well as some of their extended family, get settled in the Midwest and set up with jobs—not on farms.

The ice cream is refreshing.

Dave is full of stories. He tells me about the male calf he raised in secret as a kid on the farm. His father accidentally ran over the calf, broke his leg, and told Dave to shoot him. Dave couldn't bring himself to kill the animal at first; he raised him in secret for nine months, then slaughtered him for veal. Tenderest meat he's ever eaten, he says, because the calf barely moved. The more muscle cattle develop, the tougher the meat is.

I'm curious about his logic: How did he justify the choice to eat the calf when, months earlier, he couldn't bring himself to shoot him?

Dave doesn't respond to that question. Instead, he tells me a story he heard on a radio show about some guy who was reading Ben Franklin's journals and came upon the famous story about a turkey that got struck by lightning and died. Not wanting to waste the turkey, Franklin had cooked and eaten it, remarking upon its tenderness. How did it get so tender, Franklin wondered. Could it have been the electrocution? Whoever it was who stumbled on this anecdote decided to apply the principle to animal slaughter, and it worked. A few seconds of electrocution tenderizes the meat.

"It's business," Dave says. "I see these cows and I see business."

I guess I understand.

Dave drops me back at the gas station. I consider the trip a success. I was worried about the trans thing, but it was a nonissue. I liked hearing Dave's stories. Once he got my dad to ride a bull backward when they were kids: "I wanted to see if he'd notice." On his family's farm, cows lived out their natural lives, wandering off and dying where they died. The family buried them with a tractor hoe. This predated mad cow disease, and since they never injected them with hormones, they didn't have to worry about land or water pollution.

I'm pensive on the drive back. I've seen some cows now, and I'm not sure what I see. I see the bunks at the barn where underpaid workers rest between shifts. Those terrified, panicked hogs. That one cow at the window, chewing her cud as she studies me.

NOTE

1. Melissa Sanchez, "How a Fire on a Dairy Farm Led Us to More Than a Year's Worth of Stories About Immigrant Dairy Farmers," *ProPublica*, February 29, 2024, https://www.propublica.org/article/how-dairy-farm-fire-investigate-workers-michigan-wisconsin.

The Letdown: Lactation Suite

The difference is spreading.
—GERTRUDE STEIN, *Tender Buttons*

— 1 —
OBJECTS

AT CHURCH ONE Sunday, I'm investigating my buttons. They're sewn onto the vest attached to my blouse, and they're boxy, plastic, and nonfunctional: They button nothing. Attached by thread through an opening at the bottom of their stalks, they droop like wilting lilies, three in a row. I'm ten and the sermon is boring. I tilt a button up and trace the embossed surface with my finger. I remember being drawn in by some asymmetry or imperfection; I'm mesmerized. I pore over their ridges and fall in, oblivious to the surrounding world. With voracious concentration I tend to my buttons until I feel the aura of attention and look up to find Aunt Teresa, my cousin Beth, and my mom all in a line down the pew, observing me and clutching each other in a fight to contain their laughter. What was I *doing*? I flushed, and let my buttons go.

In a few years I would bring the same focus to my nipples. Anyone watching would have beheld a similar sight: girlish person with chin in their neck, frowning and fixated. The surface of the nipple, puckered and perforated, was like nothing else I knew. I would scrape a fingernail gently along the spongy plane, grazing it back and forth. I watched the surface knot. Then I dug into the tangle, trying to unravel whatever was there. Wince. An intense, not exactly erotic sensation, like soap in the cunt. Press my palm over it to erase the strange feeling. I would lift a tit to survey the nipple in totality. As with the buttons, I could only get so close.

Now I know the surface was punctured by milk pores. Before they were carved out of my body during chest masculinization surgery, both nipples would have had twelve to twenty of them. The surface was like cheesecloth, or a tiny colander cap. A thimble. A mesh hat. A porosity through which milk might have flowed.

MY MOTHER DID not like nursing. We're with that same aunt, Teresa, my mother's younger sister, in a Midtown hotel room, killing time before a Broadway show. My cousin Beth isn't here: She's at the beach with her two kids. Teresa loved nursing Beth, who loved nursing her kids in turn.

My mother says that with me, she didn't even try. She calls herself a bad mom because of this. Before I can react, she explains her choices: She started out nursing my older brother, who was a big child, insatiable, "a terror." Her nipples were perpetually sore, and she didn't produce much milk. She was also recovering from a difficult childbirth; it was hard to relax, trying to nurse with stitches in her vagina. After two weeks, she switched to formula. When I came along fifteen months later, my brother's Irish twin, she decided not to nurse me at all. I turned out fine—right? Nervous laughter.

I guess I assumed I was nursed, because I'm startled to learn that I wasn't. For a moment I feel an intense wave of—I think it's betrayal. Especially after she mentions that she *did* breastfeed my younger brother Derek, so both of my brothers. But not me. Was it because I was a girl? And less valued? In a rush it seems to explain everything about our relationship, and about my tenuous place in the family. The wounded child wonders, and wails.

I store these feelings for later and focus on others, like the empathetic pull at my chest. Post-surgery I'm pretty sensationless there, but hearing about her soreness is activating a phantom form of what anthropologist Sarah Thornton calls "breast perception." In her book *Tits Up*, an investigation of the cultural meanings of breasts, she describes it as "something inchoate, a vague mood linked to my gut instincts."[1]

I remember that. How my chest gave me information about the weather within and without, some of which took years to learn to interpret. How, in the lead-up to my period, my nipples dilated and chafed against the rough skin of my binder. Ugh, why do I feel so . . . oh. This again.

How they puckered in the ice-cold pool at the Y when I was a summer counselor. How they stung when one of my charges poked at the knots: *What this? What this?* I was wearing a one-piece Speedo, hardly designed to be revealing. Later, my boss beckoned me over and mumbled something I didn't quite hear. When I smiled agreeably, he repeated himself: *You need a different swimsuit.* I lowered my smile, my eyes. My face went hot from the shame.

How they blushed when a classmate lobbed beanbags at my chest in Latin class. Blindfolded, I was supposed to catch them when he tossed them (a Saturnalia game). *Put your elbows together*, he instructed. *Like this?* I couldn't get them under my tits. *No, move your arms up*. Smashing them against my chest didn't work either. I try it now and still, my elbows don't meet.

How they held impressions: the reddened trace of my seat belt, the bruise from the strap of my messenger bag.

How they flushed, humiliated, before a surgeon who reached out with both hands and squeezed like he was honking two clown horns. *Nice healthy breasts*, he said. *Now what are we doing to them?* I found another surgeon.

How they ached when I stripped off the binder. How they tingled from the drop. How I held them.

TENDER BUTTONS: Tend her buttons. Gertrude Stein's strange work of prose poetry presents a domestic catalog of abstracted nouns. Stein wrote it not long after the arrival of Alice B. Toklas, who would become her partner until her death, into her life and home. *Tender Buttons* is organized into three sections—Objects, Food, and Rooms—and the first entry is "A Carafe, That Is a Blind Glass":

> A kind in glass and a cousin, a spectacle and nothing strange a single hurt color and an arrangement in a system to pointing. All this and not ordinary, not unordered in not resembling. The difference is spreading.[2]

The entry announces the book's interest in systems arranged by likeness and difference. A carafe is made "in" (or of) glass and is also a cousin to "the glass" as an object. It is "blind"—that is, unlike the glass of a spectacle, it doesn't see. But at the same time, this difference between carafe and spectacle doesn't prevent the two from being related.

Stein is interested in how we arrange and order life into language. With *Tender Buttons*, she constructs a taxonomy of nouns, that is, subjects and objects, in domestic space. They are kinds (of words, of objects), and they are different and all different kinds. The difference branches out, makes more of itself, more kinds, makes kin.

What makes the carafe's color "hurt"? Is the glass an inflamed red or a yellowing bruise? Is its hurt owing to its singleness? I don't know. Stein's deliberately naïve prose is often rebuffed or even mocked for its supposedly "uninterpretable" nature. But in fact it's the opposite: Porous and overflowing, each syntactical unit is abundantly, excessively interpretable, inviting a feedback loop of meaning-making between writer and reader. The titular buttons suggest a kind of fastening for clothing, or switches that can be pressed on and off, like those of a telephone switchboard, as scholar Kathryn R. Kent has observed.[3] A button can be a word whose meanings flicker in various patterns as it becomes understood in relation to different surrounding words. If the buttons are tender, they have an affective dimension; they feel and are felt. Or they're meat. Or currency. These switchy buttons can be "turned on," activating what Kent calls the work's "erotic currency."[4] "Tender buttons" becomes a metaphor for the nipples and clit, as well as for words; it's a directive to "tend" the body and language at once.

I LEARNED ABOUT binders from a blog post I stumbled into while working part-time as a keyword editor at Info.com. This was 2008. Info.com was by then so outpaced by other search engines—by *the* search engine—that its main source of income had become selling data.

I was living in Chicago, in the process of sliding from femme-y to butch. I had just met Lyra, a feral genius femme writer I wanted to date. For a year I had been tentatively creeping masc-ward; when Lyra joined my book club, I lunged. Within a week, I secured my first rattail and started poking around furtively in the men's sections at Belmont Army. It's not like I hadn't heard of binding—I just didn't know where to start.

I opened the spreadsheet my supervisor had sent me. My first category of the day was BRA, which came with a list of subcategories, or "pinpoints." My task was to populate each pinpoint with the keyword queries a person might use to try to find the pinpoint. By listing search terms, I would build out and differentiate related categories. The job, in brief, was to taxonomize.

I went to work. The first pinpoint for BRA was *training bra*. I tried out keywords like *junior bra* and *youth bra* in various search engines and added the most effective ones to the spreadsheet. *Girls bra, first bra, starter bra.* Thin and usually cotton. I announced mine with pride in fourth grade by wearing a white top that let the straps show through.

Next was sports bra. I gathered keywords like *athlet* bra, gym bra, high-impact bra, high-intensity bra, workout bra, jog* bra*, using asterisks to open the words up to their other forms (i.e., *athlete, athlete's, athletic*). As a teen, I preferred mine on the looser side to avoid back rolls, a choice that left my tits swinging in an infinity sign pattern as I ran up and down the field, brandishing my field hockey stick, a thin shield. When, after a game, my mother loud-whispered that I needed a new bra, I jerked away and pretended not to have heard her. She was right. My chest was sore from this one. But the awareness that my sports bra could be seen when unseen—that I wasn't hiding anything—was unendurable. I jerked away from it, and from her.

Push-up bra: *support bra, shaping bra, lift bra, sculpting bra, how to push my boobs up, bra to make my boobs look bigger.* I remembered these. My high school years overlapped with the era of the Wonderbra, which overlapped with the era of Tyra Banks in angel wings on Victoria's Secret runways. Did I own any push-up bras? Just one, I think, strapless and purple and inching down under my prom dress.

Underwire bra: support bra, bra with wire. I'd kept my favorite, though I'd stopped wearing it: off-white, cotton, with soft wire and stretched-out cups. The underwire rose high in the center, defining separated orbs. In high school, my mother hated the cockeyed shape this bra gave me, but from my perspective it was the most functional of my bras. I could position the strap of my crochet purse between the orbs where it would stay.

I got to *compression bra*, but I didn't know what that was. Looking it up led me to a blog called the *Sugarbutch Chronicles*, specifically a post on butch bras by writer Sinclair Sexsmith. Sexsmith's number one recommendation was Title Nine's Frog Bra, a *sports bra* celebrated for its mashing strength: four barbells' worth, and popular among US butches and transmascs at the time.[5] I emailed myself the link and ordered one in black that night.

I was wearing it when Lyra and I made out in Neo, the goth club, a few weeks later. I was wearing it when I biked eight miles from my apartment to hers to leave a coded love note by her door, imagining myself the Lynnee Breedlove to her Anna Joy Springer (I had borrowed her copy of *Godspeed*). I was wearing it when we made out by the lake. I was wearing it when she revealed she had a boyfriend and that she was sorry but she couldn't see me anymore. I was wearing it when I took my heartache into Boystown and met Deb outside of Berlin Nightclub. In Deb's bed that night, it came off.

Within a year I'd worn it out, and then the Frog Bra was gone—Title Nine was sold out and could no longer source the material for it. This was devastating to many.[6] When Andrea Lawlor sent me a hand-me-down in the mail, I couldn't believe my good fortune. It was a size too small, but I wore it stubbornly until the seams popped and the elastic got shriveled and twisty. Eventually it was too worn to wear, but I kept it as a relic for many years.

Frog Bra: *the superior binding bra*. It let us leap without bouncing.

Then it was 2010, and Joey, my partner at the time, was introducing me to the Underworks men's double-panel *compression shirt*. These were full-torso undergarments designed for cis men, extra-long girdle-like tanks: Mine went all the way down my ass and the bottom edge liked to roll up. It was a whole thing, tucking your Underworks double-panel compression shirt into your American Apparel briefs, then pulling it up a notch to avoid flattening the top half of your ass.

It was hot and sweaty, but I loved the shape this binder gave me. Joey taught me to spread my tits under it for a more masculine silhouette. That's the difference: spreading. He also informed me that during sex I could, if I wished, keep my compression shirt on, an option that hadn't occurred to me and became the obvious choice. We fucked a lot in those binders, rolling around like zippery sausages, scratching and squeezing each other's nipples through the layers. Before sleep we'd take turns going to the bathroom to pull them off. We'd shuffle back in our big shirts with our shoulders protectively hunched.

That model was renamed the Ultimate Chest Binder—a nod to the brand's growing transmasc/butch clientele?—and I usually had two in rotation: one newer and tighter for dates and important days, one softer and more stretched-out for casual wear. The seamed edges had a habit of curling out or under. I washed them by hand once a week.

Then it was 2012, and the era of Binders Full of Women Writers—the secret Facebook group created after Mitt

Romney made a comment about workplace gender equality that got meme-ified.[7] The group was inclusive of gender-nonconforming writers, but it was a period of gender crisis for me: I had a drawer full of binders, but in a binder full of women, did I belong? Then again, I loved the image the phrase conjured, jumbo-sized chest binders strapping us in and smooshing us together in sweaty professional solidarity. I joined but felt furtive about it and didn't participate much.[8]

Next was the era of gc2b, a queer-run company that promised more comfortable options. I ordered my first gc2b half-binder in 2016 and went through nine over the next two years. Made of softer, more elastic material with a flattening panel sewn into the chest, they were, yes, more comfortable than the Underworks tanks, but the seams burst easily and they didn't last long.

<u>Compression bra</u>: *compression vest, compression shirt, mashing bra, masher bra, binding bra, chest binder*. This pinpoint category could have been divided into two, one for <u>medical compression bra</u>, another for <u>compression sports bra</u>, and perhaps subdivided further into men's and women's categories. But not butch or trans. Keywords for those subcategories would have had little to no value to the companies to whom we were selling it.

A few months after top surgery, I got rid of them all. I threw out the ones with popped seams and curled edges and sent the rest to a trans donation project. I wish I had written my name in them, I wish it had been more personal—like a chain letter, like a Pretty Panty Exchange.[9] Not that I wanted anything back. Just the connection.

BACK IN THE hotel room, my mom says what she hated most about <u>nursing</u> (*breastfeeding, chestfeeding, bodyfeeding, infant feeding*)[10] was the nursing bra she had to wear 24/7, with pads in case of leakage. "It made me feel like a cow."

Nursing bra: *nurs* bra, breastfeed* bra, lactat* bra, milk* bra, matern* bra, pumping bra, chestfeed* bra*. Sub-pinpoints: *maternity sports bra* and *sleep maternity bra*. Some are made for nursing, some for pumping, some both. Most have removable foam pads.

Aunt Teresa agrees, and says one issue with breastfeeding is that when your baby cries, your boobs respond by leaking milk. She amends her statement: when any baby cries.

My mom shares that after Derek, my younger brother, was born, he would wail whenever she dropped off my older brother and me at daycare. "I'd be there in the car with my breasts spurting." She weaned him after six weeks.

They're describing the chain of physiological events known as the *letdown*. (It's also known as *milk ejection reflex, breast milk release, milk flow release*.) The *letdown* can be triggered by an infant latching, by strong emotions, or, as in the examples above, by a crying baby. It refers to the stimulation of nerves in the nipples—a sensation that my friend Caitlin, six weeks into nursing, compares to "a little electric shock" or, when activated more acutely by her baby's screams, being "tasered in the chest." The nerve stimulation causes a chain reaction: First, the pituitary gland increases the prolactin, which boosts milk production and releases oxytocin, which signals the muscle cells around the milk ducts to contract, thereby squeezing milk from the alveoli into the ducts. The milk then flows toward the nipples and out—ideally into a mouth or a pump. The letdown works like a feedback loop: When the nursling latches, the oxytocin kicks in like a pleasure wash, activating relaxation and positive feelings that trigger more letdown and more oxytocin. The tingling might occur multiple times in a feeding session.

When this feedback loop works, nursing is generally a pleasant experience for both parties, and a sense of closeness is achieved along with the life-sustaining transfer of milk. When it's frustrated in some way—the infant struggles to latch, or the latch is painful, or the nursing person has difficulty relaxing due to any number of internal or external stressors (another child needs attention, for example, or *dysphoric milk ejection reflex*[11] has kicked in)—nursing can seem impossible. My mother was "tense, impatient, nervous" as a new mom (who, again, was in a lot of pain). She could never relax. "I'm a very impatient person," she says. If my dad were here, he'd confirm: "Yep. You're a VIP."

THE *LETDOWN* CALLS to mind the term's other, more widely used meaning: *disappointment*. Thornton draws this connection in her chapter on breastfeeding: "When you let someone down," she writes, "you fail or disappoint them."[12] If nursing is equated with letdown, then the mother is in a position to fail or disappoint.

When my mother shared that she did not nurse me, I was disappointed—and surprised. For decades I'd assumed we had shared this intimate bodily connection. Eyeing her chest, I had thought: How wild it is that I put my mouth there; how strange, we were once so close.

Melanie Klein's object relations theory views the *breast* as the "primal good object" which "forms the core of [the child's] ego and vitally contributes to its growth."[13] The absence of this vital core ego experience in my early life could provide explanations: for my issues with food, for the strain in my relationship with my mother. It may also explain—because my first food came not from small-bodied, large-brained homo sapiens but from large-bodied, small-brained bovines—why I'm sometimes so slow, why so many of my conversational contributions involve asking fast talkers to repeat themselves. What? Sorry, what? Sorry. My mind was made from cows.

But I'm embarrassed to be entertaining these ideas about nursing. How profoundly unfair to my mother, and my father, too, who fed me so well and so stably for the duration of my youth! And to everyone else—all the other formula babies, whose egos must be as variously formed as those of the breastfed—and their parents, who are making decisions for their infants' health and their own well-being in all sorts of social, economic, and medical circumstances, often with inadequate support.

My wise mind and my critical mind know better. I understand that "fed is best," and that for many parents, formula is freedom. I know that for many people who could or might want to, nursing is not a possibility, and that for others, serving as the primary food source for a child may feel like an oppressive, gendered division of labor. And I know—though I have to remind myself—that these two means of feeding are not mutually exclusive, that combination feeding is widely practiced. I know that the subject of infant feeding is fraught, stirring up personal and historical feelings. I know that parents are judged for nursing and judged for not nursing (this, friends, is called a *double bind*, not to be confused with a *double-panel binder*). I know that the reality of nursing rarely matches the romantic image of the serene Madonna locked in a loving gaze with her nursling. I know that pumping and nursing *and* formula feeding are laborious and time-consuming practices around which one must structure their entire life. And parenting is fucking hard.

And I know that this sense of letdown isn't really about the breast or about nursing itself, but about what they symbolize: a need for nourishment that can come from anywhere.

I suppose the most salient revelation from this conversation with my mother is that we'd never had it before. Why? Because my mother has some guilt about this. Because we tend to avoid personal topics. Because I never asked.

Now *I* feel guilty. We might have talked about it earlier if I had been in a position to chestfeed a child. My mother has been transparent about wanting more grandchildren. So far I've not produced them. I'm the letdown: It's me.

"Are you still taking that thing you take?" she used to ask me, meaning T. "I just hope you don't get rid of your, you know," she might lower her voice here: "boobs."

<u>*MALE NIPPLES*</u> (*male nip*, man nip*, men's nip**) are flatter and squintier, less round, my surgeon informed me in the consultation. They're lower and further apart. To create a more masculine look, she would stitch them back on like wider-set, more ovaline eyes.

They healed visibly passable, though lopsided and the color of grubs. In a post-op appointment, she offered to tattoo some blush into them at no extra charge, and we selected a dusty rose for the areolae, leaving the nipples a touch lighter. She'd done studies on the coloration, she explained. <u>*Female nipples*</u> (*female nip*, woman nip*, women's nip**) are darker than the surrounding areolae; <u>*male nipples*</u> tend to be lighter.

I don't know what sex my nipples are.

Actually, I do: They're transsexual.

They're smoother, flatter, and more static than they once were. I see pores, but they can't express milk. Their stalks have been snipped; the milk ducts have been shoveled out, along with the bulk of mammary tissue.[14] Though my buttons healed beautifully and are not exactly fragile, I can more easily see them dissolving on the tongue like communion wafers than sustaining an infant's latch. But I had a lover who did this thing where they rummaged around and behind both nipples to summon whatever sensation was there. They rummaged and rummaged, more and more forcefully, with their fingers and their fists, until I felt it. The threads held fast.

— 2 —
FOOD

THERE ARE TWO entries for "MILK" in *Tender Buttons*, and the second is more interesting:

> Climb up in sight climb in the whole utter needles and a guess a whole guess is hanging. Hanging hanging.[15]

Whole for hole. Utter for udder. Could a guess be a goose or a guest? The hole guest is hanging. Like a teat. Each word is a kind of word that resembles in sound another kind of word. The text floods with fluid meaning. There is no buttoning it up.

One of Thornton's goals in *Tits Up* is to reclaim certain terms—like *tits*—for women's <u>*breasts*</u>, "shifting their connotations into more affirmative, woman-owned territory."[16] Leaving aside the fact that <u>*woman*</u> is its own (hotly, often hostilely) contested territory, Thornton sees the <u>*letdown*</u> as one such term. Other cultures use different terms, she notes: Latinate languages, for example, use the language of ascension—*montée de lait* and *montata lattea,* in French and Italian, respectively, mean the rising of milk.[17] What if English speakers called the *letdown* something else, Thornton wonders, something associated not with disappointment but with nourishment?

I get what she's saying—to find a new keyword would help revalue nursing and mothers in a culture that devalues both. At the same time, this connection between nursing and disappointment feels kind of right—as though, along with the calories, enzymes, and immune support an infant needs to grow and survive, the milk letdown also infuses the child with a certain amount of disappointment-preparedness. Welcome to our broken, unjust world, the milk communicates: What a letdown.

Others have made similar cases. In her book-length argument for nursing, *The Big Letdown*, journalist Kimberly Seals Allers focuses on "the letdown around us": "the unseen commercial and social underpinnings that leave [new mothers] frustrated and confused." She's especially critical of the formula industry and family-unfriendly federal policy.[18] An Australian TV comedy called *The Letdown*, created by Alison Bell and Sarah Scheller, similarly riffs on the connections between the milk letdown and the letdowns of new parenthood, which include the challenges of nursing.[19] Both of these examples find a wellspring of meaning in the term, and in how it names the ways parents are failed by a social system that claims to want more babies—albeit a certain kind of baby, ideally white, produced from within monogamous matrimony between heterosexual, middle- or upper-class parents who are legal citizens—yet offers stingy support when the baby arrives.

I've never nursed and never will. I've never been responsible for keeping a child alive with my body, income, time, and caretaking decisions. I'm more familiar with the letdowns the queer and trans child experiences. I've been let down by a culture that kept queer and trans people largely out of sight—or, when visible, a source of fear or comedy—throughout my youth and adolescence; a culture that thrust Wonderbras at me while keeping binders hidden. I've been let down by my straight family's discomfort and illiteracy with queer and trans issues and their rejection of the aspects of my life that frustrate their categories. I've been—we've been—let down by every vicious cycle of conservative frenzy to erase queer and trans people and to "save our children" from queerness and transness—especially transness—willfully ignoring, if not openly celebrating, *because it's the point*, the harm this legislative and cultural violence does to queer and trans youth. These betrayals, too, are part of a feedback loop. Where is the Frog Bra that can mash them all?

My mother was also failed. I can't index all the ways, common and particular, that the world has let her down. But I feel confident in saying that she has been failed by a culture that devalues women's bodily knowledge and that shames women for nursing and shames them for not. By disapproving nurses and judgmental in-laws. By us, her children, when we disrespected her mom-ness and domestic work. By me and the alarmingly queer choices I've made. If only she'd nursed me. I might have turned out different—less different, that is. More like her.

IT'S A STRANGE, uninformed certainty to have had, I see now—the assumption that my mother nursed me. At the time, "breast is best" messaging was still new, and it was associated with *hippies* and *feminists*, which my parents were not.[20]

Dr. Spock, then the go-to expert for pregnancy and childbirth, "didn't really talk much about breastfeeding," my mother says. I look up early editions of *Dr. Spock's Baby and Child Care*, first published in 1945. The chapter on nursing takes up twenty-two of 504 pages and leads by addressing its perceived disadvantages, including women's concerns that it will "ruin" their figures. He is largely reassuring on this matter, though warns against "getting generally fat."[21] My mother would have been using the 1976 edition, where the chapter on breastfeeding is about the same length—thirty-six of 666 pages (my edition is a mass paperback)—but has been revised to open with its values.[22]

She doesn't remember getting information or support about nursing from her medical team, either. I ask her if there was a lactation consultant on hand, and that gives her something new to feel guilty about: "I didn't even know to ask for one," she says remorsefully. There probably weren't any, I tell her, but I don't actually know. (The profession emerged in the 1970s, I find out later; the field's first certification program was created in 1985.) She was sent home with formula.

I ask her whether she absorbed knowledge from more experienced family members. Her mother and mother-in-law were "no help at all," she says. "They never breastfed and didn't understand why I would even want to. Every time you saw them, they thought the baby was starving and needed formula." Both of my grandmothers fed their kids formula from the start, the norm in hospitals for after-birth care in the 1950s. Within their generation, formula was thought to be superior to human milk; this argument was wrong but was backed by medical authorities. Many obstetricians were so confident that mothers would not (or should not) want to nurse, they administered hormone shots immediately after childbirth to dry up their milk, often without consultation.[23]

Pumping was not really an option for mothers of the post–World War II and Boomer generations. The only *milk pumps* (*breast pump, lactat* pump, nursing pump*) were manual or made for hospitals: The first electric model, invented in the early twentieth century, weighed forty pounds. For decades, there was no perceived need for home or portable pumps because most parents went straight to formula, in part because there were no accessible pumps.[24] Another loop; another letdown.

ALL THIS MAY be old news, known history, but it's new to me, and I'm humbled by all I didn't know and haven't been inspired to find out. Now that I'm motivated, I've become fascinated by the complicated histories of infant feeding and the many factors that have contributed to rises and falls in the popularity of nursing. I've been surprised to learn how hard it can be for infants to latch, that it's not necessarily some "natural" thing our bodies intuitively know how to do, but something that may need to be learned and troubleshot, often with the help of experts.

It's not just me. "I knew none of this when I gave birth," says Caitlin, who has gone through three different lactation consultants since her baby was born six weeks ago. "Maybe I just missed the memo on when everyone learned this." By "this," she means everything from how to hold the breast to encourage latching to how to modulate her milk supply, as well as how to understand her child's oral physiology. Oh, right, she remembers. She'd signed up for a lactation webinar, but her baby arrived early, and she missed it.

The world of knowledge around lactation seems paradoxically both universal and subcultural. Most other new parents Caitlin has talked to knew as little as she did. Caitlin's feeding cycle, which now involves nursing, bottle feeding, then pumping, is two hours on, one hour off. It sounds brutal. She's trying to move out of this triple cycle and is waiting for her baby to decide if he's going to nurse. If not, fine. They'll go with the bottle.

"Some of it is just like their literal mouth and jaw muscles have to get stronger." Her baby has a recessed chin and a high palette, she starts to explain, but interrupts herself: "I'm making my baby sound like a loser." She laughs. "He's great, but he is having a hard time getting a tight enough suck, so he pops off. Some of that will get better with time, and some of it is just his anatomy." She hopes the "Suck-Swallow" clinic will help, she says. Caitlin's a comedy writer who will do great things with this material.

My friend Liza, another new parent, has had a comparatively easy go of nursing, if by easy we mean she was doing it "basically constantly, like, hundreds of times a day."

I'm frankly aghast. "How did you survive that?"

"For me nursing felt really great," she says, noting the range of hormones she got to experience and all the time she spent sitting and being still. But it was also a ton of labor, she's quick to add, quick to remind herself. "It probably has a rosy tint now."

FORMULA CAN BE expensive.[25] *Nursing*—at least the milk itself—is ostensibly free, if you ignore all the bodily and time costs. Like everyone else I've talked with who has nursed, Liza underscores these costs. Time, calories, water, disrupted sleep. Disrupted time, more calories, more water, less sleep.

Then there are the other costs: the physical and emotional stress that some people experience when nursing; wage loss sustained by those who must take unpaid time off in order to nurse. And while most health insurance plans cover pumps and lactation counseling, other costs may include *nursing bras* and *nursing pillows*, *nipple shields*, *nipple pads*, and *nipple balm*. And *milk storage bags* (*breast milk bags, human milk storage, how to store breast milk*).

I learn about the milk bags indirectly. Eating dinner with my roommate Waqia, I mention I've been revisiting Lauren Berlant and Michael Warner's article on public sex, which ends with a dom pouring milk, then food, then more milk, down a sub's throat, then inserting three fingers to induce vomiting.[26] This reminds Waqia of a performance they did where they ate white food after white food—mayonnaise, mozzarella, cottage cheese, milk—then vomited it all up. They'll send me the video of the performance, they say. It was really fun.

Their partner, Heather, also has a milk connection. Her grandfather was involved in the invention of the *milk bag*, Waqia tells me. "The milk bag?" I echo. "What's that?" It's how milk gets sold in certain parts of Canada, they say. (Also Europe, South America, Israel, and India.) Heather has written about it in the intro to her book: As an employee for Dupont Canada, her grandfather took on a project to develop more economical approaches to milk packaging. The cheapest way to package a liquid, he knew, was a plastic bag. And so the milk bag was born. Heather, a white Canadian, writes about this as a complicated inheritance impossible to disentangle from ecocide and white settler colonialism.[27]

Never having seen such a *milk bag*, I look it up after dinner to get a visual. It takes me a while to get to my target, probably because I'm searching in the US, which almost never uses them. (A milk bag requires 75 percent less plastic than the average milk jug. Of course we go with the jugs.) The top results aren't bags for dairy milk but milk storage bags meant for nursing. Like bras, there are all kinds: *disposable, reusable, plastic, silicone, space-saving, designed to attach to pumps*. Squat and donut-shaped; self-standing and stackable; some with Ziplocs, others with screw caps.

I add "Canada" to my query and reach the common milk bag, which is a plastic pillow full of milk. It's clear, thin, and jiggly, though surprisingly tough, designed to be rupture-avoidant. It resembles a wine bag but with much thinner plastic, and nothing so fancy as a spout. Heather's grandfather told a story about his colleague throwing a prototype against a wall to prove that it wouldn't break. It didn't.

My search results also lead me to a Nintendo Switch game series with two parts: *Milk Inside a Bag of Milk Inside a Bag of Milk* and *Milk Outside a Bag of Milk Outside a Bag of Milk*. I'm lured by these Steinian names, which could be entries in *Tender Buttons*; I click. The player's objective for the first game is to "help the girl buy milk, be the first to not disappoint her." A gallant mission. If only I had a Switch, I would help and not disappoint her. Alas. She's doomed to be let down.

THERE IS SO much to learn about lactation. Am I seeming naïve? Am I making it sound exotic? Do I seem—jealous? Do I wish I had explored my own potential for lactogenesis prior to reconstructing my chest? Maybe. No. I've just become absorbed in this subject. It's like at the church with my buttons. I've fallen in.

As I'm talking to my peers about nursing, I keep hearing about *The Lactation Station Breast Milk Bar* (2006, 2012, 2016), a performance in which the artist Jess Dobkin served flights of human milk to attendees. She had planned the project while pregnant and envisioned serving her own milk, but had difficulties nursing and ended up working with milk donors instead. During the performance, Dobkin served the milk samples from behind a crescent-shaped bar while inviting guests into conversation.

"They tasted very different," Dobkin, who had tried all of the samples herself, told me in an interview. "Some tasted really sweet, more like ice cream sweetness, and others tasted more sour." Some were thinner; others thicker. This isn't surprising; human milk is dynamic and changes all the time. The tastes of the donor milk were affected by various factors: what the nursing person had eaten that day, whether they collected the milk at the beginning or at the end of a feed, and the age of the child they were nursing (if there was one). "In that way," Dobkin said, the varieties of taste are "a reminder that milk is a bodily secretion."

It's easy to forget. Store-bought cow milk is so removed from its origin, most of us don't think about the bodies that made it. That's by design: It's sourced from multiple udders and blended to all taste the same. There's nothing like the *terroir* associated with raw milk, whether from cow or human.

Back in the hotel room, my aunt mentions that her daughter, my cousin Beth, stopped drinking cow milk after she had a realization that humans are the only animal who drink the milk of another species. "It's kind of gross when you think about it," Aunt Teresa says, wrinkling her nose.

But humans are not the only *MAMMALS* (*animals that*

milk, animals with fur, type of animals humans are) that drink the milk of other species. In Germany, a farm dog nursed a potbellied piglet who was rejected by her mother. In China, a golden retriever nursed two newborn Siberian tigers. These are the novelty stories that make headlines, but the examples are not so novel. I've seen cats lap up milk leaking from a cow's teats. Lactating humans have nursed puppies, fawns, piglets, monkeys. We might give goat milk to guinea pups. My foster kitten tried to suckle my nose. It's our mammalian bond. We mammals milk.

Humans, in some regions more than others, have long been entangled with cows (*female cattle, dairy cattle, milk cattle*). Some of the earliest artificial milk vessels for infant feeding were made of cow horns.[28] Some of the earliest artificial nipples for bottle feeding were made of preserved cow teats.[29] The first electric pump for human milk was invented by an engineer for a dairy milking-machine manufacturer. This kind of interspecies design exchange has also benefited cows: the *cow bra* (*udder support net, teat protector*), modeled after human bras, was developed by a Dutch veterinarian to prevent cows from damaging their teats. Most dairy formula is made with cow milk. *All over the world, babies are dependent on cow's milk for their very lives*, the narrator of a 1943 pro-dairy propaganda film booms. *It would be hard for humans to get along without our foster mother, the cow*.[30]

The English expression *letdown* comes from the dairy industry, where it describes how milk flows through the downward-spurting udder of cows. This is another reason why, in Thornton's view, the name doesn't fit the process for humans: In the human body, it's an upward and outward flow. "Couldn't this reflex be framed more positively—as a flow, uprising, or liberation?"[31] She stops short of suggesting that the bovine association is denigrating, but that seems to be the overall implication. While I've never lactated, I have been called "Megan Milks(,) the Cow," and I get it, I do: The association can be, is meant to be, demeaning. It's wrapped up in misogyny: Only women get associated with cows. In the same way that Thornton wants to reclaim "tits" and "the letdown," I want to reclaim "cow" from these derogatory meanings.

It may be just that I'm feeling defensive. As a formula baby, aren't cows my "foster mother," after all? More accurately, they might be a kind of <u>wet nurse</u> *(hired breastfeed*, breastmilk nurse)*. Before they were replaced by cows in the early twentieth century, <u>wet nurses</u> were a primary food source for US infants in families of means. Generally some combination of poor, young, single, immigrant, or enslaved, <u>wet nurses</u> were hired or forced to provide milk for their employers' or mistresses' infants, often to the detriment of their own babies' health. Many were forcibly separated from their children or compelled to abandon them to asylums out of economic desperation or shame.[32]

I learn about the professional descendants of <u>wet nurses</u>: the <u>milk sellers</u> who worked in early <u>milk banks</u> (*milk stations, breast milk reservoir, donor milk, buy breast milk, human milk, where can I get breast milk, where can I get human milk, milk network, human milk program*). These facilities, which date back to the 1910s, were sometimes called "human dairies," and from photographs, it's easy to see why. In one image, five milk sellers are seated in a row of semiprivate stalls similar to cow stanchions in a milking barn.[33] Under the careful watch of supervising nurses, the milk sellers—typically young, poor, single, and either first- or second-generation immigrants—are bent over and pumping.

I'm coming to understand how blatantly and how enduringly human milk has flowed from bodies with less to more social and economic privilege, and in this way how directly it has been involved in fortifying structural inequality. And I'm recognizing that when lactating people like my mom, who descends from working-class Irish immigrants, report feeling "like a cow," they may not be rejecting the cow so much as they're reacting to inherited histories of bodily exploitation, to the feeling of being extracted from, to becoming objects that feed.

Milk banks still exist. Most collect donor milk, though some pay their donors. These donors are typically not supervised while pumping, though they are screened for communicable disease and other health concerns. Kin to *milk banks* are *milk networks*, grassroots networks that have sprung up to support the peer-to-peer exchange of milk. Sometimes this involves money and sometimes it doesn't. In either case, *milk banks* and peer-to-peer *milk networks* both provide human milk to parents of infants who need it. They often supply milk to infants who are adopted or whose lactating parent is ill or has died, as well as infants whose parent(s) cannot or have chosen not to lactate.[34]

"That makes me so uncomfortable," a friend says, screwing up their face in disgust, when I tell them about milk banks. "Some random person's breast milk."

I understand their reaction—it's an intimate thing, eating someone's bodily fluids, and cross-feeding is no longer normalized in the US. But it used to be, and through these kinds of networks is becoming so again.

Jess Dobkin's more recent milk project, *For What It's Worth* (2023), explores the ethics and politics of milk marketplaces in the twenty-first century. The exhibition sprawls over the final gallery room of the Wellcome Collection's *Milk* exhibition. When I see it in London as part of an artist's talk led by Dobkin, I'm dazzled by the maximalism: the vibrant colors and moving pieces, the variety of materials and their textures, the scrupulous attention to detail, the play. There's no actual milk here—no liquids were allowed, Dobkin tells us—but the representations of milk gush out everywhere through other materials, such as white paracord, white fringe, and silicone tubing. The room is divided into several defined areas, each devoted to a different market for human milk. The first represents milk networks among parents via an open fridge overloaded with milk containers: gallons, quarts, *breast milk storage bags*. The fridge light flickers on and off, and a mannequin lounges, exhausted, across the top. In the side door, the *breast milk bags* are bunched together and labeled with tags that resemble posts from a milk exchange network. "SELLING EXCESS MILK," reads one, from Lowland, California. "I am selling extra milk I have in my deep freezer. I have test results if you need to see them. I don't do drugs. I do have a coffee every morning. I take long walks." Price: five dollars.

Another area represents the fetish market that has formed around the *adult nursing* (*milk kink, lactation kink, lactation play, erotic milk play*) community, here embodied by a mannequin in studded leather collar and chest harness. Knob-like (boob-like) appendages on the mirror she's holding drip long lengths of milky white fringe. At her feet, a travel bag monogrammed with *MILF* is stuffed with baby bottle nipples.

There's a workout station, too, representing the fitness enthusiasts who buy human milk to support their gains. Barbells and bodybuilding guides rest under a vertical knee-dip station; overturned protein powder canisters leak noodley tubing.

In our interview, Dobkin says this new project for the Wellcome "reignited" something for her about milk, seventeen years after the first performance of *Lactation Station*. "It never gets boring, as a subject and a substance. It's so complex and it touches on all the nodes." She rattles off a list of issues including intimacy and healthcare, equity, race, health fads, eugenics, what it means to be a donor. The installation poses questions about all of these topics. What *is* milk worth? Five dollars for a few ounces? What does it mean to assign monetary value?

Dobkin says working on the project "made me think a lot about fetish and what we consider fetish. What's the difference between how breast milk is fetishized in kink culture versus how it's fetishized by new parents? What's kink, you know? Maybe none of those uses are more valid than others."

High on one wall, one of those half-sphere balance balls used for calisthenics has been mounted, boob-like, with a tassel attached to its nipple. Above us, the tassel twitches, as if to affirm Dobkin's point.

MY MOTHER SAID the plus side of her not nursing me was that many people got to feed me. Grandparents, aunts, uncles. My dad took on most of the night feeding.

Also cows, whose milk was used as the base matter for the powdered formula I ingested, sourced from so many dams. Thank you, cows. Thank you, Mom, Dad, everyone else.

Thank you, all my other mothers, those "many-gendered mothers of my heart."[35] I'm not sure I'd claim Stein as one of them, or not without hesitation. Her language play tends to be more cerebral and abstract than the visceral writing I prefer. While I admire her audacity and the blazing originality of her work, I might say I have some trouble latching on. Then there's her collaborations with Nazi-occupied Vichy

France: To call them disappointing would be an understatement. But this return to *Tender Buttons* has been giving me something I need; it has sprayed the nourishing play of words, sounds, and meanings into my mouth.

HUMAN MILK IS, or can be, a renewable resource. The more regularly a lactating person nurses or pumps, the more milk they produce. Ideally, the feeding person is making the same amount of milk the baby consumes, and there are various tricks one can use to manipulate flow. Expressing infrequently will cause the milk production to slow and eventually stop. Pumping too much may create not only more milk than the baby needs but also a letdown that is too powerful for the baby. When the milk comes down, it's like a fire hose.

The more expressed, the more produced. I've been working on this essay for more than a year, and the milk has come down like a fire hose. I can't get it down fast enough. It's filling me up, yet I still feel on the outside of it. Outside a bag of milk outside a bag of milk. What would it mean to get inside?

— 3 —
ROOMS

IN THE FIRST season of *The Jerrod Carmichael Reality Show*, stand-up comic Jerrod Carmichael separately confronts both of his parents on camera, attempting to force some kind of accountability and repair process around the ways they have failed him as a child and as an adult. Are these confrontations righteous and revolutionary, or are they narcissistic and exploitative? Probably both, and that tension is what drives the show, which is as uncomfortable as it is riveting to watch.

In one of the later episodes, Jerrod takes his mother, Cynthia, to the Met Cloisters, a New York museum that specializes in medieval European art and architecture. He has already confronted Cynthia on the show about her religious homophobia. In response, she told him that she loves him unconditionally, but she doesn't agree with his lifestyle. Okay—he points out—that sounds like a condition.

Carmichael is known for his intimate, relaxed storytelling style: He speaks to his audience with disarming candidness about his personal life, typically while seated in a chair or on the stage floor. In his special *Rothaniel*, he comes out as gay to his viewers and describes his family's struggle to accept his queerness. A few months after winning an Emmy for that work, Carmichael was tapped to host the Golden Globes. His reality show begins with the lead-up to that night at the Globes, then tracks his life from there. We see him navigating the world not only as a newly out gay man hooking up on Grindr behind his boyfriend's back, but also as a newly very rich and highly visible celebrity who feels ambivalently responsible to loved ones from other periods of his life. The show is not simply a documentary of Carmichael's life; among other things, he uses it as an opportunity to (try to) repair his fractured relationships with his parents, especially his mother.

At the Cloisters, they're sitting on a bench in the courtyard and she is talking about her religious faith. "He [the Lord] has never failed me," she explains.

"Who has failed you?" Jerrod asks.

"Humans."

"Like who?"

"Why do you want me to name names?"

"I'm curious."

She holds his gaze a long moment and doesn't reply.

I recognize the Cloisters. I was just there, in pursuit of a Nursing Madonna (*virgo lacta*, madonna lacta*, lacta* mary*). There's one hanging on a wall a few rooms away from where Jerrod and Cynthia are sitting and talking. Nursing Madonnas depict Mary with one or both breasts bared; she is either feeding baby Jesus or spraying her glory, her milk, into the open mouths or eyes of others, usually Saint Bernard of Clairvaux, who, according to one version of the legend, was healed of an eye infection by a spray of Mary's milk. In my favorite of these images, the Nursing Madonna holds Jesus at her shoulder while ejaculating beams of milk from both breasts to the damned souls below her, whose heads bob like peeled potatoes in a vat of stew.[36]

When I found the Met Cloisters' *Madonna Lactans* in the third room,[37] I was underwhelmed. The painting is small and understated in comparison with the more spectacular examples. Painted circa 1490 by a "Master of the Saint Catherine Legend," Mary holds her breast with fingers spread wide. It's strangely high, a balloon attached to her collarbone. No milk is represented in the painting—no splendorous sprays, no perfectly arced jets, no squirts or dribbles—though Baby Jesus's loose, fluidly rendered swaddling cloth is appropriately milky.

The child grabs the nipple between his lips while gazing up at Mary's mouth. Leaning in for a closer view, I see that his facial expression appears more irritated than the serenity I might expect. He seems unimpressed, disappointed, let down. Is this all there is? This impossible tit, this milk machine, this *Mom*?

No sighting of this Nursing Madonna in Carmichael's show, though Jerrod does point out a sculpture of Mary with an older Christ child on her lap. "Aww, that's us," he says to his mother. "Aww," Cynthia echoes. "But you weren't a virgin," he says. She swats his arm.

The letdown is a rich place from which to make art, a position fusing anger and hurt. To say *You have disappointed me* expresses something about expectations. It means *I expected more from you*. Jerrod comments a few times on his need to use the camera to mediate conversations he wouldn't have otherwise. "If the cameras help me, then they fucking help," he says to his father at one point. "That's my way. And yes, I'm afraid to have these conversations without them." This approach may be unfair since he's the one controlling the narrative, and doing so from a position of more wealth and cultural power than most of the loved ones he features. But with his parents, Jerrod will always be the child.

In a joint therapy session she has agreed to attend, Cynthia tells the therapist, Kali D. Cyrus, that she would like "for [Jerrod] to not be gay." Cyrus asks: "Does it make you feel disappointed or sad?" Cynthia responds: "Maybe disappointed. That's a maybe. Not sad." Later, she says, "We can go weeks without talking. *That* makes me sad." She tears up.

"You might be the only homophobic person in my life," he tells her.

Sometimes I think: enough. Enough resentment. There is nothing my parents, now in their seventies, have said or done that is not forgivable, that is not something I can understand through the filter of their lives and the limitations of their contexts. I don't mean to excuse these limitations, or the connections to be made between paper-cut microaggressions and the barrage of manifestly hostile rhetoric and policies currently targeting trans people. But while they may exist on a continuum, these two categories are not the same. If at times my parents have let me down, they have said and done many more things that have been loving and supportive.

Jerrod: "I wish there wasn't a gap. I wish we understood each other."

I have worried I'm "using" my parents for this book, extracting—milking—from them whatever I can to—what exactly? Air our issues, my grievances, in the public privacy of the printed page? But it also works the other way around: I'm using the book to get to them. I may need it like Jerrod needs the camera. I'm interviewing them and sharing drafts with them. The book gives us a third thing to focus on, something to mediate ourselves and our intimacy through: the book as the mirror through which we make eye contact. There are many rooms to our relationship. I want to bring them into this one.

I SEND MY mom excerpts from a draft of this essay—just the passages she appears in, as she requested. (I'd asked if she wanted to see the full draft or just the relevant excerpts.) A few days later, she replies with a longish email further explaining her decision to formula feed me. She reiterates some of the reasons she's already shared with me but that I chose not to put in the draft. My thinking was that by providing the more granular details surrounding her choices, it might seem like I was implying she *needed* justification. I don't think she did. But as I read over her email, I'm realizing that without that context, the inciting "problem" of the essay—if that's what it is (I think of it more as an entry point)—is never quite resolved.

Reading it again, I worry that I've hurt her with this essay. I worry that her email is an expression of defensiveness or even, maybe, humiliation. If so, I think it's a mutual humiliation: hers over her (good! sensible! well-made!) choices being publicly broadcast, mine over showing up here as a demanding and entitled old baby.

I worry I've overemphasized the wail of the wounded child, which was, as I felt it, a momentary flare that ignited other concerns. At the same time, I worry that I deflected too quickly, shutting that kid up and closing the door on the lingering mom stuff that was surfacing. Most personal nonfiction moves from less to more intimate, and this essay has gone in the other direction. I invited you in, and I invited her in, and then it got too crowded. I had to shove you all out and shut the door so I could soothe myself by researching the complicated histories of infant feeding—about which I wrote and rewrote many pages, only to cut most of them from this final version.

Waaaah. Will I ever get this essay right?

I give my mother a call to talk over her email, ready to apologize and despair. But she's surprisingly sanguine, and I quickly realize that we've entered different rooms. The room that she's in is built on the literal details of her email. The one I'm in is the same, but it's also the basement. I'm here with my shovel, trying to dig up all of the underlying dirt and getting nowhere. Against the unyielding concreteness of her details, my shovel clangs.

She's not here for a reckoning. She just wants this stuff in the record.

When I was born, she reminds me, she and my father were in the process of moving to Kentucky from Virginia for my father's job. They had sold their house in Richmond and moved in with my father's parents for six weeks. My dad was commuting between Richmond and Annandale until the house sale closed; he was also wrapping up his duties at his previous position. "As you know, I had trouble breastfeeding [Michael] & felt I had no privacy at Ruby & Jim's trying to breastfeed so didn't even try," she wrote. "It was just so much easier bottle feeding you with all that was going on at the time."

They moved to Kentucky when I was six weeks old and Michael was sixteen months; we lived in a hotel for a few weeks before my dad's new boss and his wife invited us to temporarily move in with them until my parents could find a new house. "It was a very chaotic time in our lives & breastfeeding you was just not in the picture. I still loved you & continue to love you fiercely!!! Anyway, you can include any of this in your essay if you want but felt it was important to clarify the why & wherefore of my decisions about breastfeeding. It was the right decision for me & our little family at the time."

Very sensible and certainly right. And yes, I turned out fine.

. . . Or did I?

I wonder what she thinks.

Maybe I am a demanding and entitled old baby. But entitlement, as Elle, my sweetheart, reminds me, can be a defense against grief. If that's so, what am I grieving? I don't think it's about nursing or not having been nursed. It's about the letdown of my mother not being willing to enter the basement with me. It's about all those tiny jabs that have led up to a sense of rejection, and the reactionary rejecting in turn. It's about distance. The difference that spreads.

I can choose to be grateful for this blocked, clogged intimacy. It's why I'm a writer now, and why I do queer intimacy the way that I do.

On the phone, I ask my mom how it feels to be revisiting

the circumstances of my birth, four decades later. "It feels wonderful," she says. "I loved being a mom. Every minute of it."

Really? That's it? is what I'm thinking—She's not exasperated by my one-sided determination to interrogate our forty-three-year-old past? She's not at all concerned about what I might write? But I'm moved by her firmness on this point. I look down at the other question I've composed in my notebook: Does she ever feel grief about our relationship?

I think better of asking it. We move on to chatting about our cats, the weather, an upcoming trip. We exchange I love yous; hang up.

I leave the shovel and the room. There's more I could say, but I don't need to say it. The conversation has gone another way, and I find I'm happy with where it went.

I OPEN ANOTHER door—and another. These last rooms are not rooms my mom would ever personally go into. Her loss! They're some of my favorites.

"I am happy to say that I too have cured an eye infection," Athénaïs Nin tells me, after mentioning the Madonna Lactans's healing of Saint Bernard. We're meeting on Zoom, and she's sharing her experiences with induced lactation. The infection she cured was a partner's stye: She dribbled some of her milk on it with an eyedropper, and the stye cleared up. The healing properties of milk.[38]

Nin is a therapist, writer, and sexuality educator, and lactation is an important part of her kink life. She describes it as "a devotional practice," in that it requires pumping at least four times a day—ideally five or six—and taking medications to keep up the supply. For her, this level of dedication is tied to how she shows up in her play dynamics as a trans femme mommy. "There's so much ritual contained within it, and so much devotion—devotion to oneself, devotion to one's body, devotion to one's dynamic, devotion to one's little one." She relates it to nurturance and affirmation and envelopment. "Or if you're in a submissive role and you're feeding—devotion to one's dominant."

I learned of Nin's work through my hairstylist, who told me about a workshop on lactation play that Nin had put on in Brooklyn. I was sad to learn about it after the fact and reached out to Nin for an interview. She's game, and lovely to talk with; it's clear this is a favorite topic, and she has come prepared. She's worn a T-shirt with an illustration of a milk carton that reads *Mommy Milkers* in an Olde English script. Behind her is a wall of books and zines, with *Milk Kink Zine* vols. 1 and 2 facing outward.

When I ask what she finds exciting about lactation, she has a long list. "It delivers a lot of nutrition. It's involved in folk medicine." She refers back to the healed stye.

"You can cook with it," she goes on. "I've made caramels. I've made pudding."

Nursing someone is also a very physically bonding process, she says. She loves the closeness and the warmth. "It's about reclaiming motherly desire." This is a source of gender pleasure, as Nin experiences lactation through a trans and queer lens.

"It involves so much body and system hacking," she explains. "We're constantly hacking systems and hacking our bodies. I was a formula baby, so the idea that I'm actually feeding people with my milk—*and* I'm trans . . . that's fucking cool and meaningful and so gender-affirming for me."

"It's wholesomely depraved," she adds. "And I love anything that's wholesomely depraved."

I ask about her experience of the *letdown reflex*. "When I am feeding someone, during letdown, I hear this phrase kind of moving through my body: 'I am love.'" She pauses. "And I feel like I am. I am the very embodiment of it. I am the conduit of love and care and nurturance." She connects this feeling to her identity as an anti-Zionist Jew and the principle of the Yiddish word *do'ikayt*, which means *hereness*—the idea that "home is not a place on a map."[39]

"We don't occupy," she explains. "Home is where we are and who we are with, and the relationships that we form. I've never had a strong attachment to a physical place that I call home, but when I am feeding, it's this sense that I am providing home."[40]

I'm moved by her description of the exchange. Milk is a renewable resource; so is sex. I admire how Nin draws on both to create a sense of home.

A FEW DAYS later, I bring up *Tender Buttons* to Liza, who mentions that Stein and Toklas used the word *cow* as a code word for orgasm. I remember I have a copy of *Baby Precious Always Shines*, their selected love notes. After we get off the call, I find it and flip through.

So many cows. This one is among the most explicit:

> Just concentrated concentrated on my wife's
> cow just concentrated on my wife's cow
> just concentrated and being all concentrated
> on my wife's cow my wife will have her
> cow now as I am just concentrated
> on my wife's cow just concentrated
> just Y.D.[41]

I take the book with me across the country to Elle's apartment. She's in the middle of moving, and boxes line the walls.

On her living room sofa, I read a few of Stein's letters to her, just concentrating on keeping a straight face. "They fucked *a lot*," she says, laughing. "Do you think Alice mooed when she came?" She tries out some cow sounds. It's not *not* hot.

We head into her bedroom for the transgressive mommy scene we have planned. I am a very lucky boy. Mommy tucks me in but noooo I'm not tired yet. Mommy will give me some milk to help me go to sleep. There's no milk but the idea of milk. There's no home but the idea of home. In the erotic transfer of that idea, there's a letting down and a letting go. Together we concentrate, just concentrate, until the milk comes down.

NOTES

1. Sarah Thornton, *Tits Up: What Sex Workers, Milk Bankers, Plastic Surgeons, Bra Designers, and Witches Tell Us About Breasts* (Norton, 2024), 3.
2. Gertrude Stein, *Tender Buttons*, in *Selected Writings of Gertrude Stein* (Vintage, 1990), 461.
3. Kathryn R. Kent, "'Excreate A No Since': The Erotic Currency of Gertrude Stein's *Tender Buttons*," in *Making Girls into Women: American Women's Writing and the Rise of Lesbian Identity* (Duke University Press, 2003), 150.
4. Kent, "'Excreate A No Since,'" 151.
5. Sinclair Sexsmith, "More on Butch Bras," *Sugarbutch Chronicles*, June 24, 2008, https://www.sugarbutch.net/2008/06/more-on-butch-bras/.
6. The Frog Bra resurfaced in 2015 to much fanfare ("Holy shit the Frog Bra is back!" cheered ftmichael on Reddit; "This is actually the best day of my life," attested Dancing Diva on the item page) but was discontinued a few years later, again due to Title Nine's difficulty with sourcing the material. On the product page, the company explains

that the manufacturer made this particular fabric "on a unique loom" that is no longer in service. Fans of the Frog Bra—which include many cis women, especially athletes—continue to plead with Title Nine to bring it back: "We will fund this loom with our own money," proposes SC from Portland in 2022. As of the time of writing, new posts were still appearing every few weeks on the item page: "I would do anything to find more of these. PLEASE BRING THEM BACK!!!!" pleads SSS from Seattle in June 2024 ("Frog Bra," Title Nine, https://www.titlenine.com/p/frog-bra/320927.html).

7. At a presidential debate, Romney said: "I had the chance to pull together a cabinet, and all the applicants seemed to be men. . . . I went to a number of women's groups and said, 'Can you help us find folks?' And they brought us whole binders full of women."
8. The group has since dropped "women" from its name and remains intended for women and gender-nonconforming writers.
9. A chain letter that was circulating in the early 1990s, at least among my group of friends.
10. In this essay, in most cases, I use *nursing* or, when applicable, *lactating* to be as inclusive as possible. When speaking about specific individuals, I adopt the language they use to refer to themselves. In historical contexts prior to debates over the language politics of body/breast/chestfeeding, I default to *nursing* or *breastfeeding*.
11. Dysphoric milk ejection reflex (D-MER) is a specific hormonal imbalance in which milk letdown is accompanied by a drop in dopamine, resulting in a feeling of hopelessness, anger, depression, and nausea. Jacob Engelsman, *Lactation for the Rest of Us* (Jessica Kingsley Publishers, 2025), 31. See also Zainab Yate's *When Breastfeeding Sucks* (Pinter & Martin, 2020).
12. Thornton, *Tits Up*, 76.
13. Melanie Klein, *Envy and Gratitude and Other Works, 1946–1963* (The Free Press, 1975), 180.

14. Some people who've undergone top surgery or other forms of breast/chest reconstruction surgery can lactate. If they've been damaged in surgery, it's possible for milk ducts to repair themselves. This is rare for those who, like me, have had a double incision with nipple grafts. See Engelsman, *Lactation for the Rest of Us*, 37. Because the milk ducts run around the underarm, it's also possible for milk to be expressed from the armpits.
15. Stein, *Tender Buttons*, 487.
16. Thornton, *Tits Up*, 19.
17. Thornton, *Tits Up*, 76–77.
18. Kimberly Seals Allers, *The Big Letdown: How Medicine, Big Business, and Feminism Undermine Breastfeeding* (St. Martin's Press, 2017), 10. Throughout her book, Seals Allers investigates how the development of formula shifted cultural and medical authority from women to doctors and commercial entities in matters of infant feeding. She also addresses the limitations of the Family and Medical Leave Act, which provides leave that is unpaid and only available to employees who meet specific eligibility criteria.
19. The protagonist, Audrey, struggles with nursing and bemoans the new limits parenting places on her social life. She fights with her husband Jeremy about sharing childcare, and suffers postpartum brain fog and feelings of incompetence. Everything to do with this major life transition is (comically and seriously) hard. Audrey feels at once like a failure and as though she is being failed.
20. The early 1970s saw rates of nursing at their lowest (22 percent) in the US. By 1981, my birth year, in part thanks to the education and outreach efforts of the Women's Health Movement and La Leche League, rates had risen, especially among well-educated white women: About half of all infants in the US breastfed; the rest didn't consume human milk at all. Anne L. Wright and Richard J. Schanler, "The Resurgence of Breastfeeding at the End of the Second Millennium," *The Journal of Nutrition* 131, no. 2 (February 2001): 421–25, https://jn.nutrition.org/article/S0022-3166(22)14649-3/fulltext.

21. Benjamin Spock, *Baby and Child Care* (Pocket Books, 1946), 33, https://archive.org/details/in.ernet.dli.2015.67215/page/n3/mode/2up.
22. Benjamin Spock, *Baby and Child Care* (Pocket Books, 1976).
23. Historian Jacqueline Wolf, as interviewed in Rebecca Corey, "A History of Breastfeeding and Formula Shaming: How Did We Get Here?," Yahoo!Life, August 22, 2022, https://www.yahoo.com/lifestyle/history-breastfeeding-formula-shaming-161727806.html.
24. As breastfeeding rates rose in the 1980s, so did the number of women in the workforce. The first portable electric pump went on the market in 1988 and was invented by Elena Grant, a computer systems supervisor and nursing mother frustrated by the limited options available for mothers pumping in the workplace. See Katherine Harmon Courage, "The Sucky History of the Breast Pump," *Smithsonian Magazine*, September 12, 2022, https://www.smithsonianmag.com/innovation/sucky-history-of-the-breast-pump-180980653/.
25. In 2024, costs are a few hundred dollars a month, higher for specialized and hypoallergenic formulas. Some formula, especially prescribed formula, may be covered by some insurance plans, but this varies.
26. Lauren Berlant and Michael Warner, "Sex in Public," *Critical Inquiry* 24, no. 2 (Winter 1998): 547–66, http://www.jstor.org/stable/1344178.
27. Heather Davis, *Plastic Matter* (Duke University Press, 2022), vii–x.
28. Ian Wickes, "A History of Infant Feeding, Part IV: Nineteenth Century Continued," *Archives of Disease in Childhood* 28, no. 141 (1953): 419, https://doi.org/10.1136/adc.28.141.416.
29. Wickes, "A History of Infant Feeding," 421.
30. *Our Foster Mother, the Cow* (Frith Films, 1943; rev. 1947), YouTube, https://www.youtube.com/watch?v=zamcq8xa1Y0.
31. Thornton, *Tits Up*, 76–77.

32. For more on wet-nursing in the US, see Janet Golden, *A Social History of Wet Nursing in America: From Breast to Bottle* (Ohio State University Press, 2001); Stephanie E. Jones-Rogers, "Wet Nurse for Sale or Hire," *They Were Her Property: White Women as Slave Owners in the American South* (Yale University Press, 2019); Jacqueline H. Wolf, *Don't Kill Your Baby: Public Health and the Decline of Breastfeeding in the Nineteenth and Twentieth Centuries* (Ohio State University Press, 2001); Hannah Ryan, "Early Photographs of Enslaved Wet Nurses and Charges in the American South," *Liquid Gold: Lactation as Labor and Human Milk as Commodity in Transatlantic Visual Culture* (Cornell University Press, 2019); Marylynn Salmon, "The Cultural Significance of Breastfeeding and Infant Care in Early Modern England and America," *Journal of Social History* 28, no. 2 (Winter 1994): 247–69; and Kelley L. Baumgartel, Larissa Sneeringer, and Susan M. Cohen, "From Royal Wet Nurses to Facebook: The Evolution of Breastmilk Sharing," *Breastfeeding Review* 24, no. 3 (2016): 25–32.
33. Mathilde Cohen and Hannah Ryan, "From Human Dairies to Milk Riders: A Visual History of Milk Banking in New York City, 1918–2018," *Frontiers: A Journal of Women Studies* 40, no. 3 (2019): 143–45.
34. For more on milk donors and milk networks in the US, see Thornton, "Lifesaving Jugs," ch. 2 in *Tits Up*.
35. A phrase from Dana Ward that many of us picked up from Maggie Nelson, who cites it in *The Argonauts*.
36. Filotesi dell'Amatrice, *Madonna of Grace*, ca. 1508.
37. Master of the Saint Catherine Legend, *Virgin and Child*, ca. 1490–95, oil on wood, The Met Cloisters.
38. See Engelsman, *Lactation for the Rest of Us*, 123, for more on milk's capacity to heal eye problems.
39. Nin credits Jewish queer and trans legal advocate Andy Izenson as the source for her understanding and embrace of *do'ikayt*.
40. In a follow-up to our interview, Nin shared that she has since gotten a tattoo of the word *do'ikayt* between her

breasts, saying that the tattoo and its placement were in many ways inspired by our conversation.

41. Kay Turner, ed., *Baby Precious Always Shines: Selected Love Notes Between Gertrude Stein and Alice B. Toklas* (St. Martin's Press, 1999), 93.

Night Milk

Cynthia tells me about Maurice Sendak's *In the Night Kitchen*, which she is able to quote readily, having read it often with her kids. *I'm in the milk, and the milk's in me*, she recites. *Seems up your alley.*

I'm visiting her in Saint Louis and finally meeting her two children, who are now five and three. We're well into the pandemic, and Cynthia and her partner have had few people over. To their older child, I'm a new audience for his exuberant, arrhythmic dance moves. To the younger, I'm a strange object who has come from beyond. He will keep a wide, uncertain eye on me at all times.

The book sounds wild. Something about a boy and a massive milk bottle. Cynthia hunts down their copy, and I page through it at the kitchen table, an arm's length from two gallons of milk in the fridge.

Here's the storyline: Waking up in the middle of the night, toddler protagonist Mickey tumbles down through his house and out of his clothes into the "night kitchen" below, where he lands in a bowl of cake batter. The night kitchen into which he has fallen is a surreal dreamscape, a kitchen that is also a city. Flour sacks and jam jars double as buildings. A slender unlabeled bottle (of oil, perhaps, or of wine) stretches to the stars, the highest skyscraper.

When he drops into the bowl, three lookalike bakers, rotund and disproportionately large, mistake Mickey for milk. Gleaming with a jolly malevolence underscored by their Hitler mustaches, the bakers fold him in. "Milk in the batter! Milk in the batter!" they chant ritualistically. "Scrape it! Make it! Bake it!" One baker carries the loaf toward the oven, next to which another waits, gazing at the bread bump as if entranced. The third baker rests an arm along the top of the stove, labeled "Mickey Oven."

But just before the bakers slide him onto the rack, our worthy hero sprouts from the top of the loaf to declare: "I'm not the milk and the milk's not me! I'm Mickey!"

The bakers seem to have been well aware of this, as evidenced by their Mickey oven. But Mickey does not know that they know and so, with the unsettling confidence of a well-adjusted child, announces himself as himself: He's Mickey.

Oh, to be so sure of oneself. Oh, to know one's name! If only I shared this self-knowledge.

A more conventional story might end here, but this is Sendak, beloved for his strange worlds and surreal logics. Now that Mickey has come to understand what he is (Mickey) and what he is not (milk), he takes it upon himself to go in search of replacement milk for the bakers. First he outfits himself in a roomy jumpsuit made of batter; then he creates a Mickey-sized, batter-based airplane. Finally he grabs the bakers' measuring cup and plants it on his head, a hat. He's off to "get milk the Mickey way," which involves flying high, high, over this night kitchen to find—what's that we see? An impossibly tall bottle glowing brightly against the night sky? And what does it hold, pale and opaque?

It's milk!

Mickey dives out of the airplane and into the bottle, where his bread suit easily disintegrates. He floats, singing: "I'm in the milk and the milk's in me / God bless milk and God bless me!" After a quick, joyful swim—sensuous, even—Mickey fills the measuring cup, climbs to the lip of the bottle, and in one long, unbroken stream pours the milk into the sticky batter below. The bakers get busy: mixing, beating, baking. And Mickey, his mission accomplished, crows "cock-a-doodle-do!" He slides down the side of the glass and into bed.

THIS, CHILDREN, OUR narrator concludes, is why we get to eat cake every morning—thanks to Mickey. But who eats cake in the morning? Not me. I like to cook up an egg scramble with veggies. No milk, or Mickeys, required.

The book's assumption of daily morning cake leads me to wonder if it's not American in origin but of some other cultural provenance. A stranger in our midst—like me, to Cynthia's youngest. I'll have to keep my eye on this one.

But Americans eat all sorts of everything for breakfast, and "morning cake," I learn, is a generic category that includes the more familiar (to me) coffee cake. Anyway, I also learn that Sendak was born in Brooklyn, a Polish-Jewish American who grew up during World War II.

In the Night Kitchen was first released in the US in 1970, but it still seems deeply strange, a book from another place, and I guess it is, since Brooklyn then and Brooklyn now *are* hugely different. In any case, now that I know it's American-born, I can't unsee the Americanness. It's there in the self-satisfied white boy invoking God while floating in milk—as if the bottle he's swimming in is an ad paid for by the Dairy Farmers of America. It's in the night sky's resemblance, with its five-pointed stars, to the top-left corner of the American flag. And it's in Mickey's song, which calls to mind the patriotic hymn "God Bless America" and its associations with Christian conservatism. At the time I encountered the book in 2022, as right-wing conservatives were increasingly brazenly using "wholesome" American—i.e., white straight Christian—family values as an excuse to enact legislative and material violence against minoritized communities and people with uteruses, *In the Night Kitchen*'s glittery milk magic seemed to sour on the tongue. In early 2025, as we track the nation's swift tilt into illiberal authoritarianism, the book's milky patriotism now smells fully rancid.

But Sendak wasn't conservative or Christian. He was a weirdo Jewish artist. That he and his family lost many relatives during the Holocaust gives distressing new meaning to the bakers' Hitler-style mustaches and their menacing "Mickey Oven." And, though it has since become associated with conservative values, the hymn "God Bless America" was written during World War I (though not debuted publicly until 1938) by Jewish composer Irving Berlin, formerly Israel Baline, who fled Russian persecution of Jews with his family as a child. Berlin pulled the song's titular refrain from his mother, who repeated it often after they had arrived in the US. In this light, the song reads like the expression of a Jewish assimilationist desire to belong.

The book can be read similarly. When he springs from the cake batter, Mickey recognizes he must "mix" himself into the situation, not as milk but as a useful denizen of the night kitchen. And so he makes himself an airplane that most closely resembles a WWII-era US military fighter jet. While the hymn's refrain rings like a plea or a prayer of belonging, Mickey's "God bless milk and God bless me" is a gloat of triumph, a defiant assurance of his place in the milk of America at large.

Another friend who is a parent offers a second possibility: that Mickey's song references not "God Bless America" but a popular nursery rhyme, sung to the tune of "Hush Little Baby." There are a number of variations, but the shortest and perhaps most common is this:

> I see the moon and the moon sees me
> and the moon sees somebody I can't see
> God bless the moon and God bless me
> God bless that somebody I can't see

Mickey's syntax and cadence snap into place easily along these guiding lines. I find an online lyric video featuring a happy and slow-blinking full moon, soporific by design. Mickey's song is less lullaby, more exultation: He's awake and he's himself. He's Mickey. God has blessed him.

I find I'm jealous of Mickey. I want his confidence, his self-assured braggadocio. I want his dream and his morning cake.

Do I also want his name?

No. In the US it's so strongly associated with Disney.

The Milky Way—through which Mickey navigates—is another name. According to Greek myth, the band of light that gave our galaxy its name sprang from Hera's breast. She woke in the middle of the night and found Zeus had affixed another woman's child—Heracles—to her breast. If the child drank her divine milk, he would become immortal. Understandably upset by this nonconsensual consumption of her body, Hera pushed the child away. The milk spurting from her breast lit up the sky.

In the Night Kitchen is famous for the controversy its

illustrations provoked. Though he starts off in pajamas and later coats himself in a suit of bread batter, there are ten or so panels in which Mickey is depicted nude, most of them when he is inside the milk bottle. There's no mother figure portrayed in the book, but one can't help thinking of human milk. Is Mickey returning to infancy by diving, naked, into the milk, which may stand in for the womb? Or is he expressing autonomy by finding and enjoying this milk on his own, outside of a mother's breast?

IN THE NIGHT KITCHEN is a homosocial world. Mickey has parents, but in his dream, they are sleeping. This is true of Sendak's work generally: His stories are about children on their own, bodies encountering other bodies, contact with strange otherworlds as delightful as they are potentially dangerous. Mickey's dream initiates a sensory education, much of which is enabled by his nudity.

Mickey's skin is painted with the palest pink, subtly distinct from the ivory yellow substance within which he floats. His misrecognition as milk relies on his whiteness. This is a white child, whiter because nude. And in fact, for this fable's surreal narrative logic to hold, Mickey *must* be a milk-white child.

SENDAK WAS AN atheist, I learn.

He was also queer; he came out publicly a few years before he died at eighty-three. His partner of fifty years, Eugene David Glynn, was a psychoanalyst, and Sendak saw *In the Night Kitchen* as the first in a trilogy of books exploring childhood development through a psychoanalytic lens. Long before he came out, *In the Night Kitchen* had been challenged by parents and librarians on the basis of its gay subliminal messaging. In this reading, the milk bottle is a phallic image. When he tastes the milk—semen?—and sings, "I'm in the milk and the milk's in me," it could be read as an initiation into gay sex. I like this reading the best, mainly for its absurdity. But the enduring association of gay men with pedophilia is no joke.

I'm in the children's wing of the public library, looking for a copy of *In the Night Kitchen*. There are so many age and genre categories, and I can't find the right one. The wing is rowdy and busy, and everyone else seems to be a child or a feminine-presenting parent. I'm masked, tall, wearing an oversized denim jacket, dark jeans, and boots. A silent queer masculinity ducking down to check the call numbers on the low-sitting shelves. After a while, my nervous wandering attracts questioning, then suspicious looks. I find the book and exit quickly.

When I read *In the Night Kitchen*, I'm not the milk. I'm Mickey. But I understand that outside the book, I'm no longer Mickey. The kids are Mickey. I'm not absent mom or absent dad either; if I'm anyone, I'm the gay baker, the childless and child-hungry threat.

Back in Saint Louis, when Cynthia's youngest looks at me with alarm, part of me thinks he's right. It's true: I am disrupting the hub of their home, their flow and routine. I'm the single nonparent adult pulling Cynthia away from her family to go out, to get drinks, to gossip and talk about our dates. The child-free artist escaping responsibility and normative maturity. Though it feels true, I remind myself that it isn't. I'm rehashing insulting myths about childless queers: that we are childish and immature, playing at being adults. And I'm buying into reductive and erroneous ideas about parents: that their autonomous lives necessarily end when they have children, and that queerness and parenthood don't mix.

After a day or so, the younger one starts to warm up to me. I feel accomplished and special to have broken through, though I'm told this is his usual pattern. We make chalk art on the sidewalk. He hands me one piece of chalk and picks up another. "Orange," he tells me. "Blue."

CYNTHIA'S YOUNGEST WAILS through the night. I worry that my strange presence has disturbed him. Have I brought upsetting energies into the house? Have I introduced new germs?

He can't fall asleep, which means he can't fall into the night kitchen. None of us can. We can't fall, so we can't fly.

I hear Cynthia or her partner move in and out of his room, offering comfort. After a few hours, he settles. Together, we dream.

I fall down through the ceiling of the makeshift guest room. I fall into the night kitchen, where I catch sight of Cynthia, blurry and receding. Her partner tilts a measuring cup of milk into her mouth. Rivulets run down her chin and onto her chest. She's not the milk but the milk's in her. The boys glug their glasses with two hands.

Soon there's no more milk.

It's up to me to get it.

I need no plane. I float up into the Milky Way, rising out of my clothes. I am white, if not milk white. I am freckled and tattooed. My torso flashes silvery in the night. I'm a minnow on a mission: milk.

I stretch my body from cloud to cloud. In the distance, a sea of cloudy froth—I hear the hymn . . . *the oceans white with foam* . . . as I swim up to another layer of atmosphere.

I don't see a bottle, but I see a cow. *What's your name?* I ask her. *Moon*, she tells me. I start to announce I'm Megan, or Milks, or Mickey—I'll decide when the word pops out—but language leaves me as she rubs her belly against mine. Her udder is swollen and heavy, stretched like an overfull water balloon. Where is her calf to drain it? She nudges me, and now I'm milking. Her teats are like bristly dicks, thick and full. I don't know how at first, but I figure it out, and when I pull her, there's moonlight.

I direct the milk down, bringing it home to my friends and to their children, to the night kitchen, to the world below. I pull and pull. We find a rhythm. The cow groans with the pleasure of release. When the milk runs out, she kicks me away and trots off, swallowed up in the night. Cock-a-doodle-do. I am receiving my sensory education. My skin is alive with the cool air, the mist from the clouds, the warm glow of the milklight. My name doesn't matter. I am a body in the world: floating, falling. Awake now and ready for cake.

MAGA Milk

— 1 —

YOU ARE TRYING to write about an estrangement.

A rift. A tear in the ground.

A fault.

A difference that spreads.

A dis-ease that is political.

He is white and so are you. Freckled and prone to sunburn.

He doesn't like you. You don't like him.

These seem like your firmest overlaps.

But you come from the same source. You have more in common than you'd like.

You feel confident in assuming the nature of his dislike. It's based on the nature of your dislike, which is based on his expressions of politics. He's anti-vax. Is obsessed with Trump and the Second Amendment. He blames immigrants and trans people, for what, you no longer care to understand.

You're tired of understanding.

Maybe he's MAGA and the most predictable kind of Fox News zealot. Maybe he jokes that LA's "71 genders" are at fault for the wildfires razing the region. Maybe he has a side hustle in which he plays small roles in big film productions that pass through the region. Maybe he's played the role of a slave catcher, or a cop, or a veteran homesteader. Maybe he's told you the white men are always the bad guys in these films.

Maybe that's the last conversation the two of you have had, maybe five years ago, during which he asked you nothing about your life. Maybe he never will.

Maybe he still could.

Maybe, in the absence of contact, you've turned him into something unfair and untrue.

Maybe he's done the same to you. You're ungodly. Stay away from his kid. You're the threat from which he must protect his family.

Protect yourself. Second-person point of view gives you a shelter to hide within. A place to be submerged, less visible and exposed. More opaque (more milky). Here, you are you and not-you. Your sense of self floats upward and away while staying nearby, within reach.

You harbor fantasies: if you could just talk it out. Talk it over.

When you think about talking with him, you feel dread and alarm. This other thing: hope. And a deep heavy sadness that could be classified as grief.

Second person allows you to express these feelings with that affect associated with whiteness: what gets called emotional restraint.

It lets you do other things, too: like enact a tension between the general and the specific that contests any suggestion of universality.

Send him an email. You're writing a book about milk, about the name Milks. Would he be willing to talk with you?

Grief because: Your family was sometimes a happy place. Grief because: You once looked up to him. And he was your friend.

Grief because: You keep trying. You think.

Days pass. Weeks. Is this trying? You could give him a call, but that would be too strange.

Or too hard. After a month, you send him a second email.

THEN YOU HAVE a dream.

He is forcing your Toyota Acura up your grandmother's driveway with his truck. Your car is behind him, boxing him in, and you aren't moving fast enough. He's impatient and teaching you a lesson.

Your grandmother's house is built into a hill, with the driveway on a steep incline down to the carport from the road. To back out of the driveway, you have to reverse uphill and pause at the top to wait for a gap in the passing cars. It's a busy street, tricky to enter in reverse. He's pushing you toward it.

You rush to your car, yelling No, don't. Just wait. You'll move it. He doesn't wait. He nudges your car back with his. You manage to open the car door and get inside, the door flopping open from the backward momentum. In his rear-view mirror, he flashes a malicious grin. Now you're choked up and heaving with panic. Your hand is shaking; you drop your keys. He's going to fuck up your car. If he'd just give you the chance, you would get out of his way.

What is he reacting to? You rifle through your dream memory. Have you been disrespectful? Have you been testing him?

There is something precious in your trunk, you remember. That's why it took you so long to get in the car and get out. You needed to secure a fragile thing. If he pushes you into the road, whatever's in the trunk (you can't remember) will get crunched by an oncoming vehicle.

Is that what he wants: to crush the thing? Maybe, but you don't think so. A plot materializes, then dissolves.

Your mother stands on the carport, a witness. She's on your side, ostensibly, yelling at him. But she can't help but chuckle, too, amused at his brazenness. It's not funny, you tell her—or you try. You're in dream-state; you're trying to speak but you can't. The words are shrill in your throat, too high-pitched, a whine that's lodged as a lump.

When you wake up, you can't remember what happened. Just that you—and the precious thing—were destroyed.

THAT WASN'T REAL, you tell yourself. It didn't happen. It's not fair to characterize this person from this one quick dream. It's not fair to characterize him from the feelings that produced it. The feelings are real, but they aren't facts.

What's fact is the Lego city you built that he stomped on when you were a kid.

What's fact is the Confederate flag splayed out like a sleeping dragon in the rear window of his truck.

The Confederate license plate holder. The bumper sticker.

What's fact is him saying you "smelled Asian" when you came home from your friends' homes in high school.

You flushing red and without any adequate response.

What's fact is you infiltrating his algebra class, embarrassing him by being younger, a girl, and better at math.

What's fact is the zeal with which you overedited an essay he wrote for a class. What's fact is his rejection of all your suggestions.

What's fact is the day he helped you out by hitching your grandfather's trailer to his truck and driving all of your belongings through five states. After unloading them, he turned around and drove himself home.

What's fact is the stiffness with which you together perform a gesture that could be understood as a hug.

You pinning him down in the yard, trying to smash his head with a rock.

Did that really happen? You can't remember.

Real: the photograph of him and his wife he posted to social media, gussied up and gleaming. Happy to be forming their own family.

Real: his years of hard-won sobriety. The wine you've tossed down in his presence, convinced you needed it to get through the meal.

Real: You have been imagining watching *Get Out* with him and talking about the milk scene, in this way facilitating a conversation about milk and whiteness. The fantasy doesn't get far. But you would lead the conversation and you would win.

Not real: The two of you having a conversation in which you are able to change his mind about anything. This conversation does something other than give you that wheezy shrill lump in your throat. The STOP IT, NO, STOP, STOP THAT RIGHT NOW that you can't get out.

Not real: The two of you having a real conversation about anything, really.

Real: He doesn't drink milk. He drinks Mountain Dew.

Real: When you suddenly erupt into nonsense blips and beeps while making an elaborate salad, it feels like a trace of him. Not the salad, but the noise. The irrepressible urge to make silly sounds.

Not real: In the dream, you're screaming I hate you, I hate you. In the dream you have a ponytail and a purse.

Real: the absence of advocates. Your mom on the sidelines, not stopping it.

Real: the panic flooding you as you bolt awake, struggling to determine what's real and what's not.

— 2 —

Upon this industry, more than any other of the food industries, depends not alone the problem of public health, but there depend upon it the very growth and virility of the white race.

—THEN-SECRETARY OF COMMERCE HERBERT HOOVER, speaking to the World Dairy Congress in 1923

MY COUSIN SAYS this has happened a few times: her son's (white, woman) teacher looks at the attendance sheet, sees the name "Garrett Milks," and, though she knows him well enough to know both his names, finds my cousin's milk-white son in the middle of the room and calls him Garrett White.

MILK IS WHITE. Right?

Milk is innocent.

Milk is thicker than water.

MILK IS MADE largely of casein proteins suspended in water. These proteins cluster with calcium and phosphate to form particles called micelles. Micelles refract and scatter light, giving milk a white appearance.

So, milk is white.

Or at least it appears so when exposed to light.

Two gloved hands hold a skinny tube of what looks like frozen butterscotch.

The clue reads: "This animal's milk is fatty and becomes fattier the longer it nurses. It has a dense texture and a very 'milky' smell."

The options:

— cheetah

— golden lion tamarin

— Asian elephant

I guess Asian elephant and wonder if I know what "milky" smells like.

Correct. I'm awarded information: "Asian elephant gestation lasts about 22 months—the longest gestation period for any mammal. When a calf is born, it can weigh between 150 and 350 pounds."

I'm at home with my foster cat, Whole Milk, a rescue who's recently given birth to five kittens (now weaned and adopted out).[1] As I'm moving through the questions of this "Guess That Milk!" online quiz, I wonder how her milk would be described. The quiz is written by a researcher who manages the Smithsonian National Zoo's walk-in freezer of animal milks, and I'm struck by the range of colors in the accompanying images: Some milks are as bright as egg yolk, others like dark honey. An orangutan's milk is grayish and nearly translucent. The zoo's milk repository (the world's largest, as of 2019) contains samples shipped from all over the planet. Some appear white. Most are a shade of yellow.[2]

After five days or so, human milk transitions from the yellowy, thicker colostrum to a whiter, more fluid substance. Some has a parmesan tint, and some appears grayish, like oatmeal. Depending on where a lactating person is in their cycle, the foods and medications they've ingested, and whether their nipples are cracked or bleeding, their milk may take on hues of silvery blue, minty green, pale pink, brownish, or near black.

Cow milk is whiter. I've seen it streaming out of cows' bodies and coursing through clear rubber tubes. I've squeezed it straight from the teat and I've seen its whiteness firsthand. Pure as the glue that subs in for it in commercials. Glue that's made, typically, from cattle hooves.

A clean, crisp, light-scattering white.

IF YOU'VE SEEN *Get Out*, Jordan Peele's breakout film, you'll remember the scene with the milk. It's quick and comes near the end. We've been in the basement with Chris, the Black protagonist, who's in the process of escaping the surgery that will remove his brain so that a white man's brain can replace it, slipped into Chris's body in an odious act of body snatching and transracial drag.

Cut to Rose, Chris's white girlfriend, upstairs in her room, celebrating her family's success by scouring the internet for her next mark. As Rose enters "Top NCAA Prospects" into the search bar, she's listening to the triumphal theme from *Dirty Dancing* on headphones, unaware of what's happening downstairs. Before her is a bowl of dry Froot Loops and a tall glass of milk. She takes one small sip of the milk. Then another. Controlled, almost dainty. She uses a straw.

There are all kinds of white, but this milk is *white* white. And now so is Rose, who has transformed herself from breezy creative to something more severe: a crisp white button-down and tight ponytail, no makeup.

The house is on fire. Her father and brother are (plot spoiler) dead. But Rose's bubble of white obliviousness remains intact. She sets the glass down with the steely calm of sure victory. The joke's on her.

As I watched this scene on the film's opening weekend, my skin felt sticky, as if coated in milk. I was feeling my whiteness and my Milks-ness at once. I was feeling horrified, and I was feeling, well, fragile.

My dream was right. The fragile thing needed smashing.

In an interview about his use of milk in this scene, Peele says he was unaware of the links between milk and white nationalism when he shot it. But there is "something kind of horrific about milk," he says. "Think about it! Think about what we're *doing*. Milk is kind of gross."[3]

I MEET JOSH COHEN, a graduate scholar of religious history, at a local café. He orders a tall hot coffee, black; I get a pineapple and kale smoothie, no milk. We met a few weeks ago at a friend's birthday party: His partner waved him over after I mentioned my project. "This is Megan. They're working on a book about milk." "Really?" he said with an uncertain smile. "You're not joking?" He was working on one too: a dissertation on milk in Renaissance Spain. We nerded out on milk facts and agreed to talk over coffee.

Now Josh tells me more about his research, which explores the religious power of milk in Inquisition-era Spain. By "milk" he means human milk, not cow or other animal milks, which were not much consumed then by humans in fluid form—though occasionally infants were given sheep, goat, and other animal milks when human milk was unavailable. Josh's central argument is that human milk had cultural power in Renaissance Europe: It was seen as an instrument through which *raza* could be transmitted. Now understood to mean something akin to "race," in its original context, raza described a stain or crack in the lineage, and was used mainly to name what was seen as a core defect in Renaissance Spanish Christians with Jewish or Muslim heritage. (That is, the "impurity" of Jewish or Muslim heritage was the defect, which was raza.)

While the official religious doctrines saw raza as transmitted through genealogical "blood" (or a kind of metaphorically abstracted semen), Josh contends that in lived experience, "raza started to spread in other ways, horizontally, from body to body in the world—most exemplarily through paid breastfeeding."

Medieval and early Renaissance cultures believed that milk was blood—white blood. Josh traces this logic back to Aristotelian embryology, which proposed that a fetus was made from the combined life spirit of the father's semen and the material clay of the mother's menstrual blood, which also served as its first food in the womb. After birth, God (or sometimes Nature) sent the mother's excess menstrual blood up to the breast, where it was cooked, purified, and whitened before being expressed through the nipples. Human milk was blood that had been sweetened and purified, made white.[4]

In this way, the newborn's first meals were guaranteed to be "familiar." "Strange" milk was to be avoided. If a child suckled a "strange" wet nurse, it was thought, the alien milk would undermine the father's imprint and erode a child's original connection to their father.[5]

In Renaissance Europe, this logic was reinterpreted through Christianity. Now religious and cultural authorities—e.g., church officials, physicians, jurists, and poets—believed that a "bad milk" could, by imperiling the father's imprint, also imperil the child's Christianization. The two bloods would duke it out in what Josh describes as a "battle of bodily fluids."

Much was at stake in this battle. In Inquisition-era Spain, discriminatory statutes about blood purity (limpieza de sangre) prevented Christians with Muslim or Jewish ancestry from holding church, city, or state office. These groups were often known as "New Christians" and had either been forcibly baptized or were descendants of people who had been forcibly baptized. In contrast, "Old Christians" were "clean" of all Jewish or Muslim ancestry and were considered pure, clean, morally perfect, and raceless (sin raza), like Jesus or the Virgin Mary.[6] Many scholars point to these statutes as the origins of a modern conception of race.

Since blood held power, so, too, did milk, the white blood. Those with cultural authority urged Old Christian parents not to hire New Christian wet nurses. If they did, they risked their lineally pure infant "getting raza"—that is, "contracting the Jewish or Muslim tendencies lingering in that milk-blood."

But, as Josh says with a shrug, "People don't do what they're told." Many Christian families continued to hire Muslim and Jewish wet nurses, who were more affordable and more abundant. Christendom has long been contaminated by strange milk.

WHEREAS HUMAN MILK could become strange according to bogus Christian-supremacist ideas about ethnic and class pollution, early commercial cow milk was often literally contaminated. When the market for fluid cow milk emerged in the nineteenth century, city streets were thick with filth. In New York, tens of thousands of horses worked the city, each releasing an average of twenty-two pounds of manure and one quart of urine per day. That equine waste mixed with runoff from the carts that predominantly Black or immigrant "night soil" men used to carry off the human waste they emptied from overflowing privies. Animal carcasses—horses, rats, cats, and dogs—were left in the street for collection. Pre–germ theory, none of this was seen as a public health issue so much as an offense to the nose.

As the milk market developed, opportunities for contamination occurred at each stage. Cows' teats, often manure-caked, were not reliably cleaned before they were milked. Milk pails were left open to the elements, inviting dirt, insects, leaves, or hair to fall into the product. Dr. Hervey D. Thatcher, who invented the sealed milk bottle, traced his invention's inspiration to the moment he saw a young girl drop a grimy, well-loved doll in a milk pail; the milk merchant fished it out, shook it off, and proceeded to sell Dr. Thatcher the milk.[7] This kind of milk pollution was ordinary and unquestioned.

Until cows took over in the mid-nineteenth century, wet-nursing was a common practice in the US. Hired or forced by middle- and upper-class white families to nourish their infants, often to the detriment of their own children's health, wet nurses sustained much of the nation with their milk. Most were lower-class immigrants or enslaved Black women. As was the case in Renaissance Europe, wet-nursing in nineteenth-century America was often cross-class and cross-race. In this period, too, the practice was upset by fears of cross-contamination, here fed by growing class disparities and eugenicist sentiment. Despite its dirtiness, many families became convinced that feeding infants cow milk was safer than risking their adulteration from milk that came from a "lower" woman's breast.[8]

Meanwhile, most poor and working-class mothers continued to breastfeed—the more economical choice. But the availability of cow milk allowed them to wean their infants more quickly after birth so that they could return to work and wages. Soon many families across classes were relying on cow milk as a primary infant food source. This wasn't all bad, of course. For many women, especially those in the lower classes, taking their bodies out of the food chain was a relief.

But the resulting situation was grim. The infant death rate soared. In the 1840s, half of all infants born in the city did not survive to the age of five. Many of these deaths were linked to what was known as "summer complaint," a catch-all for cholera and other digestive illnesses that people didn't think to trace to milk that had soured in the heat.[9] These were the years before proper refrigeration and storage, before sterilization and pasteurization, before food regulation of any kind, and before the germ theory of disease was widely adopted. People didn't understand that bacteria (from insects, from manure, from unwashed hands) could enter the open pails of milk that were commonly used for milking and selling. They didn't understand that bovine tuberculosis could be transmitted to humans through milk.

They also didn't understand that cows were more susceptible to the spread of disease when kept in close quarters. City cows were kept in crowded stables, many of which adjoined city whiskey distilleries. Often, cows were fed the runoff grain husks, sugar, and water from the distillery process. A brewery cow might be tied to a stall where she would be confined her entire life, spending her days standing in her excrement and surviving on steaming brewery slop. She was given no fresh water—the brewery runoff, it was thought, provided enough. Without solid food to chew on, she might lose her teeth. Her body might erupt in ulcers. Her tail might fall off. She would be milked even when sick with tuberculosis, even when too weak to stand.

A healthy cow can live up to twenty years. These cows often died within six months.

Because it came from sick cows, swill milk (as it became known) was visually unappealing—bluish and thin. Milk merchants' solution was to add various white things—poisonous things like chalk and lye and plaster of Paris—to make it more appealing to buyers. This toxic whitened milk was marketed as "pure country milk."

In New York, it took many years and continued pressure from social reformers and journalists before the city started investigating. Brewery dairies were protected by Tammany Hall, the political machine that controlled much of the city, and Tammany Hall had a vested interest in distilleries. But eventually, arguments against brewery dairies gained traction, and public pressure led to their closure and to the passage of regulations against swill milk in 1861.[10]

This wasn't the end of what was now known as "the milk question"; rather, it ushered in many decades of debate over milk safety. Strangely, when the public started asking these questions, they weren't asking whether humans should be drinking it at all. The assumption was that cow milk was—is—good for us. Not just "good": As historian E. Melanie DuPuis has explained, milk reformers argued that it was "nature's perfect food," an ideal source of nutrition they credited to the Christian God.[11] The question, then, was how to return cow milk to its "wholesome" form.

It went undisputed: Bad cow milk was bad, good cow milk was perfect. And human milk? Take it or leave it. If you were a well-resourced white mother who—because of your own reluctance or inability to nurse—saw your infant's food source options as coming from either a cow or a woman who was poor, "fallen," an immigrant, or of color, choose the cow.

For decades, these arguments have persisted, bolstering the national reputation of cow milk as unequivocally "wholesome" and "good," something kids and adults alike should be drinking. These arguments devalue human milk and ignore bodily difference when it comes to lactose sensitivity.

Or rather, they don't ignore lactose sensitivity: They use it as proof of white superiority. "By declaring milk perfect," DuPuis notes, "white northern Europeans announced their own perfection."[12]

I'VE PUT "WHOLESOME" in scare quotes above because it's one of those dubious words, like "pure" or "healthy," that nearly always seem to demand complication. "Good." "Real." "Normal." "Perfect."

My friend Cynthia, who teaches disability studies, sends me a presentation she uses to introduce eugenics. Her slideshow focuses on the Fitter Families contests held in the 1920s by the American Eugenics Society.

I find out more about these competitions, which built on the popularity of the Better Babies movement. Initiated as a response to the nineteenth-century infant mortality crisis, Better Babies contests promoted infant health and wellness alongside eugenicist ideas of "good" and "bad" heritage. The first such competition was held in 1908 at the Louisiana State Fair, and was judged based on criteria for the most "scientific" baby. The contest caught the attention of the national magazine *Woman's Home Companion*, which created a Better Babies Bureau that encouraged women to organize similar contests in their own communities. *WHC* saw this as a "serious scientific" endeavor: to produce "healthy babies, standardized babies, and always, year after year, *Better Babies*."[13]

The Fitter Families contests aimed to improve on the Better Babies model by making them *more* eugenicist. Frustrated by the absence of attention to heredity in the Better Babies movement, the organizers designed Fitter Families in coordination with the Eugenics Record Office. This new competition, which focused on the family as a unit, took the conventions of baby contests, including judging criteria like nutrition and education, and added criteria more associated with agricultural fairs, such as a baby's breeding and genetic lineage.

The first Fitter Families contest was held at the Kansas State Fair in 1920, and was heralded as long overdue "progress." Livestock breeders had paid close attention to heredity for many years: Today, you can look up registered cattle in online databases and find extensive genetic histories (see "Milking the Bull" for more on bovine genetics). Now these principles were being applied to humans through contests that claimed to contribute to our collective knowledge of human genetic history—that is, white genetic history. The goal: perfecting the white race.

One of Cynthia's slides features the medallions provided to award-winning families. They are embossed with the figures of a white man and a white woman in Roman-style togas passing a torch to a nude and well-muscled toddler. Above them stretch the words *YEA, I HAVE A GOODLY HERITAGE*.

"Zoom in on the bottom right-hand side of slide #7," Cynthia instructs me. It's a Fitter Families Examination form from 1925, filled out by the father of the family who won the "Large" category (for families with five or more children) in Texas. This Dallas-based teacher and agricultural agent's posture is "erect," his chest is "full," and his shoulders are "firm" and "well-shaped." His skin color is "normal" (that is, normal white); points off for stained teeth and tartar buildup. His "eugenic score" is "A." What Cynthia wants me to zero in on is a line in the "Health Habits" category, where quantity of milk precedes water in priority of importance: This guy claims to drink an average of six glasses of milk a day.

THAT'S A LOT of milk! But it's not so far off from the kind of milk mania my generation grew up with. In the 1980s and 1990s, it seemed like you couldn't get through one measly episode of *Saved by the Bell* or *Fresh Prince* without seeing a

"Milk. It Does a Body Good" commercial; you couldn't read an issue of *SPIN* or *YM* without flipping past a "Got Milk?" ad; you couldn't get away from the cautionary spectacle of stooped-over women with osteoporosis. At a friend's book launch party I meet a writer named Kevin who's around my age. He tells me his mother took seriously the USDA's guidelines for children at the time—three glasses of milk a day—and decided that Kevin, who was a smaller kid, needed all the help he could get. He'd come home from school to find not one, not three, but *four glasses of milk* lined up on the kitchen counter. One by one, he pounded them, trying to get it over with as quickly as possible.

My guts are lactose-friendly and still roil at the thought. If you were someone with lactose sensitivity or nonpersistence, this milk-manic period would have been particularly difficult to stomach. For those who no longer produce the enzyme lactase, fluid milk consumption can result in gastrointestinal distress. Yet for decades, lactose nonpersistent people, many of them from racialized communities, have been coerced by USDA guidelines, school milk mandates, and white-centric ideas about health into glugging down this white stuff that has made them physically ill.

This state-supported conflation of cow milk with health and "wholesomeness" is a form of dietary racism that operates on both literal and symbolic levels. The correlation between race and lactose nonpersistence has been trotted out repeatedly as evidence for the supposed physiological superiority of white people. The positive traits that health authorities of the 1920s and 1930s ascribed to milk drinking included physical and mental strength, longevity, an appreciation for aesthetics and culture, and progressivism in science and "every" intellectual field.[14] Dairy consumption at this time was on an upswing, a way in which white Americans could react to the influx of Chinese immigrants, who were predominantly lactose nonpersistent. Milk came to represent "a seemingly intrinsic connection to white citizenship."[15]

This correlation isn't real. Lactose persistence—that is, the ability to break down lactose in the body into adulthood—has less to do with race per se and more to do with whether one's ancestors depended on herd animals to survive. About 70 percent of the world has trouble digesting lactose, including 15 percent of white people. The minority of humans who can digest milk into adulthood include people of North African, Middle Eastern, South Asian, and Northern European and Scandinavian descent. Many Africans in the Ethiopian and Kenyan highlands are lactose persistent, as are many Saudi Arabians and Himalayan South Asians. In these climates hostile to cultivating sustainable food sources, the milk of herd animals provided important nutritional support, and the human body, regardless of racial phenotype, evolved to meet the available food sources.

And lactose persistence has nothing to do with physiological superiority. It's a biological benefit only in food cultures that prioritize dairy. That the United States is saturated with dairy-based products is not because Americans need so much dairy but because the federal government has had to do something with the country's milk surplus. In 1995, the USDA created a marketing branch, Dairy Management Incorporated, whose job it has been to find creative ways of feeding this surplus to Americans. DMI develops dairy-based products in collaboration with fast food companies like Domino's and Taco Bell.[16] Take Domino's extra-cheesy American Legends pizzas, for example, a DMI-driven product: "We use six legendary cheeses brought to you by America's dairy farmers," reads the product's promotion page. "Then we give you 40 percent more." Since the majority of adult people are lactose nonpersistent, these dairy-happy menus constitute a form of food oppression in low-income neighborhoods that lack other food options.[17]

School milk mandates have been another form. In effect since 1946, the USDA's National School Lunch Program reimburses schools for student lunches. But in order to qualify, schools must provide dairy milk with every meal. In 2022, twenty-eight civil rights and health care groups joined together to write a letter to the USDA's Equity Commission, charging that the program is enacting dietary racism. Given that many of the millions of students who rely on the program may be lactose nonpersistent, the NSLP's incentivization of dairy milk, the letter argues, is "inherently inequitable and socially unjust."[18] (While the letter aimed to highlight the impact of the NSLP program on students from racialized communities, a majority of whom are likely lactose intolerant, it's worth noting that lactose-nonpersistent white students have also been affected by the program.)[19]

Evidence exists that the dairy industry and the USDA have jointly exaggerated claims about the health benefits of milk. On some nutritional guidelines that are similar to the USDA's, such as the Canadian nutritional guidelines and the Harvard Healthy Eating Plate, dairy is excluded from the recommended food categories.[20] While milk consumption is known to improve bone health in limited ways, a number of studies have challenged the industry's linkage of milk and osteoporosis prevention.[21] There is also no causal relationship between milk drinking and longevity. Japan, South Korea, and Singapore are among the top five countries with the highest life expectancy averages, as of 2024; all three display high levels of lactose nonpersistence. In fact, a 2019 study suggested that drinking milk may actually reduce longevity.[22] Other studies have shown links between dairy consumption and increased risk of heart disease, cancer, diabetes, and multiple sclerosis.[23]

Taking stock of all of this, we might wonder if we've been trolled.

IN FEBRUARY 2017, 4Chan users and neo-Nazis showed up to troll artist Luke Turner's *HEWILLNOTDIVIDE.US* installation. Developed in collaboration with actor Shia LaBoeuf, the project consisted of a live streaming camera placed outside the Museum of the Moving Image in Queens, New York. It was designed to run for the duration of Trump's first presidency, and the stream was viewable online in real time. LaBoeuf, who became the project's face (and whose name, incidentally, translates to "The Beef"), appeared on-site daily, leading whoever wanted to join him in chants of "He will not divide us." It wasn't long before 4Chan trolls caught wind, dubbed the project "cringe," and arrived on the scene to disrupt the chants with alt-right satirical catchphrases like "kek" and eardrum-splitting shrieks of "reeee."

Let me pause here and acknowledge that I, too, think this artwork is cringe. What I'm interested in is what happened next.

In the midst of this war between earnest woke leftists and alt-right chaos agents, a tall white guy ambles up one day toting a jug of milk. Staring steadily at the camera, he brings the milk to his mouth, tilts it up, and gulps. It's his thing, he says later, in an interview. Known as Milkman, he goes around and drinks milk.[24] Watching online, 4Chan trolls think this is hilarious and make memes out of him:

"Milk power!" Soon they're showing up to the live stream location with their own quarts, pints, and gallons. "Praise milk," one of them says, and pours some onto the camera, blurring the feed.

Paperboy Love Prince, a local activist who is a frequent presence at the site and who is Black, objects to the milk fever, arguing that it's racist.

The trolls think this, too, is hilarious. They lean in. "This is pure fuckin' racism, bro," they chant. "Milk, milk, milk!"

The idea was to poke fun at "the whole 'milk is racist' thing," they later explained. They did this by turning milk drinking into a race thing, taunting, "Hey you nonwhites: I can do this and you can't," between big gulps of milk. "We must secure the future of our diet and the future for milk-drinking!" That second line is a parody of the Fourteen Words white supremacist dog whistle.[25]

Watching a recording of this scene, I'm struck by how adolescent they seem as they vamp for the camera. They're performing for each other on-site and for their peers watching online. A few make some attempts to spit the milk at the camera. One guy tries to spray it with force, but it comes out as a dribble. Gross, I think. That is some swill milk.

Alt-right social media erupted in "Milk Pride" statements like "heil milk" and lambasted what they called the "Vegan Agenda"—code for a Jewish conspiracy, or maybe everything "woke"—and its army of "Soy Boys." White supremacist alt-right leader Richard Spencer added a glass-of-milk emoji to his Twitter bio. The neo-Nazi group Identity Evropa caught wind and rolled up to the camera to brandish their swastika tats and chug milk with the others.

Milk is just milk. It's innocent, benign—right?

No, it's murky and opaque, and too easily conceals whatever filth we throw in it.

— 3 —

IN RENAISSANCE EUROPE, Christian cultural and religious authorities believed that strange milk would estrange the child. Today, right-wing cultural and religious authorities believe transness will do that. Trans people curdle the milk; we do it even as we're being milked, our transness extracted from our overall humanity and funneled through narrowing, pathologizing rhetoric. We're not real. We're not real, and yet we're ruining the nation. Ruining families. Estranging other people's children through our contaminating presence. We've been cast out by right-wing scare tactics invested in deepening cultural division and mistrust. We have been poured out and polluted with something else, something unfamiliar and toxic.

I'M RETURNING TO this essay in late 2024, as Trump is poised to return to office after campaigning on blood purity rhetoric: the claim that immigrants are "poisoning the blood of the nation."

I'm thinking about white nationalism's dirty purity, its raza, its swill milk.

I feel estranged from this essay. I feel estranged from its growing estrangement from an ever-stranger and more disquieting present.

And I'm still trying to write about an estrangement.

MY OLDER BROTHER and I don't really talk.

This isn't unusual or surprising. Most people I know are estranged from one or more family members. Most people I know are queer or trans or both.

In the Brechtian sense, estrangement refers to a representation that "allows us to recognize its subject, but at the same time makes it seem unfamiliar."[26] Peele's use of milk in *Get Out* is an example of this kind of estrangement; it allows us to see things anew as they are.

Estrangement also names the experience of living at some remove from a feeling of cohesion or rightness, whether in the context of the body or the family or a sense of culture or nation or humanness. In this sense, estrangement belongs to a family of words that includes disaffection, dissonance, and dysphoria. It also has resonance with queer antisocial theory and Afropessimism, as explained by philosophy studies scholar Eyo Ewara, who proposes it as a framework for thinking the two theories together.

In Ewara's conception, estrangement is "a condition that implicitly references a shaping by the past, whether through an event or through a drifting apart in time."[27] This description understands estrangement as a kind of transition. When it's familial, it may be a movement from compulsory attachment to something more quality-contingent, or what Rin Reczek has called "democratized kinship."[28] There are varieties and degrees of estrangement, many ways to do it. It can be hard or soft. You can name it or not.

"To be estranged is not to be a complete stranger," Ewara writes. "It is to have *become* strange in ways that remain tethered to that from which one is estranged."[29]

My brother and I are estranged, but we remain tethered.

The guilt I feel for my nominal affiliation with milk and its associations with white supremacy—that guilt is similar to the guilt I feel for my association with him. It's also connected to the guilt I feel that we are estranged in the first place, as if the duty of repair were mine alone to bear.

It's not really guilt, I guess. It's shame.

After receiving my second email, Michael writes back, referring to an email he says he sent but that I didn't receive.

It's my birthday, which he doesn't acknowledge. He has reasonable questions about what the interview will be used for. I respond to his questions. He doesn't reply.

"It's not our job as artists to solve estrangement, but to feel and be in estrangement," Jess Arndt said in a public conversation on estrangement with Lara Mimosa Montes. "Part of estrangement is feeling outside of. And that also produces an inside."

This essay is some of my inside.

Blood makes kinship connections. Milk makes kinship connections. Neither is thicker than that blend of mutual care and curiosity that constitutes a nourishing relationship.

If he would just ask me one question about my life. Just one.

THIS NEXT STORY is not about Michael.

In 2023 I spent a month in a small, conservative city for a residency. In this place with its abundance of American flags and pickup trucks, I was a stranger. But when I wore cutoff T-shirts and loose shorts, I figured I passed well enough as someone like Michael, someone who might fit in.

The center kept bikes on hand for us to borrow. They were cruisers, heavy and slow, but they were something, and most days I took a bike ride for a break.

On my last full day, I went for a final ride through the city, a goodbye tour. I biked past the Ten Commandments installed on the lawn of the courthouse. I biked past historical markers for the Oregon Trail. I biked past the garage with human-sized dinosaur figurines set loose on its roof.

I biked further in one direction than I had ventured before, and I found myself in a marina. It was eerily quiet except for the rush of the river. I stood on a grassy overhang and breathed it in. I was alone, I thought, and thoughtful. I would miss this place. I breathed out. Time to go. I mounted my bike and pedaled off.

I was rounding the bend out of the parking lot when a hulking pickup came thundering down the hill. The road was broad, and we were on opposite sides; I mean there was plenty of room for us both. But as the truck approached, the driver wasn't hugging the bend—he was aiming his vehicle straight at me. I rode closer to the edge of the asphalt, giving him more space. He kept coming. Were we playing chicken? Who'd flinch first? I would. If I stayed my course and he stayed his, he'd mow me down like a tall clump of dandelions. I rode into the grass and stopped, deliberately not making eye contact. The truck roared past.

Was I paranoid? Had that really happened the way it seemed like it had?

I remembered an earlier day in this town. I had been on one of my walks, listening to a friend's podcast via earbuds, and didn't notice the SUV skulking behind me for who knows how long before some sixth sense kicked in. Seeing it, I had an uneasy feeling and cut across railroad tracks into a park area where the truck couldn't follow. It turned at the intersection and rolled off.

I had been listening to an episode on gun violence in small-town America. I attributed my uneasiness to that and walked on.

Now, biking back from the marina, once again I regretted my rainbow fanny pack. It was too gay. I'd gone into the local Walgreens looking for a small tote for precisely these wanders, and the clerk directed me to a humble Pride display on the end of one of the aisles. Hmm. You don't have anything else? Nope. He looked a little gay. I'm not against Pride rainbows, I explained. I'm just not sure I want to walk around with one. You know? He shrugged noncommittally and offered that it was on sale.

Maybe the guy in the pickup would have fucked with me regardless of my gay messaging. Maybe he was fucking with me because I was there, and strange, and fuck-with-able. Or maybe he wasn't fucking with me at all, and was just on his phone, steering loosely and not seeing me.

Maybe it was nothing.

It's only now, putting it into writing, that I recognize the parallels between this incident and the dream I had involving my brother, his truck, and my car. The feelings are real. The truck is real. I'm still unsure, maybe, what to make of the stranger behind the wheel.

NOTES

1. She came to me from the rescue agency with this name. Her kittens were named Oat Milk, Two Percent, Half Percent, and so on.
2. Jenna Pastel, "Making Sense of Animal Milks," Smithsonian's National Zoo and Conservation Biology Institute, December 20, 2019, https://nationalzoo.si.edu/conservation/news/making-sense-animal-milks.
3. Jen Yamato, "Jordan Peele Explains *Get Out*'s Creepy Milk Scene," *LA Times*, March 1, 2017, https://www.latimes.com/entertainment/movies/la-et-mn-get-out-milk-horror-jordan-peele-allison-williams-20170301-story.html/.
4. Joshua Cohen (scholar of religious studies) in discussion with the author, April 2023. For more, see Cohen's dissertation, "The Food of One's Own Blood: Educating Christian Bodies in Renaissance Spain" (PhD diss., Harvard University, 2023), https://nrs.harvard.edu/URN-3:HUL.INSTREPOS:37378137. See also Deborah Valenze, *Milk: A Local and Global History* (Yale University Press, 2011), especially ch. 3, "The Renaissance of Milk."

5. The fear wasn't just of strange nurses: The later Middle Ages were full of rumors and fables about infants raised on sheep milk, goat milk, or dog milk becoming sheepish, goatish, or canine in turn. "From this vantage point," Josh says, "Jewish or Muslim raza was understood as a lacteally transmitted disposition not unlike goatishness."
6. Within the poetry and theology of the period, the Virgin's divine purity was often linked to her blinding whiteness. In a Christian hymn from the era, Mary is described as: "inmaculado / no escurescido de sombra, / ni de raça ni negror, / ni nublado" ("immaculate / not darkened by shadow / or by raça or by blackness / nor cloudiness"). Ana M. Gómez-Bravo, "The Origins of *Raza*: Racializing Difference in Early Spanish," *Interfaces* 7 (2020): 64–114.
7. Mark Kurlansky, *Milk! A 10,000-Year Food Fracas* (Bloomsbury, 2018), 170.
8. My sources for this section on nineteenth-century New York include Kurlansky, *Milk*; E. Melanie DuPuis, *Nature's Perfect Food* (New York University Press, 2002); Kendra Smith-Howard, *Pure and Modern Milk: An Environmental History Since 1900* (Oxford University Press, 2013); and Tyler Moss, "The 19th-Century Swill Milk Scandal That Poisoned Infants with Whiskey Runoff," *Atlas Obscura*, November 27, 2017, https://www.atlasobscura.com/articles/swill-milk-scandal-new-york-city.
9. Older children and adults were also getting sick and in some cases dying: US President Zachary Taylor is thought to have died in office in 1850 from bad milk. But babies and young children were at greatest risk, especially those from poor families who did not have adequate access to ice. See Kendra Smith-Howard, *Pure and Modern Milk*, especially ch. 1, "Reforming a Perilous Product: Milk in the Progressive Era."
10. Milk purity laws were the first food safety laws in the nation and one of the first foods through which arguments over the "goodness" of food were made. DuPuis, *Nature's Perfect Food*, 10. Conversations about milk safety led to broader conversations about food safety, and eventually Congress passed the Pure Food and Drug Act in 1906,

which prohibited "the manufacture, sale, or transportation of adulterated or misbranded or poisonous or deleterious foods, drugs, medicines, and liquor."

11. DuPuis, *Nature's Perfect Food*, 113.
12. DuPuis, *Nature's Perfect Food*, 11.
13. Quoted in Francine Uenuma, "'Better Babies' Contests Pushed for Much-Needed Infant Health but Also Played Into the Eugenics Movement," *Smithsonian Magazine*, January 17, 2019, https://www.smithsonianmag.com/history/better-babies-contests-pushed-infant-health-also-played-eugenics-movement-180971288/.
14. Vasile Stănescu, "'White Power Milk': Milk, Dietary Racism, and the 'Alt-Right,'" *Animal Studies Journal* 7, no. 2 (2018): 108, https://www.uowoajournals.org/asj/article/id/275/.
15. Stănescu, "'White Power Milk,'" 107–8.
16. Andrea Freeman, "The Unbearable Whiteness of Milk: Food Oppression and the SDA," *UC Irvine Law Review* 3, no. 1251 (2013): 1252.
17. Freeman, "The Unbearable Whiteness of Milk," 1252.
18. Quoted in Brad Dress, "Civil Rights Groups, Including Al Sharpton-Led Organization, Urge USDA to Fix 'Dietary Racism' in School Lunch Programs," *The Hill*, August 9, 2022, https://thehill.com/homenews/3594330-civil-rights-groups-including-al-sharpton-led-organization-urge-usda-to-fix-dietary-racism-in-school-lunch-programs/.
19. As of April 2024, the USDA has updated NSLP requirements to be inclusive of lactose-free and lactose-reduced milk options. As of February 2025, it's unclear whether the Trump administration's anti-DEI agenda will affect the program.
20. Benjamin Levi DeVore, "The Wolves Are Guarding the Cow Pasture: Examining the US Dairy Industry's Control Over the Federal Government" (master's thesis, Central European University, 2020), 26.
21. Freeman, "The Unbearable Whiteness of Milk," 1258; Kaili Wang et al., "New Insights into Dairy Management and the Prevention and Treatment of Osteoporosis: The Shift

from Single Nutrient to Dairy Matrix Effects—A Review," *Comprehensive Reviews in Food Science and Food Safety* 23 (2024), https://doi.org/10.1111/1541-4337.13374.

22. At least among mostly white health workers. Those who consumed whole milk regularly were found to have higher risk of total mortality, with heightened risk of death by cardiovascular disease and cancer. Ming Ding et al., "Associations of Dairy Intake with Risk of Mortality in Women and Men: Three Prospective Cohort Studies," *BMJ* 367 (2019): l6204, https://doi.org/10.1136/bmj.l6204.
23. Freeman, "The Unbearable Whiteness of Milk," 1259–61. See also Anne Mendelson's *Spoiled: The Myth of Milk as Superfood* (Columbia University Press, 2023).
24. In the film he presents this behavior as apolitical, but I'm not sure how ingenuous he's being and can't find more information.
25. "We must secure the existence of our people and a future for white children." Popularized by white supremacist David Eden Lane and inspired by a passage in Hitler's *Mein Kampf*.
26. Bertolt Brecht, "A Short Organum for the Theater," quoted in Darko Suvin, "Estrangement and Cognition," originally published in *Metamorphoses of Science Fiction: On the Poetics and History of a Literary Genre* (Yale University Press, 1979) and reprinted in *Strange Horizons*, November 24, 2014, http://strangehorizons.com/non-fiction/articles/estrangement-and-cognition/.
27. Eyo Ewara, "For Estrangement: Queerness, Blackness, and Unintelligibility," *Philosophy Compass* 18, no. 3 (2023): 8, https://doi.org/10.1111/phc3.12897.
28. See Rin Reczek's *Families We Lose: Estrangement and the Democratization of Kinship* (New York University Press, forthcoming).
29. Ewara, "For Estrangement," 8.

Dear Dairy III: Chaseholm Farm (Pine Plains, New York)

August 2023

Two humans are leading twenty cattle into the barn when I walk up. "I'm looking for Sarah," I shout. One of them waves from the back. "That's me." I wait. I was expecting a short-haired Sarah to match years-old photos I've seen of her in local online profiles about her and Chaseholm, the small farm she runs in Pine Plains, New York. This Sarah has long, thick hair in loose waves under a ball cap, and she's latching the rope gate after her cows at the other end of the barn.

A third-generation farmer, Sarah Chase took over operations from her father in 2013, when she was twenty-four. Since then, she has transitioned the business to organic farming and 100 percent grass-fed cattle. She's unusual in the dairy business for being young, a woman, and queer. She lives here with her wife, Jordan; her brother runs a creamery up the road.

It's 8:30 a.m., and it's milking time, which Sarah has invited me to observe. I wait behind a thin rope that gates off the barn entrance and take note of the small chalkboard signs above each stall. On the right side, I read *Eleanor, Marge, Quick, T-Bird*. On the left: *BJK, Yolo, Viper, Queen, Lucy*. The barn stretches out; I can't see the rest from where I'm standing.

The cows know their stalls and step in. Except for Eleanor, who stops short.

"Come on, big girl," Sarah coaxes. There's a gutter in the concrete floor where the barn cleaner, a system of chain links and scraper blades, runs behind the stall, and Eleanor disapproves. With one foot, Sarah drags some hay from the stall to fill in the gap. Eleanor moves forward, stops short again. Sarah pulls more hay back until Eleanor is satisfied and steps in finally with a snort. This kind of affectionate attention is hard to imagine on the bigger feedlot farms I've visited. It's also hard to imagine the cows there being known by name.

I see why Sarah calls her "big girl." Eleanor is massive, magnificent, beautiful. Her coat is dark and glossy, ultra-black. Her legs are long and white, strong and veiny. High haunch, narrow tail.

Cow! That's what my child mind is saying. Cows! Cows! Cow! I'm wowed to be finally so close. From this vantage point, I see mostly their backsides and udders: full and taut and pale. There is something sweetly vulnerable about Eleanor's shape and demeanor, as if she is embarrassed by her size, or the fact of her pokey teats. Is that me, imposing my dysphoria? In her stall she stands patiently, reaching for hay, her neck long and remarkably flexible.

A cow near the end of the row turns out of her stanchion to snack on her neighbor's hay. This gives some of the others ideas; one backs out as if she's fixing to leave the barn. "Back in your stalls, please," directs Amanda, the other human. She retrieves the wanderers and clips them to their stalls. Then she clips everyone else.

Sarah's dairy cows are a mix of Holsteins, Jerseys, and Holstein-Jersey crosses. Compared to the farms I saw in LeMars, this one is tiny, with a herd of twenty-six, by my count. The barn's full, or nearly. A dark cat, Bearcat, darts between stalls. Another cat, Clam, creamsicle orange, hops onto the wood pane of an open window. Two dogs, a terrier and a shepherd mix, roam around.

Today is special because the farm is hosting Dairy Drag this evening. The only sign of that now is a disco ball hung from the middle of the ceiling, but soon the barn will be cleared out and cleaned up for the performance.

Amanda is milking today so that Sarah and I can chat. She rolls out a cart to set up her workstation in the center of the barn. The cart holds a bucket, a notepad, iodine solutions, a box of paper towels. She's draped a few milking pumps over her shoulder.

Amanda starts with the cows in the rear of the barn. First she brings over what Sarah tells me is a CMT paddle (short for California Mastitis Test)—a plastic tray with four shallow cups. Before milking each cow, Amanda squeezes a squirt of milk from each teat into the tray. She drops solution into all four cups, swishes it around, and makes notes.

She's testing the white blood cell counts, Sarah explains, which give an indication of the cows' immune responses to bacterial infection. The farm has been having issues with milk quality because of a recent heat wave. Cows are most comfortable when the temperature is in the seventies; they get stressed in hotter weather. Last week saw a long stretch in the nineties, and prior to that there was flooding, adding to the stress. "They've been having to tromp through water that's like, up to their briskets and certainly touching their udders," Sarah says. (Briskets, I learn later, are their pectoral muscles.) "Basically we're having an immune system spike in the herd." As a result, some of the cows have developed mastitis, a bacterial infection in the udder.

A cow's udder is divided into four discrete quarters. That means mastitis can be isolated in one quarter without spreading to the others. After testing the levels in the milk from each of the cows' quarters, Amanda attaches the magnetic sleeves of the milking pump to each teat, siphoning off any poor-quality milk into a quarter-milker container. That milk gets collected in a bucket that goes to the pigs. The good milk gets sucked up and into the stainless steel piping system installed above the stalls, which drops it into a stainless steel tank housed in the milk room that adjoins the open barn.

Amanda has an LED headband wrapped around her snapback, her ponytail popping out. She's in dark jeans and heavy boots. At any given time, she has two to four milk pumps going. Her voice is chipper, pitched up when directed at the cows.

"My cows make, at maximum, thirteen thousand pounds per lactation," Sarah says. Compared to the cows that make the most in America—about seventy-five thousand pounds per lactation—that's pretty low. "They're super chill." They're milked once a day and spend the majority of their time on the hilly pasture across the road.

Sarah tells me she's only able to do this because she sells direct to consumer and can set the price higher than what she'd get for commodity milk. Most of her cows are A2A2, meaning their milk has a particular kind of casein that makes it more digestible for many people. (A1 and A2 represent certain amino acids in the chain.) Sarah also makes and sells yogurt in-house, and she sells milk direct-market to her brother for his cheese production.

Sarah has a beef herd, too, as well as hogs. All Chaseholm meat gets sold in-house. "It's this full-circle thing," she says. "Every animal I've culled in the last eight years has been through my farm store. There's limited waste."

When I ask her what she likes most about working with

cows, she smiles at the question. She appreciates being invited to talk up the sweet side of dairy farming. Usually people go straight to the challenges.

Sarah loves cows. "The dairy cow is a funny creature because they're rather dependent on people. We've created them to be particularly unwild. They are very personable, and they've been bred for that." As we talk, BJK, the first cow on our left, lies down with a sigh. She's last in line. She'll be here a while. Some milk leaks from her udder, forming a small puddle on the concrete.

"We're in intimate contact," Sarah goes on. "I go to each cow to milk her instead of just running them through a parlor. I'm usually squeezing my body in between cows to hook up my machines, and I'll have my face on her thigh while I'm hooking her up. I really know all of them, and we're used to a lot of touch. That's a really nice thing."

This morning's milking is taking longer than usual because of the careful testing. When Amanda brings the milking station closer, BJK stands, thinking it's her turn. Archie, the smaller dog, trots over and laps up the leaked milk.

Not time yet. BJK settles back down.

Someone rolls up in a truck. In the truck bed, a man crouches, his arms wrapped around a Jersey calf with wild eyes. Sarah waves. "Bye, Barry," she shouts, a farewell to the calf. His mother rejected him, she tells me, and she's had a hard time getting him to feed on a rubber nipple. But Pat, her neighbor in the truck, will work his magic.

I ask Sarah how it's been, being one of the very few queer dairy farmers. "Bizarre," she says, but mostly positive. "I came back to the community that I had grown up in, and I had a lot of nervousness about that return. I had left as a certain kind of daughter of this place and then returned like . . . a really gay version." She laughs. "It stressed me out.

But people were able to meet me where I was at. They were more happy to have someone take over the farm than they were worried that it was a homosexual."

In 2016, the farm "got a lot gayer." Sarah had been posting Black Lives Matter signs for a while, but when the Pulse Nightclub mass shooting happened, it pushed her to put up Pride flags, too. "My farm actually did suffer after that first year of having Pride flags and BLM signs up, but ultimately it was a very good thing for my business. It created a queer culture around the farm, and that has given it a lot more than it cost."

I'm dismayed to learn that Sarah plans on reducing the herd from thirty cows to twelve. "The farm feels like it could forever take everything I have, at least the way I have it now," she explains. "I need to be smart about going forward." I'd been thinking of Chaseholm as a kind of success story—like, if anyone can save small dairy, it's queers. But no one person or farm can do that, and downsizing can mean strategy, not failure. Still, the thought of Chaseholm shrinking is sad.[1]

We wrap up our interview. "I'm getting my Bobcat out," she says. "But you're not in any danger." She chuckles, and I don't get the joke until a small forklift roars to life. She uses it to start moving picnic tables in preparation for Dairy Drag.

I stick around to watch the rest of the milking.

When Amanda nears a few moments later, BJK doesn't bother standing. "Your turn," says Amanda cheerily, tapping her on the haunch. "Finally." BJK rises. Then the milking is done.

Amanda cleans up. She pours some milk from the pig bucket into two bowls, which she gives to the cats. Bearcat laps it up enthusiastically until I get too close and spook him. Sorry, Bearcat.

The cows are all lying down now. I ask if I can follow them as they head out to pasture, and Amanda invites me inside the barn to help her. The cows sense it's time: One by one, they haul themselves upright.

Amanda shows me how to unclip a cow without putting my arm in a crushable position. Their necks are strong, she warns me. I take the right side, Eleanor's side, and it's mostly easy, except for Queen, who keeps jerking her neck away before I can unclip the chain. "Queen's a meanie," Amanda calls over from the other side. "She has one horn, and she will use it." I leave Queen for Amanda to take care of and finish up my side, timidly patting a few warm foreheads. Eleanor's my favorite, and I'm hoping we'll have a moment. But no. She's eager to head outside.

They back out of their stalls and stand in the middle of the barn. As they wait for Amanda to remove the rope gate, they lift their tails and, one by one, push out the contents of their bowels. It's almost synchronized. The shit roars out like a series of waterfalls splashing heavily onto the ground. Splursh. Splursh. Splursh. It keeps coming. I'm entranced. It's not just the sensory bonanza—the flood of gushing sounds and fecund smells, the astonishing sight of holes gaping open, one after another, and discharging a cascade of semi-solid shit. It's also the communalism. The collective decision that now is the time.

Later I'll watch the first season of the Fox reality dating show *Farmer Wants a Wife* and disdain Cassidy Jo, who dry heaves when one of Farmer Alan's steers takes a shit. "It smells," she protests. "There's some on my finger," she shrieks. "Wipe it on my jeans," Alan offers, but she thinks that's too gross. I'll be surprised if Cassidy Jo lasts another week on the farm.

I'd last. Pick me, Farmer Alan.

Amanda registers my rapt state. "They're doing good," she assures me. "This is the best time and place for it. Much easier for me to clean up." After she sends them out to pasture, she'll come back and shovel the manure into the gutter that runs behind the stalls.

I guess it's the polite thing to do, to hold one's shit until the milking is done and the sanitized equipment has been stored away.

Amanda removes the rope gate and cues the cows to exit into the barnyard. This seems to be a signal to piss. Some of the cows piss on the concrete, but most hold it for the barnyard. Their back legs bend inward as they let loose. Their piss funnels into the mulch, making small frothy ponds.

I follow, doing my best to step around the mounds of manure, but it's a losing battle. "You're one of us now," Amanda says.

She passes the baton and readies the gates. My job is to steer the cows by gesturing with the baton: a thin white wand, a fiberglass cane. If anyone straggles, I'm to tap them gently on their backside. Some of the cows gaze at me blankly, or curiously, or patiently. I don't have to do much. They know the routine.

One dawdler lags behind as the others march forward. "Go, go," I suggest, and she stares at me, nonplussed. I approach with the baton. She steps forward, eyes me, waits.

Amanda sees what's happening. "That's Lucy," she says. "She likes to go last. She gets headbutted if she doesn't." Lucy's a younger cow, and the others will put her in her place. Poor Lucy. I lower the baton and wait. Sure enough, as soon as the others have moved into the corridor, Lucy follows.

Amanda was out here earlier fencing off today's fields.

She's created two adjacent paddocks, one for day, one for night. She'll come back out around 5 p.m. and move them into the next strip. "That'll be a nice treat for them," she says.

I don't stick around for the barn cleaning. I wash the shit and mud off my boots and say goodbye. I'll be back for Dairy Drag later. I glug some water and commence the drive out to Kingston, where I'm meeting my friend Anne for lunch.

BY THE TIME I get to the coffeehouse where I thought I'd camp out until Anne gets into town, I have the beginnings of a migraine. I got up at 5:15 a.m. to make it to Chaseholm by 8:30, and while these kinds of hours might be normal for farm people, they are definitely not normal for me. Maybe I wouldn't last on Farmer Alan's ranch. No. I would adapt.

For days I've had traveler's constipation, and I'm cranky and out of sorts. The farmers market is going on across the street, so the bookstore is unusually packed. I need to pee. I need to poop. The line for the bathroom is five deep, and whoever's in there is taking forever. When it's finally my turn, I think of the cows and their collective release. Be the cow, I tell myself. But it won't come.

I leave the bathroom. I refill my water bottle. I order coffee and two pastries that I scarf down with four Ibuprofen. I feel green around the gills, lightheaded; I want to be sideways. I feel so bad that I wonder if I picked up something from the cows, or from their manure. No, it's just gut stress. What I need is greens. Yogurt. Some time alone on a private toilet. I sit and stare, willing the migraine to recede.

Anne picks me up, and we head to a café away from this chaos. After a solid, greens-heavy meal, more Ibuprofen, and a lot of water, I've mostly regained equilibrium, and Anne and I tag team it to the farm for Dairy Drag.

The barn has been transformed. No cows. No manure—well, the trace scent. The stalls are filled in with clean mulch and sawdust. The strip down the middle is now a runway for performers. Beyond the barn, there are food vendors and picnic tables, as well as a small shop with Chaseholm shirts and hats. The country queers are out, stylish in their boots and snapbacks, their brightly patterned jumpsuits. Also some city folks and some back-and-forthers. These categories aren't distinct in the Hudson Valley, especially in the summer.

Rosey's Café is serving burgers sourced from Chaseholm beef. I order one. It's delicious. We introduce ourselves to the older couple across the picnic table. They turn out to be Sarah's aunt and uncle, who tell us about how dairy has changed these past decades. Everyone used to have a farm like this, they say.

It's showtime. We pack into the barn, sitting and standing in the milking stalls. Anne and I plant ourselves behind Queen's stall, leaning against the metal bar.

The show's great; the energy's palpable, electric. The barn walls seem to quiver with the exuberance. But something's missing. Is it that I was expecting the drag to be dairy-themed and it isn't? No, it's the cows. Eleanor, Lucy, BJK, Queen, and the rest of the herd would not abide this clamor. Still, it feels strange to be hanging out in their stalls without them.

NOTE

1. In a follow-up email a year later, Sarah said the herd was down to sixteen cows, which had increased profitability and made things more manageable for her and her staff.

Tres Leches

Marigold and I are in my bed chipping away at frozen-solid popsicles with our teeth when—how did it come up?—for some reason I mention the two other Megan Milkses I know of, both of whom are, incredibly, queer.

"Oh my God, have you met them?"

I follow one on Instagram, I tell her. That Megan Milks just had a baby with her wife. The other one is not on social media, but she was the cover model for the 2011 *It's All Butch* calendar, which I discovered through a "Megan Milks" Google alert.

"Tres leches," Marigold says, cracking herself up. "That's the title of your book."

When I got the alert years ago, I ordered myself a calendar. I retrieve it now.

Photographer Debbie Boud began the *It's All Butch* project in 2010. In an interview, Boud, who is butch herself, explains, "I wanted to break the mullet-wearing stereotypes and show that we can be 'hot' too." (Here I must counter that mullets are *very* hot, but I think we know what she means.) Boud made an offshoot *It's All Trans* calendar a few years later featuring all trans men and transmasculine models.

On the cover, the Other Megan Milks smirks in a leather jacket with a cigarette tucked behind her ear. This Other Megan Milks has overplucked eyebrows like I do, left over from the nineties. She has a soft butch look like I once had, and her smoldering smize belies some discomfort with the camera, a feeling to which I relate. Otherwise we look and seem nothing alike.

Marigold snatches the calendar from my hands. "Megan Milks is hot," she comments. I shrug. Megan Milks might be family. I resist assessing her hotness.

Marigold flips through the months. February's model lifts a rose to her nose in a rented tux. July's model stands before an American flag holding a lit firecracker to her crotch. October's mall-Goth model poses next to a gravestone. I point out her early aughts faux-hawk, her skull-and-crossbones belt buckle. "This butch has hit on me multiple times," Marigold says. "Tragically, I'm never into her."

We both like November, a hunky older LHB posed with a senior dog and a disarmingly sincere smile. "This butch will take care of you," I say approvingly.

Marigold agrees. "This is the best butch."

"The Other Other Megan Milks is also queer and maybe butch?" I say. She DMed me a few years ago after someone reached out to her thinking she was me. Now we follow each other. I bring up her account on my phone and show Marigold. "I could see her being an LHB, but hesitate to assign gender identity."

Marigold laughs. "You've liked all these posts!"

Both Megan Milkses seem great. I'd be honored to be confused with either of them and hope they feel the same about me.

We chip away at our popsicles. Marigold is younger than me and the last time I suggested popsicles after fucking she smirked and said that seemed like something Joe Biden would do: Fuck a girl and offer her a popsicle. Burn. Was she calling me old? Was she calling me Joe Biden? Who doesn't like a popsicle after sex?

"Tres leches," Marigold repeats happily. "That's the title. It has to be." She puts on a storyteller voice. "The three Megan Milkses go on a cross-country road trip and fuck in a hotel room at the end." She pauses. "No, you fuck in a hotel room two-thirds in, and the rest of the book is the fallout."

"Yes!" I nod, laughing. "It'll be like my *Crossroads*." She looks at me questioningly and I'm again reminded of our age gap. "The Britney Spears road trip movie?"

I would pick up the Other Megan Milkses in my economy rental, which doesn't make sense because they live in separate states, but here we live in the same town and I get to be Britney. As we drive to . . . where? Los Angeles, to become stars? . . . we chat about our shared name. What do we think about being named Megan Milks? How has it shaped our lives? How has the name become us, and we it? Is there something queer about it, like, intrinsically? But we're all different *kinds* of queer . . . oh really? How so? What's it like to be a Megan Milks—a queer Megan Milks—in Florida, in Texas, in New York?

We wonder if we're related, and if so, how. We toss out names and dates and places. We can't find the connection, but I've packed some genealogy books for the road. I wonder if either of them are related to the late Harvey Milk—one of the first out gay politicians elected to public office in the US. (I'm not.)

I tell them about *The Grace Lee Project*, in which Korean American filmmaker Grace Lee meets and interviews a bunch of other Grace Lees. I tell them about Kyle, Texas, which has invited Kyles from around the world to come in for an annual festival in hopes of beating the Guinness World Record for the largest gathering of people with the same name. (So far, Kyle has not achieved this goal, set by the city of Kupres in Bosnia and Herzegovina, where 2,325 people named Ivan gathered in 2017.) Oh, and Phil Campbell, Alabama, which has hosted a number of gatherings of people named Phil Campbell.

Megan Milks looks this up on her phone and reads aloud from a news article: "The Phil Campbells do not have much in common besides a name, but they point out some similarities. Like the man for whom the town is named, a nineteenth-century railroad engineer, everyone is white. They also have receding hairlines and not much money."[1]

How are we alike, and how different?

Hours of conversation.

And we've bonded. We've navigated minor conflicts related to gas money, bathroom stops, and soundtrack. One Megan Milks wants to listen to Megan Thee Stallion. Another Megan Milks wants to listen to the Dead Milkmen. The third Megan Milks intervenes and adds these to the playlist they'd forgotten they created for the trip. The playlist also includes Kelis's "Milkshake," Garbage's "Milk," and Billy Bragg's "The Milkman of Human Kindness." They set it to shuffle. The peacemaker.

We hit a lull in the conversation. Megan Milks pulls out the genealogy books and pores over them, trying to determine where our lineages overlap, if at all. Megan Milks doesn't find out. Before she's gotten more than a few pages in, another Megan Milks has seized them from her hands, rolled down the window, and tossed them.

"What the hell?" Megan Milks twists around to see where the books have landed ingloriously on the side of the interstate.

"There," Megan Milks says with satisfaction. "I did us all a favor."

"A 'favor'? I was reading those," says an audibly annoyed Megan Milks.

"Who cares about lineage?" Megan Milks sings, giddy from the rush of her audacity. "We're already connected. We're already family." Megan Milks pauses to let this sink in.

Stop the car! It's the cue for a group hug. And one of us could use another bathroom break. There's a diner coming up in two miles. How about some milkshakes?

We slide into a booth and order: one large vanilla shake to share.

It arrives a few moments later, thick and goopy in a conical serving glass. The server slaps down three jumbo straws in plastic wrappers and leaves us to it.

We unwrap and insert our straws. My gaze splits, one eye on each Megan Milks, whose gazes divide similarly. Synchronized, we slurp. The cold sweetness fills my mouth and melts down my throat. I swallow.

A strange tingling takes over. The brain freeze floods my synapses, lighting them up and cooling them down. I slurp up more milkshake. There's another surge, and another. And then—and then we—we merge.

A Mega Megan Milks has formed.

La la. La la. La, we say, or think, or hear.

On the outside, we're three queers staring at each other hugging red plastic tubes with our lips. But on the inside, our thoughts and memories and genetics are blasting together and being recombined.

We're posing for Debbie's camera in 2011. We're holding our screaming infant for the first time last year. We're brushing dried mud from a cow's coat last month. We're singing along to Kelis's "Milkshake" in the car twenty minutes ago. We're suspecting it may have been some kind of spell.

We're posing for the cow while brushing dried mud from our infant's cheek. We're brushing along to "Milkshake" and holding Debbie's camera for the first time.

What's happening? we wonder. We're homogenizing, we realize. It's horrible and wonderful. The three Megan Milkses are one. There is no one more Megan Milks than us.

The throats of our straws gurgle, then clear. We're coming to the end of the milkshake.

We've reached the crossroads. From here, we'll go our separate ways. It's likely that we'll never see each other again, but we'll always have this trip and the memories we made together. We'll always be some kind of family.

It's time. As one, we release our lips' grips on our straws and—another tingling, another brain blast, this time in reverse—we return to our separate selves. Alone again. And too intimately known. Avoid eye contact. One Megan Milks pays, another gets up to find the bathroom, the third looks up the nearest Greyhound station.

I drop them off there and get back on the road.

NOTE

1. Kim Severson, "In the Town of Phil Campbell, a Gathering of Phil Campbells," *New York Times*, June 17, 2011, https://www.nytimes.com/2011/06/18/us/18alabama.html.

Skim Milks

I'm moving again: making decisions while packing up books. Into the giveaway pile with *The Road* and a surprise duplicate copy of *Sweet Valley High #1: Double Love*. Another giveaway: *Wolf Hall*, bought as a "fun" book but kind of a trudge. Trash: four tomes gathering mold behind my cat's water bowl.

I pause on a squat red paperback thunked over on the shelf, the author's name in raised lavender lettering. In the center of the cover floats a glossy black mask, the kind you might see in a ballroom scene in a TV murder mystery, transforming partygoers to glamorous raccoons. The title flounces across the bottom, curvaceously all capped, its *S*'s sensuous, the *V* thrusting upward provocatively. The letters spell *Princess of Thieves*, but the font reads S-E-X.

Katherine O'Neal's erotic romance novel *Princess of Thieves*[1] was a Christmas gift from my grandmother when I was twelve years old. It may be the first work of erotic literature to have entered my life. I've kept it nearly thirty years on one bookcase or another, usually housed on the short shelf I reserve for mass market classics and pulp like this. Each time I move I consider tossing it—trash. I haven't yet.

It was an odd, disconcerting gift. Over the years Gigi had supplied me with cheap heart pendants and suffocating nightgowns, full-sleeved with shoulder ruffles and collars like frill-necked lizards. Each year we unwrapped presents in her basement, a dark den busy with blinking lights and back slaps, balled gift wrap sailing from sofa to sofa, my older brother planting sticky bows on his head. That Christmas, I eyeballed the package's size and shape and guessed it to be a book, maybe the copy of *Jurassic Park* I'd asked for but not yet received. But as I unwrapped it to reveal the lavender cursive, my consternation rose. The book's discreet cover, I saw, was a mask for a less chaste interior illustration, where a manly man leaned a womanly woman forcefully against a wall. That they were fully clothed made the heat beating between them all the more palpably obscene.

No *Jurassic Park*—this was a romance novel. A lurid, embarrassing romance novel for adult women. Not for me.

I was in a room full of men and boys who I knew would be quick to tease. Clutching the cover to my chest, I whispered my thanks at the floor, not caring if Gigi heard me. Hoping she wouldn't. No attention, please! I buried the book in the folds of my other gift, the usual long, narrow nightdress.

I would never wear the nightgown, but I did read the book—more than once, as evidenced by the cracked, white-veined spine. More accurately, I skimmed it. In fact, I might argue that this book taught me *how* to skim. Up to this point, I would dedicatedly read each word of every book, worried I might miss some crucial detail. Even the Chapter Twos of my *Baby-Sitters Club* books—full of repeated info, the club's origins and recycled descriptions of each character—I couldn't bring myself to skip. When I found my eyes scrolling down the page, I would pause, return to the start of the paragraph, begin again.

Not so with *Princess of Thieves*. I seem to have known from the first page that I would not be reading all six hundred. I quickened my eye movements, thumbed my way through. I remember little now of the characters or the situation—only a few scenes and turns of phrase, which I recall vividly, as I do much of the literature that confused me as a kid: words I chewed on, unfamiliar grammatical structures, strange meanings I worked out through context. *Molasses* in *The Baby-Sitters Club*: Used to describe the smoothness of Logan Bruno's Kentucky drawl, it meant "dark and syrupy" (I learned from my dictionary). That a pronoun could arrive *before* its antecedent: *After saying goodbye and kissing* her *father on the cheek, Nancy joined George and Bess in the Roadster.* That the word *period* could mean something you got, like chicken pox; that the word *bust* could express not only violence (as in, *I'm gonna bust you upside the head*) or having been caught (as in, *busted!!!*) but also, via *Are You There, God? It's Me, Margaret*, the size of one's chest (as in, *we must, we must, we must increase our bust*).

Princess of Thieves was a wellspring of confusion. One could rub lips that weren't attached to a face? The pronoun *he* could be used as shorthand for a body part, like some kind of reverse metonymy? Most vividly I recall a climactic scene involving a hot-air balloon, the heroine's fabrication of desire, and my confusion over the unfamiliar usage of familiar words like *wet* and *dry*.

I understood these were not things to ask my parents about, just as I understood I should pore over this book in privacy, after bedtime, with one finger on my booklight, prepared at any moment to flick it off and plunge under the covers at the first soft thump of my mother's step. The words *flick* and *plunge* are not, in this context, suggestive. In fact it did not occur to me to *touch myself*, by which I mean *masturbate*, in the midst of certain scenes, despite the swell in my groin they induced. That's because each time I picked up the book—even now, as I return to it—my experience has been disturbed by an intruder. Popping up over the edge of the balloon basket, hair done up like Queen Elizabeth, a light liver spot on one cheek: There's Gigi. Taking in this high-risk, high-altitude scene through thick-lensed glasses, she finds me within it wherever I am and presses her purplish lips together in a grimace that may communicate bemusement or disapproval.

Caught, I remove myself from the balloon's ropes and plummet down into a flurry of flummoxing questions. What had Gigi meant in gifting me this book? Had the tags been switched? Did my brother, when passing out presents, misread our aunt's or mother's name as mine? Was I meant to be reading this at all?

I add the book to the KEEP pile, then move it to my nightstand . . . for later.

AS A CHILD, my impression of my grandmother was that she was old and primarily unpleasant. Though she had married into the Milks family, Gigi became emblematic of their rigid aloofness—old sticks in the mud, my mother would say. Next to my mom's brighter, more vivacious branch of the family tree, my father's side appeared gnarled and stiff. Unfun. Even my dad seemed to enjoy my mom's family—boisterous Irish Catholics who loved to drink and laugh—more than his own. More Anglo than Irish, the Milkses were stuffy and terse and cruel when they teased. They had a strict way of doing things: the right way. Both sets of my grandparents had grown up in the Depression, but whereas my mother's parents had, in the postwar boom, chosen indulgence and brand names when possible, my father's pinched pennies and seemed to actively devalue pleasure. *Cold*, my mother would say about them, something she has also said about me.

I can still see Gigi's slow waltz around the kitchen, her heavy steps from the fridge to the table to the stove, gripping the counter edges and dragging one leg. A ruptured brain aneurysm at age thirty had left her paralyzed on the left side of her body. She couldn't move her left arm, and she walked with a limp.

Her days were defined by routine. She showered, opened the drapes, heated the electric kettle, then made her way to the front door for *The Washington Post*. She spent mornings at the table, sipping instant coffee, bifocals slung low, newspaper spread out, licking the pad of her knobby middle finger to turn each gray page. She sat in close range of the phone, which had been fitted with a curved shoulder rest that, when not in use, stuck up like a funky antenna. When it rang, she lifted the receiver with graceful efficiency and swept it into the crook of her neck, freeing her good arm. *Mm hyello*.

Between meals, Gigi held court from the beige armchair in her living room, where she consulted the week's *TV Guide* with her bad leg propped up on a leather ottoman, napping intermittently. Her nights were spent with *Wheel of Fortune* and *Jeopardy*. *Law and Order*. *Murder, She Wrote*.

During our afternoon visits, Gigi droned on to my more or less patiently listening mother (my dad always busy weeding or mowing the lawn). Mom sat on one sofa and I sat on the other, playing with one of the dexterity puzzles Gigi kept on the end table, tilting the small box back and forth to fit the steel balls in the indentations. My brothers would be outside in the yard with my dad. Sometimes I'd join them. More often

I'd stay inside, watching the sunbeams dazzle the dust. I'd have spent the car hours reading, and if I hadn't finished my book, it was all I could think about. I measured the time with pleading glances at my mother every few minutes. *Now can I read in my room? Now can I? Now? Now?* until she gave in with an exasperated nod.

I loved to read in the room where I slept at Gigi's house, under the satiny bedspread and the heavy heat of the electric blanket. The pillows were old and stuffed with down—real feathers, I marveled. The dust left me congested. I loved grabbing a handful of the candy-coated chocolates in the kitchen, off-brand M&Ms that lived in a shallow bowl on the chest of drawers against the wall. I loved playing with the rotary dial of the telephone, catching the holes and making them sing (nonerotically). I loved her creamy green bean and mushroom casseroles. Her pancakes were too small, her cookies too brittle. The milk we drank was skim, watery, and the glasses tasted funny.

She didn't open the windows, so the air in there was fusty and clung to my skin when we left, a filmy residue, like the shadow of milk in the mouth. The house smelled old and so did she.

So does *Princess of Thieves*, now, as I open it. *She was running again* . . . Almost at once I am skimming. An alley . . . Chicago . . . red wig . . . a newspaper photo catches our heroine's eye. *Is it him?* Who? Now I have to read back to find out. Oh. *He* hasn't been introduced yet, but *he's* in New York. She catches the next train.

Within a few more skimmed chapters we learn that our American heroine, whose name is Saranda, is after Mace Blackwood, a dastardly English con man who is rumored to be the greatest lover in all of Europe. Here he is in the States, trying to lure Saranda into his bed. She's playing along, but her end goal is to destroy him. I must have skimmed over the part that explains why. Who will outcon whom, and when do the juicy bits begin? The first kiss arrives in Chapter Four, it turns out, at the top of a terrace overlooking the city, where he *impale[s] her against the solid barricade of his chest*. Back to skimming.

TO SKIM MEANS to gloss, to skip across the surface, to skitter your eyes along something. To plow forward on the hunt for the key ideas and arguments of a text, or, in the case of an erotic romance novel, the sex scenes. To read for the good stuff, leaving behind all the tedious descriptive details, the who-cares character development, the endless, insufferable dialogue. The filler scenes. According to dummies.com, to skim a text effectively, you must first know what you want. Move your eyes vertically as much as horizontally. It's "a bit like running downstairs." More dangerous—but faster. I remember my dad teaching himself to speed-read from a manual. You put a finger in the center of the page and move it down as if magnetizing the content to it. No blinking. You open your eyelids as wide as you can.

FOR A LONG time I've thought maybe Gigi just didn't *know* this book was a sexy book. That it was a fluke gift, on sale at Kmart, where she bought most of our presents. Due to her limited mobility, there was a considerable range of shelf space she couldn't access. This book may have been part of a side display, therefore accessible; she'd have chucked it in the cart and kept moving.

Maybe it wasn't so random. Maybe Gigi thought this was the kind of book I was reading in my room when I wasn't fidgeting on her sofa. I did brag about reading "adult" books. Is this what she thought I meant?

I can't help but wonder whether she chose it for me at all. Maybe someone bought it for her, and she, loath to waste money or resources, had simply needed someone to pass it on to. Or maybe no one bought it. My aunt was a manager at Kmart; maybe it had been a return or a remainder. There is a sticker on the back over the UPC code: "Please Scan Inside Front Cover / Department 71 Key 29." If the book is the key, where's the lock? (Not a euphemism.)

As I've grown older, I have wondered—maybe hoped—whether the book had been more intentional, may have *meant* something, that Gigi had meant it for me. Of her ten grandchildren, only two of us were girls, and her gifts to us were girly, affirming of our connection to one another as assigned females. The jewelry, the nightgowns. A long flowery dress. Though I'm trans now, I wasn't at odds with girl things then, not really, though I can't say I understood why they were for me.

Maybe this was an extension of that, just another normal exchange between women that I didn't understand, a secret handshake passed down from generation to generation. Erotic romance as rite of passage: my grandmother drawing me into her covert community of readers and of women. There's something reassuring about this interpretation. While I would not have sought membership in this community then, now I want it to have meant *Welcome. You belong.* Not recognizing it as such, I could not belong, perhaps have never belonged. Maybe this book was the key—Key 29—to the locked doorknob of normative gender, which, once opened, would have allowed me easier entrance into the house of the normative family. Alas! If only I hadn't skimmed.

Maybe not. Twenty pages later, Saranda and Mace are at it again: teasing, withholding, masking. He wants her; he's conning her. She wants him; she's conning him. He's lifting up her skirts, sliding his fingers inside her, his words in her ear—he breaks away. *I can't do this . . . you're marrying Winston. I* know *it, dammit. But something—some distant voice inside—keeps whispering that you belong to me.* When he takes his leave of her, Saranda discovers he's lifted her wallet.

IN THE CONTEXT of milk and butter manufacturing, skimming has the opposite meaning. There, to skim is not to hunt for the good stuff, but to lop it off, leaving the diluted remnants behind.

When I workshop a draft of this essay, someone divulges that they don't know what skim milk is. West of the Midwest, I learn, "nonfat" and "fat-free" milk are the more common terms. This likely has something to do with dairy companies trying to escape skim milk's negative connotations—even now, it's hard to find a contemporary brand selling "skim" milk. Still, the word has stuck, as has the scorn. In my research I discover plenty of low opinion for skim milk, aka "blue john milk," "water milk," "milk-free milk." Skimming means the removal of the rich, thick cream. Who wants the weak, watery leftovers?

When I started restricting my diet in the late 1990s—my high school years—I demanded my mother buy me a quart of skim milk every week. After school, I poured it over my bowl of Frosted Mini-Wheats, my one indulgence, and let it soak the square nuggets soggy. I could get away with the cereal, I rationalized, so long as the milk was fat-free.

The diet-conscious embrace of skim milk was introduced by the dairy industry in the postwar period; by my childhood in the 1980s, it held firm. The unwanted by-product of butter processing, skimmed milk was considered commercially unviable until the 1930s: It was less nutritious, harder to cook with, and not as flavorful as whole milk. After skimming off the cream, dairy manufacturers either used the leftover milk for animal feed or dumped it into rivers.

But this kind of waste during an economic depression wasn't a great look, and the sour smell it discharged when dumped didn't help. Dairy companies were pressured to come up with other ways to dispose of the substance. Among their solutions—which included the development of new casein products like glue, egg substitute, and even "milk wool"—the most successful was dried skim milk, which became a key relief food during World War II. When the war ended and the US entered a period of new abundance, the industry rebranded skim and low-fat milk neither as waste nor as relief food, but as an attractive weight-loss item. It caught on.

This brief history of skim milk maps neatly onto the history of my family. Growing up on a Depression-era farm, my grandmother drank whole milk straight from the cow. As a young woman living near the city during and after the war, she cut costs by mixing dry skim milk powder with water. Post-infancy, my dad grew up drinking powder-based milk. My generation of Milkses drank 2% fluid milk; when I started dieting, I switched to skim. Fewer and fewer people consume cow milk now; in my immediate family, only Dad does. I've stayed on-trend by switching to oat.

IN 1991, my paternal grandfather's obituary was published in *The Washington Post*, 144 words long with details of his military service and career. When she died in 2013, Gigi's obituary didn't make it into the paper but was published online by the funeral home, her life squeezed down to two sentences: the first recording her dates of birth and death; the second recording her survivors, including the "ten grandchildren" of which I'm one, unnamed. Below the obituary flows a series of uncaptioned photographs, advancing from Gigi's youth in Iowa to not long before she passed. That's it. The last public record of her existence.

Not exactly: In his *History of Milk-Milks*, my dad gives her seven pages.

Some years before my grandmother died, my mother suggested I interview Gigi and record an oral history of her life. If I insisted on being "the writer" in the family, Mom thought I should be the family historian. I was disdainful of the idea; I'm not *that* kind of writer, I said. I wanted to write wild, unruly fiction. Not anything like a family genealogy, not anything my family would read.

Later, when I asked my mother to stop tagging me in family photos on Facebook, she complained: *You don't want people to know you have a family*. Really the problem was the photos: They were unflattering, pre-transition, ugh. But she wasn't wrong: I *would* prefer to maintain a clear separation of my fuller self and my familial self. The fuller self is the me who is openly—exuberantly—queer and trans, nonbinary and a writer; the me who makes claims about my life, identity, and ambitions that have been, pretty much everywhere *but* in my family, respected and honored.Compared to that fuller self, my familial self is—if you will—skim. The best layers lopped off the top.

Perhaps it has been easy for me to take family for granted: I can trace my roots back centuries through genealogy books I've purchased online. And while it hasn't been easy being the only out queer and the only trans person in my extended family, it has never meant excision. Still, when I see my zines in the magazine rack in my parents' master bathroom, evidence that they've purchased and possibly even read them; when I see that my father has left a glowing review of my first book on Amazon ("pushes the boundaries of murder, sex, and mayhem . . . [their] emotional scenes are top-notch")—I have generally viewed these as not supportive but intrusive acts, the family crowding in on my other self, the protected self, the self I've cultivated apart from them. *You don't know that person*, I think, glaring at my most recent zine as I empty my bowels. *You don't get to know that person*. Really I'm afraid of skimming myself down again, reverting to that emptier, more diluted self.

So my mother is right. I have wanted—sometimes I still want—to leave the family behind. Not just my family, but family as an institution: a system of class and cultural inheritance that also involves the inheritance of story. I want to value friendship over family, to prioritize nonbiological forms of community and lineage—queer genealogies; knots of fabulous, fugitive thought—those other spurts and splashes of intimacy and connection that, less traceable outside of family trees, are more vulnerable to historical erasure.[2]

In writing this essay about Gigi, I am trying to know her more fully, trying to gain access to what I imagine to be her fuller self—that is, the self apart from her familial roles as wife, mother, grandmother, great-grandmother. I want to know what kind of friends she had, what kind of friend she was. I want to imagine that, had we known each other in different contexts, we might have become friends.

But familial history is what I have, what I can know, so far.

HER BIRTH NAME was Ruby Mae Benjamin. She was born outside of Denison, Iowa. September 19, 1918: a Virgo, of course. Regimented, sensible, stubbornly punctual, scrupulous with money, she was the Virgo-est Virgo I've known. Her parents were Holland and Blanche (née Kelley). She was the second of seven children.

I get on the phone with Nora, Ruby's youngest sibling; at eighty-four, she's the only one still alive, and she lives in Omaha now, not far from where she grew up. Nora's phlegmy voice and Midwestern inflections, a mix of flat vowels and subtle twang, remind me of Gigi. Their mother, she tells me, was born in Toronto. Some of the Benjamins were Mormon, and they ventured west with Brigham Young to settle in Utah and Nebraska, part of the hordes of white settlers taking over Indigenous land in the nineteenth century.

What I know of Ruby's father, my great-grandfather—whose name was Holland, but he went by Dick—is that he was a heavy drinker who gambled away what money he made, which wasn't much. It was the Depression, and farms weren't turning profits. He lost the first farm and inherited another one, probably from Blanche's family; he lost it and inherited another one. Then there was a lawsuit. It was the ramp-up to World War II, and Ruby's brother Charlie had been out playing war and shot his friend in the eye with a BB gun. When the friend lost the eye, his mother sued the family and won. The Benjamins lost their third farm and moved twenty miles down the road to Dunlap. Charlie enlisted.

My mother's assessment of my great-grandfather Dick: "If you ever saw pictures of him, he looks like a mean son of a gun. He never smiles. Always a cigarette in his mouth. He just did not look like a nice man."

I ask Nora what he was like—her father. "All I know is

he drank a lot," I prompt. "Was he a happy drunk, a mean drunk, or . . . ?" I leave the sentence open. "I was his baby," she says. "So he never did much to me." Before I can ask a follow-up, she's changed the subject.

My dad emails me a family photo of the Benjamins. My mom's assessment is right. A tilted fedora smirking over one eye, Dick looks hardened and conniving. There's the cigarette, tight in one fist.

Next to him is Blanche. Narrow and proud, made of iron, she could be the title character of Patricia MacLachlan's *Sarah, Plain and Tall*. She's staring glumly at the camera, the edge of her apron caught in the wind, as if it's ready to fly her back to the kitchen the instant the shutter clicks closed. Or maybe she'd fly to the henhouse—she raised a thousand hens a year.

In the front, Nora is small, six or seven, tall and knob-kneed, restless-seeming between Blanche and Dick. Behind them scowls Ethel, the oldest, broad and sturdy, a handsome butch farm wife who I imagine feels resentful in this frock.

Ruby is on the other side of the photo, separated from those four (her parents, Nora, and Ethel) by her four brothers. Fresh-faced and smart-looking in a striped cotton shirtdress cinched at the waist, she must be in her late teens or early twenties: an independent young woman temporarily reabsorbed into family life. In this photograph of ten people—Dick and Blanche, their seven children, plus Clyde, the eldest's husband—Ruby is the only one smiling. She's also the farthest from her father she can be.

Ruby was educated in the same one-room schoolhouse from grades one through twelve. When she was through with her schooling at age sixteen, her father found her a job at a cattle stockyard in Omaha. She spent the weeks managing the books at the stockyard—the window in her office overlooked squirming knots of braying bulls and cows. Nora would ride with her dad when he took cattle to the stockyards. While he did business, she visited with Ruby, who would take her out to a restaurant for lunch—a real treat. Ruby would send Nora home with hand-me-downs from her coworkers at the livestock exchange: "the best clothes I had as a kid."

BLINK. RETURNING TO *Princess of Thieves*, I start over, resisting the compulsion to skim. In this way, I come to understand the setup and key plot points. Saranda Sherwin and Mace Blackwood are legacy con artists. It's a family business. For generations, their families have competed to outwit each other. Undercover using the identity of a dead person named Sarah Voors, Saranda is engaged to moneyed Winston, whose family owns a newspaper that the Blackwood family (Mace's lineage) has its eyes on. Why? Dangit. I missed that part.

I should probably pull out some salient commentary the novel is offering about family, but my eyes won't stick to the words. They're falling into the groove of old habits. Get to the good parts. Don't waste time.

By page 97 it's on, and it's great. Saranda does what she has never done before: loses control. *No man had ever moved her so completely. No man had made her feel more whole. In the aftermath, she was left with a shattering truth:* It wasn't enough.

MY MOM TELLS me about Gigi's first love, something my dad and uncle have heard nothing about. When the war started, my mom says, Ruby had a boyfriend. Let's call him Sam. Sam was drafted for service and wanted to marry Ruby before he left. Ruby was sensible. She knew that marriage meant sex, meant the possibility of pregnancy. She'd seen her mother pregnant throughout much of her young life: Blanche's pregnancies were so constant that Ruby wasn't always aware of them. Her twin brothers seemed to have shown up out of nowhere—one morning, Ruby opened the oven to bake biscuits and there they were, keeping warm. She told Sam no; let's wait until you get back. Sam went and married someone else.

My mother says Gigi spoke about Sam with wistfulness, thwarted possibility, all the what ifs of an alternative love and life path. What if she had agreed to the marriage, stayed in Omaha waiting for her soldier's return? What would that life have been like? Would they have been happy together? Would her life have been fuller, easier, bigger? Would they have been more deeply and richly in love? It's difficult to imagine Gigi in the role of pining romantic . . . then again, she did give me this romance novel. Nora, when asked, says Ruby took the job in DC "to get away from the boyfriend." That's all she knows.

The job in DC came about when an Army recruiter showed up in Omaha in 1939 or 1940, or maybe '41 (my dad's not sure), looking for women to work in the war effort. Ruby jumped at the chance to leave home. She and her friend Cece took the train east and rented a room with two beds from an Army widow. They pushed the beds together and lived there with three other women, five total. Some of the women worked night shifts, my dad says, and the others worked day shifts, so they rotated who slept in the beds. I don't comment on the queer potential of this setup.

Ruby—she'd be twenty-one or twenty-two at this point—was assigned a job in Arlington Hall as a typist for the

Department of War, later the Department of Defense. Fastidious and efficient, she quickly rose in the ranks to become one of the best typists in the pool. "All the official correspondence that went to the higher-ups in the Army," my dad says, "the generals and the DOD and all that, they had her type them up." I don't know what to make of this detail, that apparently my grandmother had her hands and eyes on several years' worth of sensitive war correspondence. It was a point of pride for her. After she quit working, her supervisors gave her the typewriter she used when she worked there.

Before my dad inherited it, Gigi's typewriter lived in the downstairs master bedroom in her house. I remember the map of the world that hung over the headboard of the bed, colored thumbtacks marking the places my grandparents had traveled—and I remember this machine. Heavy. Serious. The satisfying cash-register ca-ching of each return. I think of it while I'm typing this on a loud portable keyboard, and of the freedom I had as a kid—to play, to invent, to type, to read. Though this may only speak to the limits of my imagination, I imagine Gigi, on a strict farm schedule, had little comparable experience.

IT'S NOT LONG before Saranda is charged with murder (she didn't do it!); and Mace is nearly hanged by the town for "putting on airs." Both characters outsmart their situations. At this point Saranda admits to herself she is in love with Mace. This is complicated because in the past Mace's brother Lance (also a con artist) raped her and killed her parents. Mace looks like Lance, and he has no idea the kind of terror his brother inflicted on her.

I'm lost. I'm skimming forward, skimming backward, but I keep missing important context. The next time a character named "Blackwood" shows up to roughly manhandle Saranda, I'm worried it's Lance and not Mace. But it's Mace. I infer this because now he's pausing the scene and asking, tenderly, *Did someone hurt you once?* She cries, trembles. He understands. Doesn't realize it was his brother.

Then Lance *does* show up. She clocks him in the head, races to Mace. In the rain they make love tenderly, and she is washed clean of Lance's abuses. *Coming together*, Saranda observes, *was like discovering the true and hidden self.* Has Saranda been skimming herself too?

We're only two hundred pages into a five-hundred-page book. Minutes later Mace and Saranda are fighting again.

AT THE WIDOW'S home where they lived, Ruby and her roommates were not allowed to host men, but a colleague, Ep, held occasional mixers. Ruby met my grandfather Jim at one of these mixers, a winter holiday party.

Jim had returned to Arlington in 1946 with a Purple Heart and a Combat Infantry Badge. *We had better keep Ruby away from Jim*, their mutual friends joked, but did not succeed. What, I ask, was meant by this comment—was my grandfather a quote-unquote *ladykiller*? Though they've repeated this story for decades, neither my dad nor uncle can explain.

Jim and Ruby's courtship advanced swiftly: Jim proposed on Valentine's Day, and by March they were married. It was a quick postwar wedding, not unusual for the time. They were both in their late twenties and wanted to settle down and build a family. In her wedding photo, the last in her obituary's photo stream, Ruby is elegant in a knee-length satin wrap dress with sensible heels; Jim is solid and imposing in a boxy suit, crimson tie peeking out. They look happy, like they've won. Next to Ruby, a young woman—perhaps her roommate Cece?—appears to bounce with nervous joy. Her smile is a quivering thing, alive even in stasis. I want to know more about her.

The end of one life, the beginning of another. Ruby moves out of the widow's house and into a two-bedroom duplex with Jim. Though her job pays more, she quits to be a housewife and mother, and soon enough they're pregnant.

Two years after giving birth to my uncle John, Ruby suffers the stroke that leaves her paralyzed on the left side of her body. She's thirty years old. At the time she is in Maryland, at what we called "the cottage," a humid lakefront property inherited when Jim's father died and (in my memory) overrun with mosquitoes and daddy longlegs. They ride an ambulance from Annapolis to Georgetown in DC. "Today they'd have gone in and operated on her brain and fixed it," my dad says, referring to the doctors who treated her. "And then given us a PT, a physical therapist, to fix the stroke. She'd probably have recovered a hundred percent."

In 1949, her doctors don't have much to offer. They give her medication and tell her she'll live the rest of her life in bed. "So she comes home from the hospital and she does that for about a week, I guess," my dad says. "Then takes the pills, flushes them down the toilet, gets up, and starts carrying back on with a normal life." She manages the house and sells products for Amway, a multi-level marketing company, from home. Eventually she gives birth to three other children: first Joe; then my father, Tom; then Mary Ellen.

"She didn't like to think that she had a disability," my mom says. "It didn't stop her from doing anything." I don't remember Gigi talking about herself as disabled, though she definitely was and didn't try to hide it. She made use of numerous accessibility tools designed for people with limited mobility. She outfitted the phone with a mount. She took her cane everywhere—shiny and black, hooked at the grip. She drove with the help of a brodie knob installed on her steering wheel to support one-handed driving. When she had visitors, she asked them to loosen the lids of any new food items in jars. She had a plastic cuff with a handle that she slid over her milk cartons for easier pouring.

MACE AND SARANDA join some sort of traveling troupe. Saranda is performing as a "Gypsy" who can read minds. Mace is also an acrobat? (Runs in his family.) Eventually they are held up by a group of "Pawnee braves" who pin Mace against the wagon. They want a woman—any of the women. Noble-when-it-counts Mace won't let this happen and convinces them his ponies are a better prize.

WHEN THEIR FOURTH child arrives, Jim and Ruby buy a house in Arlington, a two-story home built into a steep hill. Jim keeps the front yard well manicured—mulched beds, an apple tree. He plants a magnolia tree that as far as I know is still there. The side hill is where three generations of Milks would go sledding when it snowed. In the backyard, which is vast and open, they cultivate a garden. Ruby cans vegetables and makes jams.

She types her correspondence on the same typewriter she brought home for her job. For decades she will keep up a round-robin letter exchange with her four former roommates from the widow's place in Arlington. Cece sends a letter to Ruby, who adds her own letter, then sends both letters on to the next roommate, Dorothy, who adds her own and sends on to Bernice, who adds her letter and sends to Grace, who sends all five letters back to Cece. Then Cece takes out her old letter and puts in a new one, and so on around the circle. "Those five women all stayed in touch," my dad says, "until they got in their eighties and nineties and started dying off." None of these letters have been preserved, or if they have, I can't get to them. I've finally gotten to the good part, and the textual history has vanished.

SARANDA TELLS MACE the whole sordid tale after an encounter with an abandoned child triggers memories of her own abandoned child—the product of Lance's rape—whom she left in an orphanage after trying and failing to love him. The child died of pneumonia. Now that she's told Mace everything, she can't look at him without seeing Lance, and suddenly Mace has the same problem. He dwells in his own misery, drinking and warning her away from him—*before another Blackwood brother forgets himself and rapes you too.* Yeesh. Then there's a "Mexican bandit." Yeesh again. Mace shoots him in the face, which explodes. More yeesh. And by *yeesh* I mean, *this content is beyond "problematic"* or, *what the fuck*.

Next, a tornado. Which provokes a stampede of cattle, sending them straight at Mace. When Saranda gets to him, he is lacerated, bruised, nearly dead. This time, when he moans at her touch, it is a different kind of moan: one of *pain*. Saranda gets lost; Mace disappears; they each think the other is dead. As if the author hopes to redeem herself for her earlier racism, she now sends a vaguely imagined group of Native Americans to heroically rescue both protagonists.

I was right, as a young person, to leap past this rapeyness and racism. On Goodreads, *Princess of Thieves* has thirty-two ratings but only two text reviews. A five-star review declares, "One of the best books I've read about con artists!" A two-star review sums up, "Predictable but in the way that most romance novels are predictable." The average rating is 3.2.

MY MOTHER SAYS I didn't get along with Gigi, which is surprising to hear. I wonder who she thinks I got along with. I thought Gigi was frustrating and my time with her largely boring. But I wasn't in conflict with her.

My mom thinks we didn't get along because Gigi didn't like girls. "I just don't think Ruby likes girls," she said, her slip into the present tense suggesting an old refrain. Neither of us acknowledges my transness. "You know, she's just not a girl person."

Ruby's only daughter, Mary Ellen, resented her, my mom says. They resented each other. "Ruby wanted to have a girl because she thought if she had a girl, she would help her in the house. And of course Mary Ellen"—whose brothers didn't have to do any housework—"wasn't having that."

The Milks household was strictly gendered, my grandfather the patriarch. For dinner Gigi would assemble an array of condiments and olives in the center of the table. We'd sit down and Granddad would study the table. "It was like he'd look for the one thing that she had not put out," my mom says, and Gigi would gasp—"What do you need, Jim, what do you need?"

"And then she'd have to jump up, her handicapped self," Mom goes on, and get the one tiny bottle she'd forgotten to put on the table. "That used to infuriate me. You know, she was like the servant."

In high school—this must have been my senior year—Gigi joins us at our house for Thanksgiving. After we've eaten, my mother is clearing the dining room table. From the kitchen, she asks where I am, why I'm not helping with the dishes. I'm still finishing my dessert. Or drinking coffee. Something. I'm not trying to not help. Dad, at the head of the table, answers, "She's in here sitting on her derriere." I retort, "Yeah, and so are you." Across the table Gigi widens her eyes and makes an *O* with her mouth, girlishly scandalized, waiting to see what the father will do. He and I sit on our derrieres. I don't remember who gets up first.

THE BIG QUESTION of the novel is: Who's conning whom? The answer is no one. The con is racism, is whiteness. The con is gender, is romance, is love. The con is family: the notion that love and money should be founded on bloodlines, the assumption that our families know us best and what's best for us.

I try to imagine what it would look like if we stopped conning each other and approached familial intimacies in more fullness. Many of us have tried this; maybe you've succeeded. I've tried. But I've found that any pull toward another path is short-lived, not unlike my attempts to reapproach this novel: Despite my best efforts, my eye muscle memory kicks in, dragging me back to familiar grooves.

I LIVED WITH Gigi once, during winter break my third year of college. Two notable things occurred.

The first was this: As I was helping her fold laundry in her room, Gigi asked me when I was going to get a boyfriend. Deflecting, I asked her when she was. The tone quickly shifted. *I've had enough sex in my life*, she said forcefully. *I want a woman.*

I was gobsmacked. What?

I wanted to know more; I wanted to know everything. I wanted to ask: *Why* do you want a woman? As a companion? A nurse? A caretaker? A lover? A friend? And: What kind of woman? And: What was sex like for you? But my habit of skimming with family could not be undone. When I needed to ask real questions, by dint of never having done so, I couldn't.

A few days later, the other, more upsetting thing happens. It's January, 6 a.m. I wake up for my publishing internship, put on a long cargo skirt and my stretchy three-quarter-sleeved sweater set. I get the coffee going and then open the door to grab the newspaper, something I've been doing each day. This morning the paper isn't on the stoop but on the sidewalk, so I have to actually step out and grab it. As the door clicks shut behind me, my heart thumps. The lock wasn't turned—was it? It was. It is. And I'm standing barefoot and coatless in the cold.

I ring the doorbell. My grandmother is taking her shower at this point, on the same side of the house as the door. From outside I hear the water cut off. *Megan?* she warbles shrilly. *I'll be right there.* It takes her some excruciatingly long minutes to pull herself out of the shower and out of her room, down the long hall to the front door. When she does she is naked—buck. Nude but for a yellow hand towel draped modestly over one shoulder, partially covering one breast.

The sight is a shock: I've seen so few naked bodies at this point. Waxy cadavers only, via a summer anatomy class, and movie stars. Nothing like this slumped shape, all skin folds, glasses, and cane. Shivering and mortified, I can barely get out my apology but make sure to look straight at her face. *I knew you would do that*, she says, snippy but not unkind. Then she turns around and limps slowly back the way she came.

Ten minutes later I hear unsettling gargling noises from her room. *Gigi?* I call, and I wait outside her door. When she doesn't answer, I barge in. She's at her vanity, shaking. Seizing. I step behind her and hold her up as she falls back, then guide her soft body onto the plush carpet. I call 911.

When the paramedics arrive, she is out of her seizure, dazed. The EMTs, both men, are concerned about her nudity. *Let's get some clothes on you*, they say, and they turn to me to fix the situation. Gigi has laid her outfit for the day on the bed, so I grab her underwear and get to work, trembling. *Sorry, Gigi*, I whisper. She is responsive, but slurring. She refuses to go to the hospital. *I don't want to go*, she says, a plaintive tone creeping in. They help her into the chair, which she presses herself into defiantly, as if daring them to try to move her. *I'm not going.*

I don't go to my internship that day, instead staying home with Gigi, who is grumpy about her changed routine. She does not let me make lunch or dinner. We don't speak of this day again. When I mention Gigi's seizure now to my parents, it's the first either have heard of it. Evidently neither Gigi nor I thought it worth mentioning at the time.

IN MY RESEARCH, I learn that to many farmers, skim milk was not just the unwanted by-product of butter-making. These farmers saw it as valuable, a cost-cutting, protein-rich supplement for their livestock. When it became sought after by chemurgists who wanted to use it for casein products, these farmers went to battle with factory managers over its fate. So skim milk may not have been the con I thought it was.

I started this essay with the idea that to skim milk is to take away all the good stuff. That to skim a text, or a self, or another person, is necessarily to betray it, or them. But there are plenty of good reasons to skim. We can glean a lot from a little; a surface read can be enough. And it's rare that we need or want to know everything. That a lover like Mace can locate and surface Saranda's *true and hidden self* is the basic fantasy of romance. As if the self could be whole. As if the self could be a static thing, to be known, to be consumed, drunk in full.

I started, too, with the assumption that Gigi's familial self was as thin and diluted as mine. I am coming to understand that I may have been wrong.

Just as I'm giving up on the search for Ruby's round-robin friends, Nora sends me three old, weathered photo albums, one of which is devoted to them. It opens to a set of six square black-and-white portraits of young women against the same arboreal background. Ruby is off-center and sweet-looking with dark lipstick, a shot of coiled hair peeking out from under her white turban head wrap. Next to her is that charismatic woman from Ruby's wedding photo, wide, bright smile and teasing eyes. *Dorothy Sprinkle?* is written next to her in ballpoint pen. A separate note in Nora's handwriting regrets she doesn't know everyone's full names, but she's made some guesses. The others, on each corner of the page, are labeled *Blanche Koski Smith*, *? maybe Bearnice Sprinkle*, *Grace Koski Anderson*, and *? Grace*. One of the Graces must be Cece, I think.

I try to find them online, but it's impossible—I'd be surprised if they lived past Web 1.0, and they would all have different names if they did, married names. Like Ruby—who became a Milks—who became Gigi to me.

Half of the album documents what seems to be a summer vacation with the fervor of someone who's just gotten their first personal camera; every moment is a photo op. The next set of photos captures what looks like Dorothy's wedding. In my favorite image, Dorothy, Ruby, and Grace-or-Cece are posing on the stone entranceway of some unknown building. Dorothy is seated with Grace-or-Cece stretched out sideways on her lap. On the right side of the photo, Ruby straddles Grace-or-Cece's knees, a wide-legged, uncomfortable-looking pose—I imagine Dorothy insisting Ruby join the photo at the last minute, and Ruby awkwardly obliging, unsure how to seem fun. Everyone is touching: Dorothy's cradling Grace-or-Cece, who is reaching toward Ruby, whose palm is on Grace's thigh. Where Dorothy and Grace-or-Cece are laughing at the camera, Ruby's expression is serene, her face in profile. Her eyes are shut; if they were open, they'd be gazing at Dorothy.

I could do more research: seek out these friends' descendants, see if they have copies of their letters. Talk to other family members, see whom they recognize. But that gaze—that imagined gaze—is all I need. The rest I'm happy to skim.

And maybe the simplest version—that Gigi had given me the gift she had meant to give me—is the truth. After all, even if it had been on sale at Kmart, a book among books, she picked this one. For me.

MAKING GOOD ON my promise to send a draft of this essay to my parents before publishing, I sit down with it and revise for five hours with their feelings in mind. This means cutting out or adjusting some of the more resentful content, some ungenerous, arguably bratty sentiments here and there. I prune out some of the sexy material, too, with the goal of making as comfortable as possible the uncomfortable experience of reading a piece of writing in which they are portrayed. Though I know, for example, that the ending will stay the ending in the final version, I decide they don't need to read it now, or ever.

How fitting, I think. I'm skimming the piece down.

I was nervous that this editing process would compromise my integrity as a writer, but in fact, it significantly improves the essay. The writing feels lighter now, released of venom. A lot of what I cut wasn't even true, or at least not complicated enough.

I send them an email contextualizing the essay—"It's as much about me as it is about Gigi"—and attach the file. I feel great all day. I have done the hard work. It was good work. I feel good.

My mom sends a nice email response. She finds the essay poignant and amusing, and jokes that she wants to borrow *Princess of Thieves*. I'm relieved. Dad will send me some corrections to things I got wrong tomorrow.

Later that night, I close Word and a box pops up: "Do you want to save the changes made to Princess of Thieves12_for Mom and Dad.docx?"

I didn't. But I did. I sent them the unedited, unsaved version, because I turned off AutoSave months ago, I forget why, but I had some good reason. I sent them the full version, which wasn't full, or fully true. Many of the statements in it were propositions I was still entertaining. When you type a thought or feeling into a sentence, does that make it true? No. It makes it a sentence, which can be revised. A lot of those sentences did not hold up to the test of time, or new moods, or logical scrutiny.

I'm mortified, but they've already read it. Neither of them has attested to any hurt feelings, but I can only assume they are hurt. I was hurt on their behalf when reading the earlier, less sensitive version. I'm kicking myself. I send them a panicked, embarrassed email. They don't really respond with much.

I guess they're okay.

My dad replies with a confirmation that Grace-or-Cece is Grace. No response to my inquiry about his emotional reaction.

Well, the skimming is mutual. And we understand more of each other than we let on.

I'VE REACHED THE climactic hot-air balloon scene. It's a trust test. Mace, a *cad*, wants only for Saranda to admit to wanting him, needing him, so he takes her up in a hot-air balloon. "Do you trust me, Princess?" asks the best lover in all Europe. "Do—you—trust—me?"

"You know I do," she responds, unaware of his plan to take her up in the air—in the *sky*. Her biggest fear, by the way, is of heights.

"*Oh no*," moans Saranda when she sees the balloon. "I'll die." She turns to leave, but Mace tightens his grip. She kicks her legs frantically. Mace tosses her in and turns the flame up without paying. "Stop, thief!" shouts the merchant, but they're up, up, and away. Chapter break.

Saranda freaks out, huddled on the floor of the wicker cabin. "You son of a bitch!" she screams. "You said I could trust you!" Mace responds that she can. "Look around you. We're fine." He grabs her by the waist and lifts her up, making her look down. She panics. He threatens to slap her. He tries to take her mind off her fear by stroking her slender thigh. She scoffs. He grins wickedly and vaults up onto the edge of the basket like Peter Pan, tipping the balloon to the side.

This is when she tricks him, a tactic to make him stop scaring her. "Have you ever made love in the skies?" she wants to know. Intrigued, he asks if that's an invitation. "Come on down here and find out," she lures.

Our heroine is strategic: Unable to admit she is too scared to look over the side of the basket, she twists around on the floor, declaring she is hot for him, needs him, now. "You're wet?" he asks, suspicious. "You'd better not be lying."

Even as Mace "takes possession of" her mouth, Saranda cannot forget her fear. She feels "as dry as a month-old bone," a description, I remember, I could not understand as a kid. I remember this next sentence too: "She knew if he came inside her now, it would be like penetrating sandpaper." I studied this line, trying to determine whether *penetrating* was used as a verbal or adjectival and wondering what precisely the difference would be. Then later the sword imagery. "You're so hard, it makes me tremble. Like a sword of tempered steel." His words are *lewd*, her caresses *wanton*, her impulses *unholy*—my god! She administers oral sex until he reverses roles, which is when he discovers: She's "as dry as dust." Interesting.

"*You little bitch*," he rasps. Orders her to take off her clothes and—gently and sensuously (to her surprise) kisses her everywhere. "You can't escape me," he murmurs. "Sooner or later, your surrender will be mine for the taking." Pretty soon he is awakening longings and lifting one of her legs, then the other, above the lip of the basket, weaving her limbs into the ropes.

I'm waiting for the ballast to run out—they have only four bags, this was part of the setup, a detail it seemed important to pay attention to. But such danger does not arise: only the danger of unnegotiated domination. "Just remember this the next time you're tempted to pretend," Mace tells Saranda before eating her out. "If I come like this," she gasps,

"I shall fall." He lets her down and brings her to a shattering climax. Then he turns her around and enters her from behind, forcing her to look down to the farmlands below. "Isn't it incredible?" he asks. Yes, she pants; comes again. End chapter.

This time I get myself off while I'm reading, and it's like I'm closing a loop that's yawned wide, stuck open for all these years. Incredible, I think, and come back to the view. There she is, again, it's Gigi: on my laptop screen, grinning out from her obituary page with that inscrutable twinkle in her eye. I return the gaze, the smile. We've gotten to the good part, I think. I click away.

NOTES

1. Katherine O'Neal, *Princess of Thieves* (Bantam Books, 1993).
2. This depends on the family, of course, and on the friendship: Many families have been cleaved or stomped out through enslavement, incarceration, deportation, coercive adoption, or genocide; some friendships have been celebrated and historicized.

Dear Dairy IV: Chaseholm (Again)

Tuesday, March 26, 2024—Day 1

The barn door sticks. I force it open and tamp down my buoyancy to match the quiet energy inside. Sanitizing water swishes through the steel pipes that run along the inner barn walls. The beat is meditative, hypnotic.

I'm back at Chaseholm for a "work exchange." That is, I had proposed a two- to three-week period where I might contribute some vaguely conceived "work" in exchange for an apprenticeship in dairying. My thinking was that two or three weeks might give me the time to actually become useful to the farm. Maybe there was some big repair project they could use an extra pair of hands on? (Not that I had any construction experience.) Or maybe I could just move some manure around. I'm able-bodied and a fast learner. Let me clean the barn. I had no idea what to propose, what "help" might be needed, and I think we all knew I'd only be in the way. I just wanted to get further inside a dairy farm, as inside as an outsider could get.

Sarah graciously counter-proposed three half days "to start." And here I am.

I wave, apologetic. I'm late, and I've been loud. Sarah tells me to hang back. She's introducing two new cows bought from a neighbor who just shut down his farm. The new cows are nervous, twitchy, which agitates the others. Anything new makes cows nervous, and there's a lot of new energy today, including me.

A wide-eyed Jersey approaches the foremost stall and halts when she sees me. I'm awed by her gaze, these dark, deep, sensitive pools beholding me. She steps backward, turns to Sarah questioningly. I shrink into the corner and avert my eyes. At Sarah's coaxing, she moves forward.

Wait, isn't this Eleanor's stall? But this isn't Eleanor. I don't see her among this crew. Maybe she's been dried off, or maybe I'm not recognizing her. I'll ask when I get a chance. It turns out no one's in their usual stalls. This cow, Solange—I can tell from the tag attached to her left ear—is wide in the belly, pretty far pregnant.

Sarah introduces me to Dan, the herdsperson who's milking today. Together they clip the cows into the stalls.

I inquire after Queen and Lucy and Eleanor, the three I remember best from my August visit. Queen, the one-horned meanie, has been dried off as she nears her next birthing, and she's with the dry cows in a different herd. She's still mean; Sarah thinks she's probably responsible for a gnarly injury to someone else's udder. Lucy's here, with the green collar. Still the runt of the group. Hi, Lucy. Majestic big-girl Eleanor passed away in October. I'm sorry to hear this.

My first task is to brush the cows using a toothed metal currycomb. Sarah demonstrates how to enter the stall, first by resting a hand on a haunch to let the cow know I'm there. I get into it, scrubbing caked mud and manure from Solange's fur. Sarah brushes another cow across the way, keeping an eye on me and making conversation. She tells me I can brush the udder, too.

"Really? It's not sensitive?"

"Maybe go gentle, but yeah. Think about how all this caked dirt and manure must pull on the hairs."

I go back to brushing Solange. She's so warm. It's near freezing outside, but with my hands on her belly, I'm fine without gloves.

Yolo is leaking, and Clam the cat positions herself under the thin stream. Right now Yolo's nursing and producing more milk than her calf needs, so the farm will take milk from one quarter of her udder and leave the rest for the calf. She stands through the whole process, as if she knows she's not long here. And in fact, she's the first to be guided out.

Dan invites me to try stripping Lush. He's pre-dipped her with an iodine solution that cleans the teats. Now I'm supposed to dry each teat and test their milk by hand. I put on latex gloves and squeeze the most prominent teat. "Each one is different," Dan says. "Try them all." It takes me a few goes to get my hand moving the right way, fingers pressing in and down in a wave to activate the letdown. But soon I squeeze out a few squirts from each teat, and he's right. The front left is best in show. The other three, shorter, are harder to pull.

I thought this would seem like more of a moment. Maybe the climactic moment: At last, Megan Milks the Cow. The teat flesh feels rubbery and squeezy. The milk spurts hot on my hands. I aim it in the small blue testing bucket we're using to check the milk for mastitis prior to milking. Ha, I said "we." It doesn't feel like an arrival, exactly. More like I have a lot to learn.

Dan slips the four arms of the milking machine over Lush's teats. As that machine runs, he pulls another one off Sparrow, a nearby Holstein, then dips her teats in a burnt-orange iodine solution that's thicker and more syrupy than the sterilizing solution—"like barbecue sauce," he puts it. It acts as a barrier to the outside world, helping to prevent infection.

We bring Yolo back to a small barnyard to rejoin her calf. She calls to her, and the calf stands obligingly but doesn't know what to do after that. Another cow, Morgane, is here too, due any day. Behind us, Lev the bull paws and groans, letting us know who's boss. Dan leaves me here with instructions to fill up the water tanks while he tends to something else. Then we unclip the rest of the cows and watch them line up and move into the barnyard, gathering around the hay. Lev joins them.

Anne asked me to record some cow sounds for her podcast, but the most prominent noise in the barn was the steady beat of the vacuum pumps pulling the milk up and into the metal pipes. I noted a few soft grunts, some tail swishes, the heavy shuffle of hind hooves. Occasionally Lev's groans.

Down the road with the beef herd, it's another story. These cattle have split into two groups, one at the top of the hill, the other at the bottom. At the sight of Dan and me barreling in on an ATV, the lower group forms a line up the lane to join their neighbors. Lots of cow sounds now: mothers calling for their young, letting them know it's time to queue up, it's lunch time. Cows in the upper group—mostly British Whites—greet the cows in the lower—mostly Red Devons.

We adjust the fencing. We roll over the bale rings from yesterday's hay and drop them around today's fresh bundles. Dan lets the cattle in.

These cows don't have their horns burned off, I observe. Dan says the farm lets them keep them, though most farms don't due to risk of injury. Horns help cattle regulate heat in their heads, which is important in colder climates. Unfortunately, the two abattoirs Chaseholm uses to process their animals just changed their policies to accept only cattle with shorn horns. The farm will have to figure something out.

Right. These cattle aren't pets, they're business. They're bodies to feed, and feed well, so that they become the best food they can be. That's what we're up to with this hay on this hill. This new abattoir problem is concerning. The slaughterhouse shortage has been an ongoing national crisis, exacerbated by the COVID pandemic, and in the past few years, Chaseholm has had to go further out to process their meat. A new horn policy gives the farm yet another aggravation to deal with.

It's a common misconception that only bulls and not cows have horns. But cattle differ from other ungulates such as deer, among whom only the male animals are horned. With the exception of a few breeds like Angus and Hereford, most cattle develop horns unless they're shorn or the nubs burned away.

Dan tells me a neighbor visited the farm recently and was appalled to learn that these horned cattle were female: "What are they *doing* over here?" Since Chaseholm is a queer-run farm, his first inclination was to assume these cows must be genetically engineered hermaphrodites.

We laugh over this story. Heifers are more valuable than steers. If it were possible to engineer steers who could make milk, it *would* solve some problems for the industry.

Dan notices two yearlings on the lam, heading toward the open fence at the entrance. He mounts the four-wheeler and drives off to guide them back, zigzagging behind them like a sheepdog until they step over the (not-electrified) fence and rejoin the herd.

Cow time is different, slow. Consumption and digestion

are ongoing processes. Pasture-fed cattle graze six to twelve hours a day, and they're always ruminating, working their intake over and over inside their bodies. I'm as curious about them as they are about me. Observing them is like meditation; my mind goes blank.

I SMELL LIKE a barn. I forgot to hose off my boots and have brought a thick stink into my rental car. I'm hungry and dazed from the sun. My GPS isn't catching service, so I just start driving, hoping I remember how to get back to Red Hook. I don't.

Wednesday, March 27, 2024—Day 2

Today I got to hug a nervous cow named Brenda.

And I stripped a lot of teats.

I yanked some; squeezed some. Just when I'd think I had the hang of it, I'd come up against a finicky one.

Dan praised my comportment. You're calm and confident, he said. Those are good qualities around cows. I beamed with pride.

Lev the bull's job is to sniff the urine for pheromones. According to Dan, when he smells them, Lev becomes quite the perv. His eyes roll back and his upper lip curls up. He lets it waft in. When he detects a cow in heat, he'll try to mount her upward of ten times in three days.

Thursday, March 28, 2024—Day 3

I'm a slow driver on these roads. This morning I'm late and feel bad about it. Pretty sure Sarah and Dan don't care. I worry they're sick of babysitting me. I'm "working" but not. Getting a free education in dairy while slowing everything down with my clumsiness and an endless stream of questions.

I milk a cow named Fuss. The whole process. Pre-dip. Clean and strip. Attach the milk pumps. Remove the milk pumps. It's a *J* movement. You break the suction and stand up, and the milk pump comes with you.

Post-dip. Say thank you and give her a pat on the haunch.

The milk tank is full, almost to the brim. Most of it will be going toward yogurt.

Milking Lucy, I have trouble with one teat, and she whips her tail at me, irritated. It stings my cheek and reeks of manure.

With the beef herd I get to be the gatekeeper, pulling the gate down and back up so Dan can go in and out with the tractor to set up the hay.

I record a short audio diary for Anne. One of the yearlings suckles when she's not supposed to. If Dan were here, I bet he'd say her mom is being too nice. Another yearling, a bronze named Sycamore, joins me at the fence line. Yet another yearling steps up next to her. They stare inquisitively, drinking me in. Pretty soon there are ten or twelve yearlings and cows observing me serenely as I record, not far from the fence. The fence is usually electrified, but now, while we work, it's not. This is the first moment I feel something like fear. They could easily barrel through this thin rope and charge me. But they just stand there, mild and unmoving except for slow blinks and chewing their cud.

Dan unloads the hay from the tractor and joins us. "Nope," he says, watching the yearling suckle. "You're too old for that." He shakes his head. "Mom's being too nice."

Another calf tries to suckle another dam, but she moves away, preventing the calf from reaching her udder. Undeterred, the calf circles around to the other side. The mother turns again, now facing her calf. She lowers her head and frames her calf with her horns. The calf stops for a moment, then backs up and goes again for the udder. The cow trots away, leading the calf to the bale ring. Here—eat this instead.

SARAH WAS RIGHT: Three half days of work is enough. I've completed my mission. I've made contact with cows, and I've even milked a few. I understand better what dairy life is like and why people stay committed to it, and I've gotten some sense of the complicated forms of care and love that can exist between humans and cattle. Now I'm ready to return to my routine.

I want to give back, so I buy things, and I leave with a haul of Chaseholm products: raw milk, yogurt, a few cheeses. Ground beef, pork tenderloin, chorizo. Some coffee. A Chaseholm cropped tee. I'm bringing it all with me to my friend Diana's, as a thank-you for letting me stay with her the next few days. She's delighted at the array, especially the dairy. The cheeses are exquisite, she declares, and we get into the yogurt too. Diana makes herself a cappuccino with the milk and pours some of the steamed milk into my empty mug to try. The smell of the barn comes back, and I realize what that odor is: not just manure but milk. A smell like the body, close.

I see the cow. I smell the cow. I hear her soft snorts and low groans. I feel her warmth and her coarse, dirt-roughed hair. I honor the cow. I drink the cow and I taste the barn, the animal in my mouth.

The Squeeze

Come; let us squeeze hands all round; nay, let us all squeeze ourselves into each other; let us squeeze ourselves universally into the very milk and sperm of kindness.
—**HERMAN MELVILLE,** ***Moby-Dick***

— 1 —
SQUEEZE

LATE IN HER life, my grandmother—Gigi—introduced a new family ritual at Christmas. It was usual that every year she handed out holiday cards with cash tucked inside, a crisp ten or twenty for the kids, maybe more for the adults. When I was in my mid-teens, though, she switched things up. Fanning out the cards, she asked the nearest grandkid to pick an envelope. She coached them first to read the recipient's name out loud, then to give that person the card—and a hug. The hug was required; the hug was the point. The Milkses were not a particularly demonstrative crew, and she wanted to encourage more warmth. The hug was expected to be "real," that is, close and tight, a bona fide squeeze. If it didn't satisfy this condition, the audience would say so—*that wasn't a real hug, you can do better than that*, etc.—and the hugger would try again. Upon being adequately hugged, the hugged person would pluck the next card and give it, with a hug, to its recipient. And so on. In this way Gigi bribed us into a hug chain. I remember cheers and applause, roars at seeing certain men hug each other. I remember the quiet anticipation—and my own hope, dread, nervousness—as we waited to hear our names. It was coercive, yes, and uncomfortably performative, but mostly I experienced it as sweet. We staged these hugs each year until Gigi died. Then we largely stopped gathering as a family.

"MORE AND MORE I'm identifying with cows," I tell Svetlana, who's over for dinner. I've made us tacos with squash, onions, and ground turkey, overcooked. I force a bite down; she douses hers in hot sauce. "I feel so extracted from." I mime squeezing milk from my lower abs and chuckle to mask the self-pity.

Svetlana has just traded in the freelance life for her first real day job and is finding the adjustment challenging but right—she needs stable income and employer-sponsored health care. I'm teaching three classes at two institutions, prepping to coteach at another school over my break, editing academic manuscripts, filing occasional book reviews, and trying to finish writing this book. Now that my paychecks at two schools are biweekly and half as much, my bank account seems to rise and fall with one breath, and I can see more clearly how scarcely my income is covering my financial needs. Prices are rising. I'm feeling the squeeze. The crushing pain of my reality. *Is this it?* reorganizes into *This is it*. I've been applying to tenure-track jobs for ten years. What else can I do? Edtech? UX? . . . ?

The problem is collective, experienced collectively: a

political economy that prizes our productivity but not the quality of our lives. I have a lot; I have enough. I have ample food and clean water. Stable housing. A home free from interpersonal and state violence. Multiple jobs, multiple income streams. Health care. Flexibility. A net. I eat all the time; I support my production. I'm producing as much milk as my body can make. It's not enough. It's too much. I'm getting sick from the stress; I can feel it. Can't sleep, can't stay asleep. Squeeze a squirt of CBD oil under the tongue. It knocks me out but leaves me groggy in the morning, less focused, takes more time to do my work. Coffee, more coffee. More sleep aids. More coffee. More work. Migraine. Sick. Then injured.

APARNA IS SQUEEZING the muscles around my knee, pressing her fingers in and sliding them upward. The fronts of my quads are tight and she wants to release the tension. Everything's connected, she says. The muscles protect the knee. I'm here for physical therapy, recovering from a bilateral knee injury. It's our second session; she squeezed me in today since I'll be gone next week. For what, she asks. A manure expo. A what. It's a research trip. I'm working on a book about milk.

She asks if I'm making a case against dairy. No, it's personal essays. I occasionally drink milk and sometimes eat beef. She's Hindu, she says, and cows are sacred in India. It's unthinkable to consume them.

I'm on my back, and she's pressing into my hip flexors. As if the pressure has pulled loose a lever in my throat, I ramble on about a documentary I watched on cow vigilantes in India.[1] She nods absently, focused now on my other hip. Have you seen that movie about the woman who made the thing for cows? she asks. I forget her name but she's played by Claire Danes.

Temple Grandin?

Yeah, that's it. Claire Danes is incredible.

I've just ordered a few of Grandin's books, but I didn't know about the biopic. We try to remember if she invented the squeeze chute for cattle *and* the squeeze machine for people with sensory disorders, or was it *just* the thing for humans, which was based on the cattle chute. We decide it must be the latter and we are right.

I watch the film *Temple Grandin*.[2] It's the summer of 1966, and Temple, an autistic teen en route to college in the fall, is staying with her aunt and uncle at their Arizona ranch. One day, Temple sees a handler guide a steer into a steel structure made of red bars. He pulls a lever and the front clangs shut, locking the steer's neck in place. Another lever presses the sides of the structure inward, squeezing against the steer's body. The clangs are loud, frightening—farm people call this "clatter"—to Temple, to the wild-eyed steer, to me. Then quiet. Temple is astonished. "What happened to it?" she asks the handler. "It calmed down!"

He shrugs. "They just like it. It gentles them." A vet tech pops the needle of a syringe into the animal's haunch and releases the vaccine. The handler pulls back the levers, and the steer trots loose.

Danes won awards for this role. To prepare, she studied Grandin's speech patterns and mannerisms, as well as video footage from her adolescence. Grandin consulted on the film. But biopics are the genre in which acting most seems like an android's mimicry, and to me, Danes's performance sits somewhere in the uncanny valley. Or maybe the issue is the direction, the camera—so many close-ups on her widened eyes and ugly crying. Look at her act! Look at her act autistic!

But Grandin felt Danes captured her with astounding accuracy. "It was like entering a weird time machine," she told media.

Temple relates more to cows than to people. An unexpected change in the environment inside her aunt's home upsets her. Frantic, she escapes the house, racing toward the chute and clambering inside it, stomach down. Her concerned aunt rushes after her. Temple begs Aunt Ann to close the gates on her. Ann is dubious, but finally: clang. Temple relaxes. She's in the squeeze.

THE OTHER KIND of squeeze machine is the milker.

Hand milking involves squeezing the teat high up on the udder between the thumb and first finger. While those fingers "trap" the milk, the remaining fingers squeeze downward in a wave motion to force the milk out. The milking machine works similarly, clenching and unclenching the teat to express the milk. When the udder runs dry, the machine falls off, or the cow, in discomfort, kicks it free.

I DON'T KNOW when or how my knee issue started. Maybe it was overextension in a particular position, in sex or yoga. It may have been the beta blocker I started taking every few days to combat public speaking anxiety: it helped me think more clearly when my mind was squeezed up in stress. The pills achieved the goal—they calmed me down, they gentled me—but they also slowed my whole circulatory system, turning me into an inflated Gumby, grinning and floaty. After class one day, my legs went rubbery on a few flights of stairs. Was that a side effect of the beta blocker or a sign of the thing itself, i.e., of some unknown injury? I don't know.

When I biked to the Kings County courthouse for a jury summons the next morning—madly, furiously, I was late, it was a busy week, and I resented this *one more thing*—I flung my legs in tight circles, enjoying the numbness, the jointless feeling of freedom. I biked hard. When I arrived and dismounted, I felt two pops in the backs of both knees. Concerning, but I was late. I had already postponed this grand jury summons once; I couldn't miss or I'd be *in trouble*. I locked up my bike and floated carefully into the courthouse.

I argued my case on the grounds of my teaching schedule, obtained my certificate of completion, and then, ignoring the knee pops, biked home. The next day, as planned, I did a HIIT class, moving through the stations on shaky legs. That night I went to a party, as planned. It was a third-floor walkup, and I could barely make it up the stairs. I could not have or be fun at this party. All I could think was: It's starting. The joint issues and osteoarthritis that run in my family. Should I be drinking more milk? I wondered. Would that help the plan not change?

THE SQUEEZE CHUTE scene is based on an episode in Grandin's life, and I'm impressed with her young insight, her understanding that what she needed was the embrace of a mechanical structure. "At first there were a few moments of sheer panic as I stiffened up and tried to pull away from the pressure," she writes in *Thinking in Pictures*, "but I couldn't get away because my head was locked in. Five seconds later I felt a wave of relaxation, and about thirty minutes later I asked Aunt Ann to release me. For about an hour afterward I felt very calm and serene." The squeeze machine smothered her anxiety like a heavy blanket on flames. "This was the first time I ever felt really comfortable in my own skin."[3]

Cattle relax in the squeeze chute for reasons similar to Temple's. Prey animals who often graze exposed and vulnerable on open fields, cattle are sensitive creatures. Their vision has evolved to scan their surroundings constantly. They don't like rapid movements, loud noises, or other surprises. The pressure of the squeeze chute may be a relief from exposure and ambient overstimulation. Maybe it also reminds them of being in the inner circle of a protective herd.

As a kid, Grandin couldn't stand to be touched. "I wanted to feel the nice social feeling of being held, but it was just too overwhelming." Although the squeeze machine was intense at first, she was in control—not at the mercy of, for example, her overaffectionate other aunt who hugged too hard and too long and wore "horrible" perfume.[4]

I have not faced the profound challenges with touch, language, and human interaction that Grandin has, but I have autistic tendencies enough to find relief in the clarity of her alienation. I can be a clumsy hugger. I go in too hard or not hard enough. I can't seem to predict whether any given person is a back clapper, a chest protector, or a cheek-to-cheeker with loosely draped arms. Some people do a split-second touch and release; some people linger. Some people pivot for a side hug. Some bury their chests and lead with their shoulders; others go all in for the full chest-to-chest. A hug may be aspirational, questioning: This is the kind of intimacy I want with you—might you want it too? Sometimes a back rub. Sometimes one hand grazing the shoulder blade. As a culture, we've reached more awareness around seeking consent before gathering someone up into a possibly unwanted embrace. Some hugs are denied. Their recipients reject them; they don't like hugs or they don't like you. Or they don't like the prospect of contracting COVID or other illness. Sometimes an elbow tap is best.

At a writers' conference years ago, I told myself to be

bold, to go in strong with the hugging. Stop being so standoffish. When I met up with a butch friend I hadn't seen in ages, I went in aggressively; I spread my wings, a hawk going in for the kill. I was insistent on proving something to them, to myself. I wanted to show them through firm bodily contact how much our relationship meant to me. I pushed my chest into theirs, gripped their lats between my biceps, and squeezed.

I once witnessed John Darnielle walk up to pint-sized master guitarist Kaki King on stage after she opened for the Mountain Goats in Chicago. Or maybe they'd performed a duet. He loved her, she was amazing, and he demonstrated his appreciation by taking her in his arms and lifting her off the ground. "All of her talent, all of her command as a musician, he just diminished it," my girlfriend at the time lamented. That girlfriend taught me how to cuddle, something I did not intuitively know how to do. I would sit stiffly next to her on the sofa while watching Oprah (she loved Oprah), and she would lean into me and arrange my limbs around her. The cuddling was both overwhelming and relieving; at once, I felt melted and more solid. When my arm grew numb, I let it.

I did not lift my butch friend off the ground, but when I brought my chest to theirs, it felt as though I was forcing together two repelling magnets, and I understood suddenly, surely, that I had breached a boundary. We stepped back and stared at each other with dismay. Their cheeks were flushed. I was mortified. We didn't speak of it. The next day at the book fair, they took me aside and, without directly addressing the earlier incident, taught me what they called the butch hug—you go in off-center with a clap on the back. We practiced a few times until I could execute the back clap at an appropriate level of pressure: firm, but not a smack, letting the palm linger for a moment—that's the hug part. You hug with the hand. The butch hug.

I share this story with a lover as an example of a lesson I have learned about hugs. They're surprised at how much thought I've given to this—hugging is not a problem they have. They're skeptical of "the butch hug" as a gendered, imposed category. It's true, I realize: I know lots of butches and mascs who love a close embrace, and I've loved closely embracing them. I guess by calling it a butch hug, my friend was, without personalizing it, telling me how to approach hugging *them*, one specific butch, and I appreciated the spirit of generosity and intimacy with which they shared this.

Maybe the casual hug is too quick to find the right pressure between two bodies with all of their histories of touch, as well as the specific degree of intimacy that exists, or could, between them. Often we feel this out *through* the hugging.

During my stint in the milking barn at Chaseholm Farm, I got to squeeze a nervous cow named Brenda. When it was her turn to be milked, Dan, the milker, instructed me to hug her; he said it might help calm her down. I stationed myself against Brenda's side, facing away from her head, then circled my arms around her belly and squeezed. She blew out air and danced a bit. I murmured sweet nothings as Dan slipped on the milking tubes. Brenda leaned into me. It was true, I thought proudly, what Dan had said earlier. I had excellent cow comportment.

I remembered that cattle like firm touch, so I held Brenda harder, too hard. I felt her rib cage expand and contract between my arms, straining against or testing the hold. It may be absurd to think my marginal strength could have bothered, much less panicked, a twelve-hundred-pound cow.

But she started coughing. When I relaxed my hold, she leaned into me again. And as the milk machine squeezed and tugged, Brenda and I eventually found the right hug.

TEMPLE GOES TO college and is overwhelmed. To survive in her new environment, she takes two hard plywood boards and constructs her own squeeze machine to help her deal with overstimulation and overwhelm. You lie on your stomach, pull the lever, and the machine angles in to give you a full-body hug.

Temple loves her squeeze machine and uses it all the time. Her normie roommate finds this weird and complains to the RA. Temple is made to see a psychiatrist who will evaluate her to determine whether she is using the apparatus for appropriate or inappropriate ends.

> Psychiatrist: So when you got in your machine did it make you *feel* like a cow?
> Temple: No, I didn't feel like a cow.
> But it gave you pleasure.
> It made me feel good. Gentle.
> The hug made you feel good?
> Yes.
> But you don't like to be touched by people.
> No.
> Do you like to touch yourself?
> (Temple brings her fingers to her arm experimentally.)
> Touching myself's okay.
> But when the squeeze machine touches you, it feels better.
> Yes.
> It gives you release?
> Yes, there is release.[5]

The psychiatrist orders the machine to get dumped.

Temple is devastated but not defeated. A few days later,

she goes back to the dean and proposes a scientific experiment to determine the effects of the squeeze machine on human sensory experience. He agrees.

She asks her peers to try out the apparatus and report back, collecting their responses as data. Some find it claustrophobic. Others find the sensation interesting and mildly pleasurable. Some, like Temple, find it deeply relaxing. By demonstrating its use value through data, Temple wins back the privilege to build a new machine. She also gets placed with a new, more compatible roommate.

She writes: "I would have been as hard and as unfeeling as a rock if I had not built my squeeze machine and followed through with its use. The relaxing feeling of being held washes negative thoughts away. I believe that the brain needs to receive comforting sensory input. Gentle touching teaches kindness."[6]

I BREAK FOR an online onboarding orientation at a Brooklyn art institute, one of three schools where I'm scheduled to teach next semester. (We'll call this one BAI.) After the orientation, there's a short meeting with the union, now the third union to which I belong—each school's part-time faculty union is different. Our reps go over the unit's history and the timeline for the next contract negotiation; they explain the complicated promotion process. During the Q&A, another new hire expresses concern over the division of ranks in her department, wondering why so few of her peers have been promoted. Another says they thought they'd get health benefits sooner.

I'm grateful to have more stable status at another school, which I'll call Graff, because it sounds like I won't get it at BAI. Our union at Graff went on strike two years ago in what became the longest part-time faculty strike in US history. We watched bitterly as the administration of our socially progressive university hired a union-busting legal team and trotted out every union-busting strategy in the books. But eventually, the administration caved and we got most of the contract improvements the union asked for, including a pay hike that inflation seems to have already outpaced.

I get off the call. I debate whether to drop the one class I'm assigned to teach at Barnett, which pays the least per credit hour of the three schools. Barnett's part-time faculty union is in contract negotiations, but leadership is weak and self-interested, and we don't expect much. I don't want to manage four classes—I know from experience that it's too much for me, especially when they're spread across three schools. But it's a better problem to have too many classes as opposed to too few, and I worry one of my two classes at BAI will be canceled due to low enrollment.

I weigh the options. If I drop the class, I'll have more writing time; keep it, I'll make more money; but not much more. Enrollment caps are up again. That means more grading. If I drop the class, I could take on more academic editing, a side gig where I get paid by the word. I can predict that future. Feeling precarious, I'll take on too much. I'll fly through the pages with an eye on the clock; retain nothing and have to start over. Tuck 30 percent away for taxes and then it's what. Grocery money. Which I'll need.

I open my yearly royalty statement and feel tricked. I tricked myself into thinking I could buy a new laptop with the extra cash. Nope. I'm stuck with this relic from 2013, speakers blown, four keys dead. The Bluetooth speaker and portable keyboard will have to be enough. Save up, save up. My maintenance bill swells by forty bucks, then ninety, then two hundred. Electricity goes up 12 percent; gas goes up 19. The price of eggs, 66. The price of milk, 27. I'll hold on to my fourth class for now.

THE ARTIST Tiona Nekkia McClodden has worked with the cattle squeeze chute as an art object, painted black. It's part of her installation *Hold on, let me take the safety off* (2019), which juxtaposes objects associated with queer BDSM culture (leather jacket, leather boots) against objects of modernism and industrial design (a Breuer chair, the cattle chute). McClodden's BDSM repurposing of the chute renders this industrial object chillingly sexy: Sleek black, cool steel, it's menacing and hot. Titled *The Full Severity of Compassion* (2019), the chute's associations with cattle make manifest the origins—slaughter—of the leather jackets, leather boots, and pieces of leather hide that McClodden has draped around the gallery.

In their book *Dragging Away*, Lex Lancaster has read this installation through the lens of readymades and queer abstraction. McClodden is autistic. *The Full Severity of Compassion* invites us, Lex writes, to think about both "the violence done to animals exploited by the livestock industry [and] the violence of normative expectations of affective and relational behavior."[7] But the squeeze chute also promises comfort, containment, and support. McClodden's artwork suggests that "structures of support might also always carry the potential for material violence." At the same time, "the severity of a hulking minimalist structure can also . . . enact something like compassion or care."[8]

I think of Grandin and her slaughterhouse designs. In North America, nearly half of beef cattle are moved through handling facilities that Grandin has conceived. Severity in compassion, compassion in severity: Grandin's slaughter facilities are built with the goal of keeping cattle calm. "People ask me all the time whether the cattle know they are going to be slaughtered," she writes. "What I have observed over the years and at many meat plants is that the things that frighten cattle usually have nothing to do with death. It is the little things that make them balk and refuse to move, such as seeing a small piece of chain hanging down from an alley fence."[9]

Grandin's facilities feature curved single-file alleys with solid sides that prevent cattle from becoming agitated at the sight of humans or other objects moving beyond the walls. Their narrow design encourages advancement in single file; this is how cattle move in herds. "Each animal has its head on the rear of the animal in front of it," Grandin explains. "They remain calmer when they can touch each other."[10] Touch gentles them. They're obedient, docile as they approach the man who will place the bolt gun on their gentle foreheads, and, with his finger on the trigger, squeeze.

"Many people do not believe me when I tell them that cattle slaughter can be really calm, peaceful, and humane," Grandin writes. "In some plants, the cattle remain absolutely calm and the employees are very conscientious. At one large plant, 240 cattle per hour quietly walked up the ramp and voluntarily entered the double-rail conveyor restrainer. It was as if they were going to get milked."[11]

At the word *voluntarily*, I balk: These cattle didn't know what they were volunteering for, or that this march would be their last. But a calm procession to slaughter is considered more humane than a forceful one. It's more economical, too: Less stress means better meat quality. When she introduced her early designs, this was the argument Grandin used to persuade beef producers who didn't much care about reducing discomfort for animals who were about to die anyway. "Stress is punishing on the body," Grandin reminded them. The more agitated a cow is, the tougher the beef. "When animals go running through a working facility, they crash into fences, gates, and other animals, and risk falling down or becoming injured. Every bruise directly affects meat quality. Old bruises cause localized areas of tough meat. Fresh bruises at the meat plant cause huge losses because the bruised meat must be cut out and discarded."[12]

In its severity, compassion is full.

At first, diminishing animals' stress may seem to conflict with maximizing production. In fact, these are parallel goals. On some feedlot dairies, cows spend so many hours eating, lining up to be milked, and being milked that they can't get the ten to twelve hours of rest and sleep they need.[13] This stresses their bodies, which reduces milk production. Less stress, more production, whether milk or meat.

"SQUEEZE! SQUEEZE! SQUEEZE! all the morning long." All this squeezing reminds me of the chapter in *Moby-Dick* titled "A Squeeze of the Hand," in which Ishmael rhapsodizes about squeezing the congealed fat of the sperm whale. Known as raw spermaceti, the substance Ishmael is handling has been harvested from a whale head; he's squeezing it by hand into oil that would be used for lamp oil and in cosmetics, leatherworking, and textiles. One whale head can yield almost five hundred gallons of spermaceti. When raw, it's said to smell like raw milk.

Ishmael's squeezing takes him over, driving him almost to delirium. "I squeezed that sperm till I myself almost melted into it; I squeezed that sperm till a strange sort of insanity came over me; and I found myself unwittingly squeezing my co-laborers' hands in it, mistaking their hands for the gentle globules."[14] With the squeeze comes closeness, a homosocial and homoerotic intimacy that he milks. "Come; let us squeeze hands all round," he entreats. "Nay, let us all squeeze ourselves into each other; let us squeeze ourselves universally into the very milk and sperm of kindness."[15]

I, too, have a tendency to give myself over to work, and sometimes find myself spun into a frenzy similar to Ishmael's. The squeeze of too much work can be relieving. It's how I made it through lockdown. It's how I've made it through heartbreak and grief: climb into the machine, deflect everything else. It's a way to pass the time. It's a way of resting without rest. I can stay still, yet moving through tasks for which I'll get paid. It's a sustaining feeling, soothing, to produce, to make of oneself a product that generates income.

I must be doing something wrong for these frenzies not to lead to sociality, eros, "kindness." Rather, what happens is that I'm alone. And almost at once, the work becomes too much. The machine morphs from soothing squeeze machine to mean milker, something extracting that I need to kick free.

I'M REASSURED BY my program director at BAI that my underenrolled class won't be canceled, so I initiate conversations with my chair at Barnett about dropping my one class there. I'm sad to let it go—it's a creative writing course I designed myself—but the pay is low, enrollment is high, and four writing classes, two of them new course preps, is too much when this book is due in four months. I need to choose time over money. Less stress, more production. I draft an apologetic email to my chair and hit send.

APARNA DRAPES HEATED blankets over my legs and I feel held and contained. Relaxed. Quieted.

She massages the muscles of one leg, then the other. I feel the healing. She shows me exercises that will strengthen my knees: one on my back, one on my belly, another a hamstring stretch, a half-cow pose. It's not the knees themselves that we're working, she reminds me, but all the muscles and ligaments they're held by and connected to. She monitors my attempts and adjusts me. I'm to do them while I'm out of town on my research trip, she instructs, and to come back in two weeks with my report.

— 2 —
SQUEEZE (DEAR DAIRY V: NORTH AMERICAN MANURE EXPO, JULY 2024)

WHEN I PULL into the lot at Patterson Farms, I'm greeted by a giant inflated cow. She's a Holstein, and she's attached to the ground with stakes. It's a beautiful day in Auburn, New York—hot, bright, and blue. Gazing balefully onto an ungrazeable field, the cow's a stoic sentinel drawing attendees to the registration table for this year's North American Manure Expo.

I step into the short line. I'm an outsider here, and nervous, but I'm less stressed than I might have expected, probably because a new crush hit on me a few days ago and I spent the drive listening to lovey-dovey pop music the likes of which I shall not name.

A staffer hands me a tote bag filled with goodies: a small notebook, some brochures, and a cardboard cow mask stuck to a popsicle stick. Behind the registration tent are other tents where sessions will be held on topics like soil compaction, greenhouse gas mitigation, and strategies for avoiding road damage. Beyond, there are rows of gleaming field equipment: lime-green tractors, cherry-red tankers, applicators, coiled hoses.

It's the expo's twentieth year. Created by the Professional Nutrient Applicators of Wisconsin (PNAW), the North American Manure Expo was born from frustration. The story goes that PNAW had approached local farm fairs repeatedly with proposals to do manure application demos; they were either told no or slotted in at the last hour of the last day due to worries about odor. Frustrated, PNAW took things into their own hands and organized a field day devoted entirely to manure. That first event brought out an enthusiastic showing, so PNAW made it an annual expo. With the partnership of University of Wisconsin Extension, the expo expanded into a two-day national event that travels to a different location and partners with a local committee each year.[16] This is the first time it's been in New York—lucky timing for me.

Manure management is a major concern for dairy producers. A lactating cow might drop between 100 and 150 pounds of manure a day; a heifer, about 50 pounds. On small farms, most of that manure goes directly onto the grass. But it's a get-big-or-get-out industry, and as dairies have increased their numbers of animals, they've had to figure out what to do with all that excrement. Most larger farms use manure pits. In North America, suggested capacity for manure storage is one million gallons per one hundred cows per year.[17]

Such mass quantities of waste can have harmful environmental impacts. Because manure emits methane gas, it's a significant contributor to the greenhouse gas (GHG) emissions that are warming the planet, and methane is a particularly worrisome GHG. Though it makes up only 11 percent of all GHGs, methane's impact on warming is intense: Compared with carbon dioxide (which makes up a hefty majority of GHGs), methane is more potent by 80 percent. Of total US methane emissions, enteric fermentation (i.e., cattle burps) contributes about 25 percent; manure management, about 9 percent.[18] Manure can also pollute water sources, resulting in bacterial contamination, unwanted algal blooms, and fish kill. And its infamous odor isn't trivial: It's polluting and can cause respiratory and other health problems in humans and livestock.

At the same time, manure is a valued resource that can be used as or converted into fertilizer, feedlot bedding, biogas, bioplastics, and more. Manure is a fluid and flexible substance, like milk.

I pick up my free T-shirt and head to the bus for my morning tour. The expo runs on farm time: I'm ten minutes early and one of the last people on. I settle into an open row and hope no one sits next to me. No one does, and then I'm sadly alone. My friend Madsen was supposed to be my expo buddy, but he had to bail last minute to finish edits on his film. I take a look at my new T-shirt with its "Top 10 Rejected Manure Expo Slogans" on the back. "If applying manure is an art, just call me Poocasso." "Wet or dry, we let it fly!" "Manure: It's what's for fertilizer." Those are my favorites.

The bus starts up, and our guide, a senior associate for Cornell's PRO-DAIRY Extension program, sends a stack of flyers down the rows and goes over the info. "As you can see, Aurora Ridge [the first of two farms we'll visit] uses an anaerobic digestion system with a plug-flow digester for biogas recirculation . . ." I examine the map of this system and try to make sense of what she's saying. On our right, the Finger Lakes.

When we arrive twenty minutes later, we're at a sprawling farm complex on verdant hills. Co-owner Jason Burroughs greets us as we gather around him on the grass. "I like to say I manage both ends of the cow," he jokes.

Aurora Ridge Dairy houses 2,500 cows and 1,315 heifers who, combined, produce something like 400,000 pounds of solid waste every day.

WHERE DOES ALL that manure go?

Come with me on this journey. Imagine we're part of a pile of manure. We're being squeezed out of the backside of a dairy cow who eats, sleeps, and shits in a feedlot barn at Aurora Ridge Dairy.

We're about to go through many stages and take a number of forms.

Our first form will be sloppy. We pile where we land, flattening into a watery and irregular blob on the ground. In the outside, which is new and cold, we cool.

We breathe, releasing fumes.

After a while, an automated scraper approaches and drags us along the concrete to a grate with thin slits. We drop down through the slits, draining into a collection pit with all the other piles. What a sensual harmony, this pile of piles. All of us have become one.

Next we get pumped into an anaerobic digester many yards away. It's airtight and hot in here, a return to our origins. But compared to our twenty to thirty days inside this large tank, our time in the cow's gut was a flash. There, we gathered. Here, we disperse. Bacteria eat away our pathogens and kill most of our smells. It can be turbulent, but the turbulence helps us breathe. We are emitting a powerful gas.

Our biogas emissions can be used for many things, from electricity and heat to bioplastics and vehicle fuel. Here at Aurora Ridge, we get converted into electricity. Zap—We power the milking machines. We power the conveyor belts. We power the anaerobic digester that makes more of us. We power the whole dairy and some of the neighbors too. In this form, we are mighty and radiant. We hum, pleased with how far our power can reach.

Meanwhile the rest of us—the leftover, digested us—gets pumped into another facility and dumped into the top of a screw-press separator.

Here in the separation barn, the screw-press squeezes out all our moisture. The solid part of us watches as the press diverts the liquid part of us into an outlet faucet. Liquid, we drain away through another metal grate in the concrete floor. Whee woo whee. We're flowing rapidly through a pipe that leads us into a manure lagoon. It's hot in here. Dark. With most of the oxygen squeezed out, the air is tight.

Over time, we are dispersed and amalgamated. We pool and burble, gather and rest. We decompose. Time ceases to exist. It's a relief, after having been pumped and dumped and squeezed from the separator, to relax. We stretch and expand, breaking down, commingling. The movement of the agitation boat periodically disrupts our calm, but we grow to enjoy the ripples, which permit us to spread still farther. Farther and farther. Aaah.

Until we're pumped into a tanker and injected into tilled soil. The era of dissolution has ceased. Our next task is to fertilize.

Back in the separation barn, the solid part of us—the leached remainder—is plopping out of the machine to amass in a green wheelbarrow. A worker wheels us over to a conveyor belt and dumps us out to spread and dry. The belt carries us up and into an adjacent storage facility. There, we move along close to the ceiling until we hit a barrier that diverts us into empty space. We drizzle down in a stream of fine sand, gradually forming a conical pile on the ground. We're parched and miss our moisture. But it feels good to return to the group.

Eventually a worker shovels us into another vehicle that transports us back to where we were born.

In the feedlot barn, we're shoveled out again on top of other, soiled bedding. Here we will rest and be rested upon.

A cow approaches. Another joins her. Is either of these cows "our" cow? Does "our" mean anything anymore? Who is "us"? We've been split and separated, squeezed and dried, remade and repiled. We can't recognize ourselves in this new form, much less the creature whose body made us. No matter. She wouldn't recognize us either.

The cows lower themselves onto us, heavy and warm. The compression is relaxing. We welcome the squeeze.

THE MANURE LAGOON at Aurora Ridge is covered, so we can't see the contents, but it looks like a giant recessed swimming pool, albeit a pool one would not want to take a dip in due to the smell, the poisonous gas, and the risk of losing consciousness and drowning in goop. The cover is impermeable to avoid runoff with precipitation, Burroughs explains. It's designed to collect rainwater that the dairy can recycle and contribute to its water usage. This storage facility has a nine-million-gallon capacity, our flyer tells us, and the total installation cost was $662,700, some of which was covered by state and federal grants.

From here I can just barely see the cows on the other side of the solid-liquid separation facility—white dots lining up for their morning milking. Burroughs emphasizes the circular nature of all of this. After milk, manure is the second most important product the dairy's cows produce. With manure, "we can make our own bedding, make our own electricity." The biogas the dairy converts from animal waste is more than enough to generate electricity for the entire complex; the surplus is sold to the local utility grid, powering something like three hundred homes in the area. The liquid manure gets used as fertilizer, which, he says, saves millions of dollars in spreading costs. In exchange for taking methane gas out of the ecosystem, the farm also generates carbon credits with a value of (at minimum) $49,000 annually—an amount that can vary widely depending on market fluctuations.

AT LINCOLN DAIRY, our second stop, the stench of the separator barn nearly knocks me out. I inhale, step back involuntarily. My senses swim. The fumes are rancid: hard-boiled eggs gone chemically foul. I don't know why these off-gases are harder to take in than those at the other site—maybe this barn is not as well ventilated. I find a less noxious space to observe the river of brown, bubbling slurry flowing out to the nearby lagoon.

LIKE BURROUGHS OF Aurora Ridge, most farmers understand that everything is connected. Healthy soil makes healthy feed makes healthy animals, and a healthy animal makes a good product at the end. But as eager as some farmers might be to switch to more eco-conscious infrastructure, many are still paying off debt from the infrastructure they installed decades ago, after the industry shifted toward Concentrated Animal Feeding Operations (better known as CAFOs) in the 1970s and '80s. That shift was expensive: It required constructing bigger barns, silos, maybe a milking parlor—and manure pits fuming with methane.

To pay for all this infrastructure, the industry pushed farmers to take out multiyear loans or even sell off parcels of their land. Maybe a farmer wants to install something like Aurora Ridge's pricey anaerobic digester, but they're still paying off the million-dollar loan they took on to build CAFO infrastructure two decades ago. Maybe another farmer decides it's time to downsize and go back to pasturing, but because they sold off chunks of their land years ago to pay for a manure pit, they no longer have the acreage or fencing to do so. That farmer might, like so many of their peers, choose to sell the farm.[19]

The primary goal of dairy farmers is to make milk. To make milk, they grow animals. To grow animals, they grow crops to feed them. They're tending the land and the animals at the same time.

When I think about how producers manage this on CAFO farms, I waffle between respect and revulsion. On the one hand, the sustainability efforts that dairies like Aurora Ridge support are astoundingly efficient and resourceful: They reduce carbon emissions while producing energy, bedding, and fertilizer. On the other hand, this huge, elaborate operation employing hundreds of thousands of dollars of equipment seems like a lot of extra steps, given that the bulk of manure goes toward crops that will become cattle feed. It's like the million-dollar version of letting the cows shit where they graze.

But these cows don't get to graze: It's not efficient to herd this many cows from pasture to barn two or three times a day to be milked. And downsizing is not really viable: Most milk buyers and processors would rather contract with one large dairy farm than hundreds of small ones.

But cows should get to spend some portion of their lives on pasture. Open-air grazing brings them joy.[20]

But animal joy is not the main objective. Efficiency is.

DAIRY FARMERS AREN'T just tending the land and the animals, or paying off their CAFO loans. They're also facing multiple demands from the public and the state around animal welfare, soil and water quality, and labor conditions. Meeting those demands costs money, but farmers can't charge the customer more to cover those costs.

This is because farmers have no agency over the price of their product. The USDA sets the price of milk based on the trade prices of butter and cheese without factoring in how much it costs to raise and milk cows or pay workers.[21] The current price of milk has dropped 55 percent below its real value.[22] In 2023 the selling price for a hundred pounds of milk was around $15.50: "roughly $3 above where it was 40 years ago." At the same time, operating and equipment costs have steadily climbed.[23]

It's a basic economic problem—operation costs exceeding income. Whether or not farmers make a profit is out of their control, so they work hard to squeeze as much milk as they can out of their operating costs.

"THE FIRST THING I'm going to tell you is this: Do not go in the hole," fire safety instructor Tom Basher admonishes us. I'm back at the expo now at a confined spaces safety demo.

"If you think you *need* to go in the hole, do not go in the hole. If you think you *have* to go in the hole, do not go in the hole." He pauses, letting this sink in. Some attendees are cracking smiles, appreciating his showmanship. He holds the pause; he's serious. "But if you're going in the hole, here are some things to do so that nobody else has to go in the hole after you."

"The hole" is any confined space, but in the context of this demo, it refers to the opening of a liquid manure spreader—one of those enclosed, tubular tankers with a steel pipe running along the top. The former assistant chief of the Ithaca Fire Department, Basher has responded to calls involving tanker accidents, and he says that in most cases, there's not much emergency personnel can do without risking their own lives. The internal environment of a manure tanker can be lethal, he explains. At high concentration levels, the hydrogen sulfide gas in the tanker eats oxygen and corrodes steel. Breathing it in for just one second can knock a person out. Between 1975 and 2022, 497 incidents of manure storage accidents were reported in the US; of these, 296 were fatalities.

Nathan Doody and Tyler Memory went in the hole. They died in a liquid manure tanker in Kirkland, New York, in June, just seventy-seven miles and a month ago from where we are now. Doody[24] went in to retrieve a piece of equipment that had tumbled in. He passed out and fell in. As he attempted to save his friend, Memory fell in, too.

With the help of a volunteer from the audience, Basher demonstrates how to make a harness with a few lengths of webbing and a carabiner. "It's not enough to have a harness, though. You need a return rope so that your buddy—because you *always have a buddy*—can pull you back up." In case you slip. In case you lose consciousness and release your grip on the ladder. In case you fall in and start to drown.

DEAN PIERSON WENT in the hole—that is to say, into debt. In 2010, in Copake, New York, he shot all fifty-one of his dairy cows, then he shot himself.

ON ANOTHER DAIRY farm not far from here, migrant laborers were found living in squalor in a converted barn with cockroaches, mice, and exposed electrical sockets and lightbulbs. Another hole.

HOW DO I squeeze this all in.

— 3 —
SQUEEZE (DEAR DAIRY VI: DANFORTH JERSEY, JULY 2024)

NEW YORK'S HILLY landscape has made it a friendly topography for dairy. The land plots that have divvied up the state are relatively small, harkening back to colonial-era royal land grants of one thousand acres per headright. Such plots have proven ideal for small farms. But CAFOs and consolidation have doomed many of those small farms to closure. In the early 1970s, when the drive to go big started taking hold, there were about twenty-one thousand dairy farmers working in New York.[25] As of 2022, there were three thousand.[26] At this point, only the larger farms can be efficient enough with their operating costs to turn a profit. The smaller farms have gotten squeezed out.

"Our way of life is really dying," says Shannon Finn, a

sixth-generation dairy farmer in Jefferson, New York. I've driven east from the manure expo to join Finn on her seventy-acre farm, Danforth Jersey, which her family has run since 1817. "I think it's a great shame, personally, because I am so attached to my cows." She has forty, all Jerseys, which produce milk with the highest butterfat content of any breed. The farm is known for its butter, which gets sold under the brand name Cowbella.

As many other farms in the area expanded into bigger, CAFO-style dairies, Danforth Jersey resisted that urge. "I feel like the only way you can really have a relationship with your cows," Finn says, "and know them individually and give them the best life as an animal, in my point of view, is on a small farm. I just personally feel like, if I was a cow"—she laughs—"this is the way that I'd want to live."

Me, too. It's beautiful here. Finn's cows spend most of their lives on pasture, out in the fields day and night except in the winter, when they sleep in a barn. No manure pit here: The majority of the cows' excrement lands directly on the grass. Manure in the barns gets collected and distributed onto the fields with a small spreader.

Finn brings me into the milking barn and introduces me to some of her favorites: Oregano and Gummy Bear and Cola and Kaboom. The click and hiss of the milking machines is hypnotic. I haven't seen Jersey cows up close, and they're gorgeous—golden caramel with cream snouts.

Finn works with a nearby creamery during the summer to make Cowbella butter, which has the advantage of being freezable. The rest of the milk she sells as a commodity to the milk truck. "The price is horrible," she says. "It doesn't even come close to covering the cost of production on a small farm like this."

She tells me about the period in the early 2000s when small farmers were told to go value-added—that is, to set up their own processing plants to make their own products, like butter or cheese, that farmers can retail themselves instead of selling all their milk to the milk truck where they have no control over the prices. "It is not the way," she says. While there is often sufficient demand for such products to make them seem more viable than commodity milk, the costs of processing and marketing are so high that farmers get stuck in another slim margin. It's almost miraculous that Danforth Jersey has made it work as well as they have. Finn's farm has had success because butter from Jersey cows who graze is rare and "very, very special." The color is a vivid yellow, "like sunshine coming out." Cowbella has loyal customers and fans among chefs and foodies. But the journey was a "very difficult road."

"It's like this snowball effect. You get into it with this idea that you've got this budget—thinking 'that's not so bad, is it?'—then all of a sudden Ag and Markets comes in and says, 'Oh, you can't do it that way, you've got to do it this way.' Every single thing is another ten thousand dollars you've got to throw at it. And then, you're in this position where you're like, 'Well, we're already so far in. We can't stop now. We've got to keep going. If we stop now, we're going to lose all the investment that we put into it.' It literally has felt like pushing milk uphill."

Many of her neighboring farmers have transitioned out of dairy. Some tried producing hops—there was a hops bubble for a while—then there was a hemp bubble. But the area lacked the infrastructure to process either product.

Now some farmers are working in maple syrup; some are trying agritourism. "You can do a bunch of stuff and spread yourself really thin and kind of make it work, but nothing has come through that is an answer. The next thing that everybody's talking about is solar power and wind power—but we're very skeptical that anything is going to be enough."

Finn believes the problem for small dairy farmers is that the drive to unionize failed. "That's really our downfall," she says. "If we had unionized back when everyone was on the same page, things could be very different. We'd have a lot more control over milk pricing. But now we don't, and everyone is fractured because everyone does things so differently."[27]

If her husband did not have a solid off-farm job, she acknowledges, she would not be able to keep the farm running.

"It splinters families," Finn says of the dairy industry. "That financial stress. All of a sudden money is the through line of your family structure."

That's what happened in her family. When her grandfather died, there was no one to run the farm, which the will split between Finn's mother and uncle. Her uncle wanted to sell off the herd, but Finn, who was working in theater, was considering jumping back in. When she found out her uncle had sold the majority of the cows without telling her or her mother, she rushed into action. "I hung on with tooth and nail to the young stock—so the calves, the heifers, the cows that were not salable. We held on."

The family hasn't been the same. "My uncle and I haven't spoken since 2016, when things came to a head. The stress of those huge financial factors is very difficult on families."

Finn has no plans to sell the farm, but her family applied for easement status a few years ago, and the approval has finally come through. That means Danforth Jersey will continue to be used as farmland even if she and her family eventually decide to sell. As more and more small farms go under, a lot of that farmland is getting moved out of agriculture, with much of it getting bought up by developers and second vacation homeowners. "Farmland really needs to stay in farming continuously," Finn explains. "That land needs to be worked." Otherwise it goes fallow, which impacts food supply. The easement program is the state's response to what is becoming a potential food crisis. But because agricultural easements can decrease property value, it's not an uncontroversial solution.

As we wrap up our interview, Finn leads me into a storage space and offers me a frozen tube of Cowbella butter to take with me. When I get home a few days later, I'll thaw it in my fridge and spread it thick on my morning waffles. It's the most buttery butter I've tried. In its richness I can taste the freshness of the grass, the clean rush of the air, the sunshine, the animal joy.

NOOB THAT I AM, I grieve the death of smaller dairies, especially after spending time on a few and seeing firsthand how clearly loved and well cared for the animals are. And I confess, there is something that pulls on my heartstrings about the endurance of the family farm.

But then I think about the role of the farm—and livestock—in the invention and acquisition of private property in the US. I think of the farm's entanglement with the violence of settler colonialism and its supplanting of Indigenous agriculture. I think about how the arrival of cattle led to the decimation of bison, a key food source for many Native tribes. I think about how early European immigrant farmers were granted free—i.e., stolen—land, and about how clearing the land for agrarian purposes was a major element of the colonial project of nation-building at the expense of tribal communities' ways of life.[28] I think about how that land has been passed down and passed down, accruing in value, such that the vast majority of family farms in New York (and beyond) are (still) owned by white people of European descent. "Vast majority" may even undersell it: 98 percent of American farmland is owned by white people. In the US, the family farm has always already been a white enterprise, which is precisely why and how it has endured.

To state it plainly, only certain kinds of families have been authorized to hold on to the land they have tended. Much of the agricultural land in the country, especially in the South, has been worked by enslaved Africans and African Americans and later by Black sharecroppers who had no real shot at land ownership.[29] Nor do the predominantly Brown migrant workers—many of whom lost their own farmland in the wake of NAFTA—who work it now. The bulk of our food supply depends on these migrants; it's appalling and foolish how readily so many Americans want to expel them.[30]

— 4 —
SQUEEZE

MY CHAIR AT Barnett hasn't responded to my email, and I'm starting to sweat. Am I going to have to teach this fourth class? I guess I can do it, but the idea constricts my chest. It's unusual for my chair to be so late in replying, so I check my sent box to make sure I actually sent off the email.

It laughs at me from my Drafts folder. I send it now with a preface apologizing profusely for the mishap, acknowledging that we now have just a few weeks before classes start, and letting her know I have a friend who just got hired in a different department and who might be interested in taking over the class.

She replies immediately, with such severe compassion I almost cry, and asks me to put her in touch with my friend.

I'M SOMETIMES IN the hole for short stints, usually at the end of August, when my summer savings have dried up. Mostly I live a comfortable life, now that I have some measure of job security at Graff, where I became eligible for health care after two and a half years of teaching. Things could certainly be more comfortable, or maybe what I mean is "more humane."

In 2022, my union at Graff kicked off the milk machine; we'd been squeezed enough. We were on strike for twenty-five days. Part-time faculty at this school make up 80 percent of the faculty body. We are the school, and the school did not want to pay us—not until students and their parents got involved, backing us up. (What they pay for tuition, after all, is exorbitant.) Then we got most of what we asked for.

Now Barnett's part-time faculty union is in contract negotiations. Because of these negotiations, Barnett has instituted a hiring freeze for adjuncts. This means my chair has limited options to cover the class I'm trying not to teach.

My friend Y wants the class; it aligns with their interests. Because they've already been onboarded through another department, it should be easy enough to bring them on—we think. A few days later, Y decides that if they take on this new class, they'll need to drop the class they were initially hired to teach—to do both, they'd have to quit their (other) part-time job, which they don't want to do. I backchannel with Y, counseling them on how to handle this; because of the freeze, the situation is sensitive.

The provost says it's up to Y's department, and Y's department is not happy. They accuse my chair of poaching their adjunct, and they will not grant permission for her to hire Y, who is now receiving angry and condescending emails from senior colleagues. Wow. I can't believe these tenured faculty have so little compassion for adjuncts. Or I can. I'm reminded of the last union-sponsored adjunct faculty gathering I attended, cosponsored with great self-satisfaction by this same department, where the raffle prize I won was a five-dollar gift card to a local coffee shop. I couldn't even pretend to thank them.

I resign myself to teaching the class I'm scheduled to teach if my chair can't find anyone else. I made the mess; I'll be self-sacrificial. I don't want to leave my chair in the lurch, and sure, fine. Extra money is nice.

AT MY AIRBNB, I do my knee exercises. Squeeze the hamstring and pull my exercise band. I pack up my bags and drive home, the whole time wondering how I'll squeeze all this into one essay. I'm not sure I can.

My chair emails again, letting me know she's been approached by an adjunct from another department who's had a class canceled and is looking to pick up another one. She'll hire this adjunct to cover my class. I'm relieved. One less big squeeze on my time. But I worry for this other adjunct, who has just a week to prep. May the union get her and everyone else a better contract.

Nope. Or, sort of. The union wins only a 33 percent hike, spread out over five years. Wages were so low to start that this adds up to not much. Not sustainable. Not enough.

—5—
SQUEEZED

MORE AND MORE I'm identifying with cows. Prices are rising. I'm feeling the squeeze. The problem is collective, experienced collectively. Aparna is squeezing the muscles around my knee. She asks if I'm making a case against dairy. I'm on my back and she's pressing into my hip flexors. Yeah, that's it. I watch the film. Temple relates more to cows than to people. The other kind of squeeze machine is the milker. I don't know when or how my knee issue started. When I biked to Kings County courthouse for a jury summons, I argued my case. The squeeze chute scene is based on an episode. As a kid, Grandin couldn't stand to be touched. At a writers' conference years ago, I told myself to be bold. I did not lift my butch friend off the ground. Maybe the casual hug is too quick to find the right pressure. I remembered that cattle like firm touch. Temple goes to college and is overwhelmed. Temple loves her squeeze machine and uses it all the time. She asks her peers to try out the apparatus. I break for an online onboarding orientation. I'm grateful to have more stable status. I get off the call. I weigh the options. I open my yearly royalty statement. The artist Tiona Nekkia McClodden has worked with the cattle squeeze chute. I think of Grandin and her slaughterhouse designs. At the word *voluntarily*, I balk. In its severity, compassion is full. Squeeze! squeeze! squeeze! all the morning long. Ishmael's squeezing takes over him, driving him almost to delirium. I, too, have a tendency to give myself over. I must be doing something wrong for these frenzies not to lead to sociality. I'm reassured by my program director. Aparna drapes heated blankets over my legs. She massages the muscles of one leg, then the other. When I pull into the lot at Patterson Farms, I step into the short line. A staffer hands me a tote bag. It's the expo's twentieth year. Manure management is a major concern for dairy producers. Such mass quantities of waste can have harmful environmental impacts. I pick up my free T-shirt. The bus starts up. Come with me on this journey. Our first form will be sloppy. We breathe, releasing fumes. After a while, an automated scraper approaches. Next we get pumped into an anaerobic digester. Our biogas emissions can be used for many things. Here in the separation barn, the screw-press machine squeezes out all our moisture. Over time we are dispersed and amalgamated. Until we're pumped into a tanker and injected into tilled soil. In the feedlot barn, a cow approaches. The manure lagoon at Aurora Ridge is covered. From here I can just barely see the cows. The primary goal of dairy farmers is to make milk. I waffle between respect and revulsion. But cows should get to spend some portion of their lives on pasture. But animal joy is not the main objective. It's a basic economic problem—operation costs exceeding income. The first thing I'm going to tell you is this. The hole is any confined space. Nathan Doody and Tyler Memory went in the hole. Dean Pierson went in the hole. How do I squeeze this all in. New York's hilly landscape has made it a friendly topography for dairy. Our way of life is really dying. Finn brings me into the milking barn and introduces me to some of her favorites. It's like this snowball effect. Many of her neighboring farmers have transitioned out. Now some farmers are working in maple syrup; some are trying agritourism. It splinters families. That's what happened. The family hasn't been the same. Finn has no plans to sell the farm. Noob that I am, I grieve the death of smaller dairies. But then I think about the role of the farm—and livestock—in the invention of private property. To state it plainly: only certain kinds of families have been authorized to hold on to the land they have tended. My chair hasn't responded to my email. It laughs at me from my Drafts folder. I'm sometimes in the hole for short stints, usually at the end of August. In 2022, my union at Graff kicked off the milk machine. Now Barnett's part-time faculty union is in contract negotiations. My friend Y wants the class, it aligns with their interests. I resign myself. I'm relieved. One less big squeeze on my time. Nope. Or, sort of.

— 6 —
RE-SQUEEZED

MORE AND MORE
I'm feeling
the squeeze
that's it
find the pressure
firm
squeezing takes
work
I'm reassured
pumped
and injected
time squeeze
squeeze time
make milk
resign myself
releasing
the relief

— 7 —
CURTAIN CALL

TEMPLE GRANDIN'S SQUEEZE machine retails for $7,000 to $8,000.

These days, it's also known as the hug machine. There are other kinds of hug machines now available, too.

I'm looking these up because I'm planning on hosting a hug party as one last stab at generating material for this book. I might want to have a squeeze machine on hand; maybe I'll see about renting one.

The hug party will also be a milk party. I'll prepare a buffet of dairy and nondairy items to serve. I'll have a milk/mylk bar. Milky Ways. Cheese platter. Tres leches. Kefir and yogurt shots. And Lactaid. Something for everyone at this hug/milk party, during which I'll extract hugs from all who've graced these pages: Mom and Dad and Michael and Derek. Ryder and Diana and B and Hugo the aggressive ram. The Georges. Aunt Teresa and Beth, Athénaïs and Elle and the Madonna Lactans. Liz, Carley, Madsen, Svetlana, and Anne. Sarah and Amanda and Dan. Luma and Claude. Second cousin Dave. Gigi. Gigi's girlfriends. Marigold and the other Megan Milkses. Aparna and Shannon and Temple. Brenda, the nervous cow.

My cat Whole Milk, whom I've recently adopted, will skulk around, getting in everyone's way and sampling all of the milks.

I'll offer stickers for my guests to wear, indicating the level of contact they're comfortable with: Please Hug Me; Ask First; No Hugs. I'll recreate my grandmother's envelope exchange. Instead of money, the envelopes will each contain an index card with a discussion question written on one side. The questions will be about intimacy, kinship, and milk, everything from *Tell us a story about milk* to *What's your relationship to the term "chosen family"?* to *Why do you hug the way that you do?* As we snack on the dairy and nondairy items, each guest will draw a card and find and embrace (or not) the recipient, who will open the card and read their question out loud.

We'll talk. We'll really talk. We'll talk and connect. I'll take notes about our conversations. Notes that I might later squeeze into the book.

It's party time. I press a button on a remote and a boob emerges from one wall. I press another button and the boob starts leaking an unidentifiable white substance. It's a taste test. Guests who correctly guess the substance get to take home one of the many cow-related items I've accumulated over the past three years—the cow mask, the vintage milk coin, the Cow parfum from Zoologist.

I press another button and the bathtub fills with milk. What kind of milk? Take a dip and find out.

Meanwhile I invite my guests to continue hugging each other—hug and talk, talk and hug . . . and here my fantasy begins to skip. As if all we need are hugs. As if one good squeeze could seal our fissures, make us whole, make us family. As if we could agree on what family is or what we want it to be.

Sick of hugging? Take a turn in the squeeze machine. Settle inside, grab the lever, and pull. Please respect the six-minute time limit. I'm looking at you, Temple. (Also Brenda and King George.) When your time is up, I invite you to write down your reactions on one of these index cards and drop it into the bottom half of a milk gallon I've cut for this purpose.

And when you have written down all your reactions, when all the cow items have been distributed, when the boob is drained of its substance and all the Milky Ways are gone, you will depart, leaving me alone with Whole Milk and still more material. I'll read the written feedback; I'll reflect on my notes. I'll make more notes. I'll crawl into the squeeze machine of the essay. I'll write it all out and I'll squeeze it all in. The essay will hold it together and press it down, press it dense.

Milk springs from my skin—it leaks from my pores. Let it flow. Squeeze and pull. Squeeze and pull.

I milk as much as I can until I milk myself dry.

And now I release the lever, and I climb out.

NOTES

1. *Holy Cowboys*, directed by Varun Chopra (2022). The film follows one of several cow protection groups emboldened under Narendra Modi's Hindu nationalist government in 2014 to kidnap cows and unleash violence against beef-eating Muslim farmers.
2. *Temple Grandin*, directed by Mick Jackson (HBO, 2010).
3. Temple Grandin, *Thinking in Pictures: My Life with Autism* (Vintage, 2006), 59.
4. Temple Grandin and Catherine Johnson, *Animals in Translation: Using the Mysteries of Autism to Decode Animal Behavior* (Scribner, 2005), 118.
5. *Temple Grandin*, directed by Mick Jackson.
6. Grandin, *Thinking in Pictures*, 85.
7. Lex Morgan Lancaster, *Dragging Away: Queer Abstraction in Contemporary Art* (Duke University Press, 2022), 132.
8. Lancaster, *Dragging Away*, 132.
9. Grandin, *Thinking in Pictures*, 167.
10. Grandin, *Thinking in Pictures*, 179.

11. Grandin, *Thinking in Pictures*, 167.
12. Temple Grandin, *Humane Livestock Handling: Understanding Livestock Behavior and Building Facilities for Healthier Animals* (Storey, 2008), 1–2.
13. Emma Ternman et al., "Rapid Eye Movement Sleep Time in Dairy Cows Changes During the Lactation Cycle," *Journal of Dairy Science* 102, no. 6 (2019): 5458–65, https://doi.org/10.3168/jds.2018-15950.
14. Herman Melville, *Moby-Dick* (Penguin, 1992), 456.
15. Melville, *Moby-Dick*, 456.
16. Kirsten Workman (cochair, 2024 Manure Expo), in discussion with the author, July 2024.
17. "Manure Management," The Dairyland Initiative, University of Wisconsin School of Veterinary Medicine, https://thedairylandinitiative.vetmed.wisc.edu/home/housing-module/adult-cow-housing/manure-management/.
18. EPA, "Inventory of US Greenhouse Gas Emissions and Sinks, 1990–2022," US Environmental Protection Agency, EPA 430-R-24-004, https://www.epa.gov/ghgemissions/inventory-us-greenhouse-gas-emissions-and-sinks-1990-2022.
19. Much of this discussion of CAFO farms is informed by an interview with Phoebe Schreiner, executive director of the Center for Agricultural Development and Entrepreneurship.
20. Or at least, that's how their tendency to gallop and buck when released onto pasture after a long winter indoors tends to get interpreted by humans. In the Netherlands, communities gather to celebrate this moment, a tradition called the koeiendans ("cow dance"). See Maisie Tomlinson, "'Are Those Cows Jumping for Joy?': Eye Whites, Hoof Kicks, and Qualitative Behaviour Assessment," *Discover Society*, August 7, 2019, https://archive.discoversociety.org/2019/08/07/are-those-cows-jumping-for-joy-eye-whites-hoof-kicks-and-qualitative-behaviour-assessment/.
21. Milk prices are set by processors—that is, the companies (such as Dean Foods, Cabot Creamery, etc.) who bottle it or use it for cheese, butter, or yogurt. Processors base their

prices on the regional base prices for milk set by the USDA. The USDA bases those prices on the Chicago Mercantile Exchange's trade prices for butter, cheese, dry whey, and powdered milk. What happens is that the manufacturers of dairy products (who are typically the processors) report to the USDA how much they were paid for butter and cheese. The USDA inserts those numbers into a formula that spits out the price that processors must pay dairy producers—a formula that doesn't at all take into account operating costs.

22. While federal subsidies and other grant programs exist that help mitigate the impact of price volatility and declining returns for producers, the USDA purposefully keeps milk prices low to support US exporters' competition on the global market. Such subsidy programs have generally favored large factory farms, exacerbating the problems of milk overproduction and methane emissions from manure management.
23. Marcela Valdes, "What a Crackdown on Immigration Could Mean for Cheap Milk," *New York Times*, October 15, 2024, https://www.nytimes.com/2024/10/15/magazine/milk-industry-undocumented-immigrants.html.
24. Actual name.
25. William Serrin, "Shifting Trends Trapping New York Dairy Farmers," *New York Times*, April 5, 1982, https://www.nytimes.com/1982/04/05/nyregion/shifting-trends-trapping-new-york-dairy-farmers.html.
26. Joshua Solomon, "New York Farm Trends Mirror National Movement on Bigger Farms," *Upstate United*, February 18, 2024, https://upstateunited.com/news/albany-times-union-small-farms-decline-in-new-york-especially-dairy/.
27. Dairy farmers in New York State did unionize once, forming the Dairy Farmers' Union in 1936 in response to milk dealers slashing prices. The DFU went on strike first in 1937 and then more successfully in 1939, when, after nine days of picketing, they convinced dealers to raise the price for milk by almost 50 percent. The DFU was an active and effective force for farmer advocacy between 1937 and 1941,

when it was dissolved due to red-baiting and conflict within the organization. In 1957, another union, the Farmers Union of the New York Milkshed, went on strike for a few hours, until the intimidation of farmers by state troopers caused the union to call it off. For more, see Thomas Kriger, "Syndicalism and Spilled Milk," *Labor History* 38, No. 2–3 (1997): 266–86. These were not the first New York milk strikes, I should note: State producers have a long history of striking, beginning with the Orange County Milk War of 1883.

28. For more on the history of early farmland in relation to private property, see "Alchemy of Farmland," ch. 2 of Sarah Mock's podcast *The Only Thing That Lasts*, Ambrook Research, March 23, 2024, https://ambrook.com/research/podcast/chapter-2-the-only-thing-that-lasts-alchemy-farmland.
29. See Brea Baker's *Rooted: The American Legacy of Land Theft and the Modern Movement for Black Land Ownership* (One World, 2024) for more on this history.
30. See Valdes, "What a Crackdown on Immigration Could Mean," for more.

RESEARCH NOTES and ACKNOWLEDGMENTS

The family histories in "No More Cows" and "Skim Milks" were informed by genealogical research conducted by Grace Croft, Robert G. Yorks, John Milks, and Tom Milks. "No More Cows" was also informed by interviews with Tom Milks, Mary Milks, and William Milks, and by email survey responses from other family members. For "Skim Milks," I also drew on interviews and emails with Tom Milks, Mary Milks, John Milks, and Nora Van Cleave. Thank you to Tom and Mary Milks for reading drafts of both essays, and to Nora Van Cleave for the photograph albums of Ruby.

I first learned of Lonesome George, who appears in "Milking the Bull," through a talk given by Nicole Seymour at the Unthinking Sex, Imagining Asexuality conference at Simon Fraser University in Vancouver, Canada, in April 2019.

"The Letdown" is indebted to Caitlin Kunkel, Liza Harrell-Edge, Jess Dobkin, Athénaïs Nin, and especially my mother Mary Milks, as well as many friends who have informally shared their nursing experiences with me.

Thank you to Joshua Cohen, whose generously shared milk knowledge helped shape the direction of "MAGA Milk."

Thanks to Shannon Finn, Phoebe Schreiner, and Kirsten Workman for taking the time to talk with me about the dairy industry, and to Jay Klemundt for speaking with me about his advocacy work on behalf of dairy farmers.

I'm grateful to Sarah Chase, Dan George, and everyone at Chaseholm for welcoming me to the farm and teaching me how to milk cows (and more), with additional thanks to Sarah for being open to multiple interviews. My thanks to Ryder Cooley for their tour of And-Hof, and to Dan Benjamin for showing me around two Iowa farms.

"Night Milk" previously appeared in the *SomaFlights* special issue of *Michigan Quarterly Review*, guest edited by Petra Kuppers and Vidhu Aggarwal. My thanks to the editors.

Research and writing were supported by residencies at Crosstown Arts and Kimmel Harding Nelson Center for the Arts. Travel to the North American Manure Expo was supported by a Lang Faculty Opportunity Award from Eugene Lang College of Liberal Arts at The New School.

My thanks to my agent Rach Crawford, who helped shape this project in important ways in the proposal stages.

I have been blessed to work on this book with the incomparable Jeanne Thornton as my editor, who didn't flinch—even responded with enthusiasm!—when I sent in a thirteen-thousand-word heap of an essay doing tentative things with taxonomies and Gertrude Stein. Thank you, Jeanne, for reading and rereading these essays so closely and smartly and with such openness to experiment and re-visioning.

I am also grateful to Lauren Rosemary Hook, Margot Atwell, and everyone at Feminist Press, especially Lucia Brown, Rachel Gilman, Tyler Kristin Hubbert, Alicia Lim, Rachel Page, and Drew Stevens.

I am once again floored by Xander Marro's creative genius: Thank you for this dazzlingly weird and somewhat unsettling (that is, perfect) cover design.

This book would be much less of itself if it weren't for supportive feedback from five writing groups (not all at once) and other friends who helped me discover what various essays wanted to be. Thanks to Dia Felix and Amber Dawn; Caitlin Kunkel, Carley Moore, Hazel Jane Plante, Casey Plett, and Craig Willse; Dodie Bellamy, Maxe Crandall, Hedi El Kholti, and London Pinkney; River Encalada Bullock, Jess Goldschmidt, Jonah Groeneboer, and Maya Suess; Jess Arndt, Jibz Cameron, and Carolyn Pennypacker Riggs; Laura Mae Northrup; Anne Elizabeth Moore; Cynthia Barounis; Lauren Russell; and Liza Harrell-Edge.

Thanks also to Waqia Abdul-Kareem, Cecilia Berkovic, Erica Cardwell, Cecily Chen, Mari Collazo, Maya Deane, Svetlana Kitto, Liz Latty, Mev Luna, zavé martohardjono, Goldie Peacock, Wade Rosenthal, and everyone else who has talked milk with me these last few years.

BIBLIOGRAPHY

Arndt, Jess, and Lara Mimosa Montes. "On Estrangement." Conversation at Pacific Northwest College of Art as part of PNCA Low-Residency MFA Program Winter Residency. Portland, OR. January 5, 2024.

Baker, Brea. *Rooted: The American Legacy of Land Theft and the Modern Movement for Black Land Ownership*. One World, 2024.

Baumgartel, Kelley L., Larissa Sneeringer, and Susan M. Cohen. "From Royal Wet Nurses to Facebook: The Evolution of Breastmilk Sharing." *Breastfeeding Review* 24, no. 3 (2016): 25–32. https://pmc.ncbi.nlm.nih.gov/articles/PMC5603296/.

BBC Earth. "Tracking Giant Galapagos Tortoises." March 23, 2019. YouTube. https://www.youtube.com/watch?v=rEp6pkkYOgE.

Bradway, Tyler, and Elizabeth Freeman. "Kincoherence / Kin-aesthetics / Kinematics." In *Queer Kinship: Race, Sex, Belonging, Form*, edited by Tyler Bradway and Elizabeth Freeman. Duke University Press, 2022.

Brooks, David. "The Nuclear Family Was a Mistake." *The Atlantic*, March 2020.

Cohen, Mathilde, and Hannah Ryan. "From Human Dairies to Milk Riders: A Visual History of Milk Banking in New York City, 1918–2018." *Frontiers: A Journal of Women Studies* 40, no. 3 (2019): 139–70. https://doi.org/10.1353/fro.2019.a747119.

Corey, Rebecca. "A History of Breastfeeding and Formula Shaming: How Did We Get Here?" Yahoo!Life, August 22, 2022. https://www.yahoo.com/lifestyle/history-breastfeeding-formula-shaming-161727806.html.

Courage, Katherine Harmon. "The Sucky History of the Breast Pump." *Smithsonian Magazine*, September 12, 2022. https://www.smithsonianmag.com/innovation/sucky-history-of-the-breast-pump-180980653/.

Dairyland Initiative. "Manure Management." University of Wisconsin School of Veterinary Medicine. Accessed August 2024. https://thedairylandinitiative.vetmed.wisc.edu/home/housing-module/adult-cow-housing/manure-management/.

Davis, Heather. *Plastic Matter*. Duke University Press, 2022.

DeVore, Benjamin Levi. "The Wolves Are Guarding the Cow Pasture: Examining the US Dairy Industry's Control Over the Federal Government." Master's thesis, Central European University, 2020. https://www.etd.ceu.edu/2020/devore_benjamin-levi.pdf.

Ding, Ming, Jun Li, Lu Qi, et al. "Associations of Dairy Intake with Risk of Mortality in Women and Men: Three Prospective Cohort Studies." *BMJ* 367 (2019). https://doi.org/10.1136/bmj.l6204.

Dress, Brad. "Civil Rights Groups, Including Al Sharpton-Led Organization, Urge USDA to Fix 'Dietary Racism' in School Lunch Programs." *The Hill*, August 9, 2022. https://thehill.com/homenews/3594330-civil-rights-groups-including-al-sharpton-led-organization-urge-usda-to-fix-dietary-racism-in-school-lunch-programs/.

DuPuis, E. Melanie. *Nature's Perfect Food: How Milk Became America's Drink*. New York University Press, 2002.

Engelsman, Jacob. *Lactation for the Rest of Us*. Jessica Kingsley Publishers, 2025.

Ewara, Eyo. "For Estrangement: Queerness, Blackness, and Unintelligibility." *Philosophy Compass* 18, no. 3 (2023). https://doi.org/10.1111/phc3.12897.

Freeman, Andrea. "The Unbearable Whiteness of Milk: Food Oppression and the SDA." *UC Irvine Law Review* 3, no. 1251 (2013): 1251–79.

Frith, Emily Benton, dir. *Our Foster Mother, the Cow*. Frith Films, 1943; rev. 1947. YouTube. https://www.youtube.com/watch?v=zamcq8xa1Y0.

Golden, Janet. *A Social History of Wet Nursing in America: From Breast to Bottle*. Ohio State University Press, 2001.

Gómez-Bravo, Ana M. "The Origins of *Raza*: Racializing Difference in Early Spanish." *Interfaces* 7 (2020): 64–114. https://doi.org/10.13130/interfaces-07-05.

Grandin, Temple, and Catherine Johnson. *Animals in Translation: Using the Mysteries of Autism to Decode Animal Behavior*. Scribner, 2005.

Grandin, Temple. *Humane Livestock Handling: Understanding Livestock Behavior and Building Facilities for Healthier Animals*. Storey, 2008.

Grandin, Temple. *Thinking in Pictures: My Life with Autism*. Vintage, 2006.

Jackson, Melanie, and Esther Leslie. *Deeper in the Pyramid*. Banner Repeater, 2018.

Jackson, Mick, dir. *Temple Grandin*. HBO, 2010.

Jones-Rogers, Stephanie E. *They Were Her Property: White Women as Slave Owners in the American South*. Yale University Press, 2019.

Kardashian, Kirk. *Milk Money: Cash, Cows, and the Death of the American Dairy Farm*. University of New Hampshire Press, 2012.

Kent, Kathryn R. *Making Girls into Women: American Women's Writing and the Rise of Lesbian Identity*. Duke University Press, 2003.

Kriger, Thomas. "Syndicalism and Spilled Milk: The Origins of Dairy Farmer Activism in New York State, 1936–1941." *Labor History* 38, no. 2–3 (1997): 266–86. https://doi.org/10.1080/00236649712331387098.

Kristeva, Julia. *Powers of Horror: An Essay on Abjection*. Columbia University Press, 1982.

Kurlansky, Mark. *Milk! A 10,000-Year Food Fracas*. Bloomsbury, 2018.

Lancaster, Lex Morgan. *Dragging Away: Queer Abstraction in Contemporary Art*. Duke University Press, 2022.

Lopate, Phillip. *The Art of the Personal Essay: An Anthology from the Classical Era to the Present*. Anchor, 1995.

McGarvie, Josiah, dir. *The Dividers*. Brisbane Documentary Company, 2023.

Melville, Herman. *Moby-Dick*. Penguin, 1992.

Mendelson, Anne. *Spoiled: The Myth of Milk as Superfood*. Columbia University Press, 2023.

Miles, Margaret. *A Complex Delight: The Secularization*

of the Breast, 1350–1750. University of California Press, 2008.

Moss, Tyler. "The 19th-Century Swill Milk Scandal That Poisoned Infants with Whiskey Runoff." *Atlas Obscura*, November 27, 2017. https://www.atlasobscura.com/articles/swill-milk-scandal-new-york-city.

Nagish, Ashitha. "Secret Nazi Code Kept Hidden by 'Milk' and 'Vegan Agenda.'" *Metro*, February 21, 2017. https://metro.co.uk/2017/02/21/secret-nazi-code-kept-hidden-by-milk-and-vegan-agenda-6463079/.

Nicholls, Henry. *Lonesome George: The Life and Loves of a Conversation Icon*. Macmillan, 2006.

Obladen, Michael. "From Swill Milk to Certified Milk: Progress in Cow's Milk Quality in the 19th Century." *Annals of Nutrition & Metabolism* 64, no. 1 (2014): 80–87. https://doi.org/10.1159/000363069.

O'Neal, Katherine. *Princess of Thieves*. Bantam Books, 1993.

Pastel, Jenna. "Making Sense of Animal Milks." Smithsonian's National Zoo and Conservation Biology Institute. December 20, 2019. https://nationalzoo.si.edu/conservation/news/making-sense-animal-milks.

Peele, Jordan, dir. *Get Out*. Universal Pictures, 2017.

"PHF/DC King George 725." Cattle Visions, February 22, 2017. https://cattlevisions.com/phf-dc-king-george-725/.

Reczek, Rin. *Families We Lose: Estrangement and the Democratization of Kinship*. New York University Press, forthcoming.

Ryan, Hannah. "Liquid Gold: Lactation as Labor and Human Milk as Commodity in Transatlantic Visual Culture." PhD diss., Cornell University, 2019. https://doi.org/10.7298/pw6h-yh88.

Salmon, Marylynn. "The Cultural Significance of Breastfeeding and Infant Care in Early Modern England and America." *Journal of Social History* 28, no. 2 (Winter 1994): 247–69.

Sanchez, Melissa. "How a Fire on a Dairy Farm Led Us to More Than a Year's Worth of Stories About Immigrant Dairy Farmers." *ProPublica*, February 29, 2024. https://www.propublica.org/article/how-dairy-farm-fire-investigate-workers-michigan-wisconsin.

Seals Allers, Kimberly. *The Big Letdown: How Medicine, Big Business, and Feminism Undermine Breastfeeding*. St. Martin's Press, 2017.

Serrin, William. "Shifting Trends Trapping New York Dairy Farmers." *New York Times*, April 5, 1982. https://www.nytimes.com/1982/04/05/nyregion/shifting-trends-trapping-new-york-dairy-farmers.html.

Severson, Kim. "Got Milk? Not This Generation." *New York Times*, April 4, 2023. https://www.nytimes.com/2023/04/04/dining/milk-dairy-industry-gen-z.html.

Severson, Kim. "In the Town of Phil Campbell, a Gathering of Phil Campbells." *New York Times*, June 17, 2011. https://www.nytimes.com/2011/06/18/us/18alabama.html.

Sexsmith, Sinclair. "More on Butch Bras." *Sugarbutch Chronicles*, June 24, 2008. https://www.sugarbutch.net/2008/06/more-on-butch-bras/.

Sherwood, Harriet. "Choosing Pets over Babies Is 'Selfish and Diminishes Us,' Says Pope." *The Guardian*, January 5, 2022. https://www.theguardian.com/world/2022/jan/05/pope-couples-choose-pets-children-selfish.

Smith-Howard, Kendra. *Pure and Modern Milk: An Environmental History Since 1900*. Oxford University Press, 2013.

Solomon, Joshua. "New York Farm Trends Mirror National Movement on Bigger Farms." *Upstate United*, February 18, 2024. https://upstateunited.com/news/Albany-times-union-small-farms-decline-in-new-york-especially-dairy/.

Stănescu, Vasile. "'White Power Milk': Milk, Dietary Racism, and the 'Alt-Right.'" *Animal Studies Journal* 7, no. 2 (2018): 103–28. https://www.uowoajournals.org/asj/article/id/275/.

Stein, Gertrude. *Tender Buttons*. In *Selected Writings of Gertrude Stein*, edited by Carl Van Vechten. Vintage, 1990.

Stewart, Hayden, Diansheng Dong, and Andrea Carlson. "Is Generational Change Contributing to the Decline in Fluid Milk Consumption?" *Journal of Agricultural and Resource Economics* 37, no. 3 (2012): 435–54. https://doi.org/10.22004/ag.econ.142354.

Stewart, Hayden, Fred Kuchler, Diansheng Dong, and Jerry Cessna. *Examining the Decline in US Per Capita Consumption of Fluid Cow's Milk, 2003–2018*. ERR-300, US Department of Agriculture, Economic Research Service. October 2021. https://doi.org/10.22004/ag.econ.327183.

Sunshine Muse. "Breastfeeding America: What We Know." *MomsRising*, August 1, 2017.

https://www.momsrising.org/blog/breastfeeding-america-what-we-know.

Suvin, Darko. *Metamorphoses of Science Fiction: On the Poetics and History of a Literary Genre*. Yale University Press, 1979.

Ternman, Emma, Emma Nilsson, Per Peetz Nielsen, et al. "Rapid Eye Movement Sleep Time in Dairy Cows Changes During the Lactation Cycle." *Journal of Dairy Science* 102, no. 6 (2019): 5458–65. https://doi.org/10.3168/jds.2018-15950.

Thornton, Sarah. *Tits Up: What Sex Workers, Milk Bankers, Plastic Surgeons, Bra Designers, and Witches Tell Us About Breasts*. Norton, 2024.

Tomlinson, Maisie. "'Are Those Cows Jumping for Joy?': Eye Whites, Hoof Kicks, and Qualitative Behaviour Assessment." *Discover Society*, August 7, 2017. https://archive.discoversociety.org/2019/08/07/are-those-cows-jumping-for-joy-eye-whites-hoof-kicks-and-qualitative-behaviour-assessment/.

Turner, Kay, ed. *Baby Precious Always Shines: Selected Love Notes Between Gertrude Stein and Alice B. Toklas*. St. Martin's Press, 1999.

Uenuma, Francine. "'Better Babies' Contests Pushed for Much-Needed Infant Health but Also Played Into the Eugenics Movement." *Smithsonian Magazine*, January 17, 2019. https://www.smithsonianmag.com/history/better-babies-contests-pushed-infant-health-also-played-eugenics-movement-180971288/.

US Environmental Protection Agency. "Inventory of US Greenhouse Gas Emissions and Sinks, 1990–2022." EPA 430-R-24-004. https://www.epa.gov/

ghgemissions/inventory-us-greenhouse-gas-emissions-and-sinks-1990-2022.

Valenze, Deborah. *Milk: A Local and Global History*. Yale University Press, 2011.

Wang, Kaili, Xu Zhao, Sijia Yang, et al. "New Insights into Dairy Management and the Prevention and Treatment of Osteoporosis: The Shift from Single Nutrient to Dairy Matrix Effects—A Review." *Comprehensive Reviews in Food Science and Food Safety* 23 (2024). https://doi.org/10.1111/1541-4337.13374.

Watson, Julia, and Sidonie Smith. *Reading Autobiography: A Guide for Interpreting Life Narratives*. 2nd ed. University of Minnesota Press, 2010.

Wickes, Ian. "A History of Infant Feeding, Part IV: Nineteenth Century Continued." *Archives of Disease in Childhood* 28, no. 141 (1953): 416–22. https://doi.org/10.1136/adc.28.141.416.

Wright, Anne L., and Richard J. Schanler. "The Resurgence of Breastfeeding at the End of the Second Millennium." *The Journal of Nutrition* 131, no. 2: 421–25. https://jn.nutrition.org/article/S0022-3166(22)14649-3/fulltext.

Yamato, Jen. "Jordan Peele Explains *Get Out*'s Creepy Milk Scene." *LA Times*, March 1, 2017. https://www.latimes.com/entertainment/movies/la-et-mn-get-out-milk-horror-jordan-peele-allison-williams-20170301-story.html/.

Yate, Zainab. *When Breastfeeding Sucks*. Pinter & Martin, 2020.

PHOTO © ZAVÉ MARTOHARDJONO

MEGAN MILKS is the author of *Margaret and the Mystery of the Missing Body*, finalist for a Lambda Literary Award in Transgender Fiction; *Slug and Other Stories*; and *Tori Amos Bootleg Webring*. They coedited *We Are the Baby-Sitters Club* with Marisa Crawford and have published criticism in *4Columns*, the *New York Times*, and *Bookforum*. They live in Brooklyn.

THE FEMINIST PRESS
AT THE CITY UNIVERSITY OF NEW YORK
FEMINISTPRESS.ORG